THE END OF TRANSGRESSION IN JAPANESE WOMEN'S WRITING

This book argues for a new articulation of the ways in which transgression is theorized in contemporary literature by Japanese women.

Exploring the rhetorical and discursive mechanics of literary "bad girls" from fiction produced during the millennial turn (1990–2010), the book contends that women writers today deploy truant, unruly, restless, and aggressive female protagonists not to challenge the status quo but rather to reaffirm it. While Japanese women's fiction has long been invested in cultivating an uncomfortable politics of opposition through "unladylike" themes such as sex, sexuality, and violence, the book argues that today authors turn to such acts of defiance to quietly advocate for the primacy of Japanese social order. Showing how transgression has not only lost its political and disruptive valence in contemporary women's fiction, this book further reveals how discourses of dissent can be retooled to promote a conservative worldview.

A fascinating literary analysis which reads Japanese literature in relation to the receding value of rebellion today, this book will be of huge interest to students and scholars of Japanese literature, gender, and cultural studies.

David S. Holloway was Assistant Professor of Japanese at the University of Rochester, USA.

THE END OF TRANSGRESSION IN JAPANESE WOMEN'S WRITING

Gender, Body, Nation

David S. Holloway

Routledge
Taylor & Francis Group
LONDON AND NEW YORK

Designed cover image: David S. Holloway

First published 2025
by Routledge
4 Park Square, Milton Park, Abingdon, Oxon OX14 4RN

and by Routledge
605 Third Avenue, New York, NY 10158

Routledge is an imprint of the Taylor & Francis Group, an informa business

British Library Cataloguing-in-Publication Data
A catalogue record for this book is available from the British Library

ISBN: 978-1-032-13983-8 (hbk)
ISBN: 978-1-032-13984-5 (pbk)
ISBN: 978-1-003-23180-6 (ebk)

DOI: 10.4324/9781003231806

Typeset in Galliard
by KnowledgeWorks Global Ltd.

CONTENTS

PREFACE AND ACKNOWLEDGMENTS

A preface is usually the author's domain, an additional space for preliminary information about the subject and its significance, the author's background or expertise, and similar details. David Holloway's draft manuscript for *The End of Transgression in Japanese Women's Writing: Gender, Body, Nation* was accepted for publication shortly before his sudden death on June 25, 2021. In the wake of this loss, Rebecca Copeland and I prepared David's manuscript for publication on his behalf. As David's former mentor and dissertation advisor at Washington University in St. Louis and a frequent collaborator of David's, Rebecca had read earlier versions of this manuscript. I was also familiar with David's work as his colleague in the Japanese program at the University of Rochester. Rebecca and I benefited from the expert copyediting skills and advice of David's close friend, Rio Hartwell. Nina Cornyetz, who also had opportunities to work with David and read an earlier version of this manuscript, generously agreed to contribute an Epilogue; it deftly contextualizes David's comprehensive analysis of the dynamics of transgression, illuminating *The End of Transgression*'s contributions to Japanese literary studies and literary history more broadly. In these circumstances, this preface is an opportunity to explain our approach to finalizing David's manuscript and acknowledge all the other individuals who made this process possible. It is also a chance to complement the Epilogue with a brief but heartfelt appreciation of David's legacy beyond his scholarship, as the singular friend, teacher, and colleague we also will remember.

This book would not have been possible without the guidance of Stephanie Rogers, Publisher for Asian Studies at Routledge. From the start, Stephanie encouraged and supported our plan to finalize David's manuscript. By immediately acknowledging this as an unprecedented situation for everyone involved, she made it easier for us to work with the challenges posed by our limited knowledge of David's vision for this publication. Stephanie also arranged for the press to cover the cost of creating the book's index. We are indebted to David's family for granting permission to prepare David's manuscript for publication. David's mother, Sandra Holloway, and his aunt, Leticia Amick, also helped choose the book's cover illustration, which we chose from a folder of David's photographs that he had compiled to consider for another publication. Gloria Culver, Dean of the School of Arts and Sciences at The University of Rochester, generously provided funds to cover preliminary copyediting before submitting the manuscript to Routledge. While still under consideration at Routledge, David received two excellent peer reviews of his manuscript with useful suggestions for optional revisions. Except for choosing a slightly more specific title, however, we ultimately decided to adhere as closely as possible to David's original manuscript to avoid making changes, even inadvertently, to his argument.

This decision guided every step of our process. We made in-text edits to tighten chapter structure, remove redundancies, and ensure consistency and clarity across chapters. Rebecca and I have known each other since our first day as graduate students at Columbia, but she is the literary scholar between the two of us, with a well-established reputation for her scholarship on and translations of works by Japanese women authors. Collaborating on each chapter, we reviewed the manuscript twice before submitting it to Routledge, once before and once after Rio Hartwell's more comprehensive copyediting. Rebecca made the most substantive edits and wrote the chapter abstracts. I reconciled the formatting, finalized the bibliography and notes, and made mostly mechanical edits. Ryan Prendergast and John Givens, David's close friends and colleagues in the Department of Modern Languages and Cultures, University of Rochester, assisted in ensuring Rebecca and I received David's most recent files to work with. If David were here, I know he also would thank them (and, I am sure, many other friends and colleagues at the University of Rochester and beyond) for their support and camaraderie as he worked on completing this manuscript.

In the few cases where Rebecca and I hit an impasse—an inconsistency or textual ambiguity that left David's final intentions in doubt—we kept any revisions to a minimum. The only major edit that we made was to excise the epigraphs that David had chosen for each chapter to comply with Routledge's publishing guidelines. We debated adding them as an appendix, but they lost their intended impact in list form, untethered from their corresponding chapters.

This book is an important cornerstone in David's accomplishments, but it is only part of his legacy. With his passing, we lost a brilliant scholar who was just coming into his own voice, but we also lost a compassionate and talented human being. As a first-generation college student, he was sensitive to differences, whether in appearance, gender, or economic and social status, and he was aware that privilege is accompanied by a sense of responsibility to give back to society. His active participation as an instructor in the University of Rochester Education Justice Initiative, teaching Japanese literature and culture to incarcerated students at Five Points Correctional Facility was just one example of his generosity to volunteer his time to support others in need. In addition to his significant contributions to the intellectual community at the University of Rochester, supporting the Japanese and the Gender, Sexuality, and Women Studies programs, he cultivated a deep network of friends, colleagues, and students who appreciated his collegiality and his generosity of time and spirit.

I have folders for emails that sustain ongoing conversations with friends that I augment and revisit over time. David's folder remains active thanks to the ongoing relevance of work, sustained by exchanges from mutual colleagues, acquaintances, and, especially, his former students. Nevertheless, it was too difficult to reread David's own emails until recently because they are so redolent of his distinct mannerisms and voice, always succinct and carefully composed in a way that recalls the thoughtfulness of handwritten correspondence. In them, a friendly greeting precedes a message with substance, invariably ending with "Sincerely, David." At first, I thought these were niceties that would fade with time, but David was a remarkably consistent correspondent. Eventually, I learned that what I first understood to be rote formality was David's genuine and thoughtful way of communicating. I grew to appreciate the consistent clarity of his voice. I now recognize this consistency as a rare gift.

Looking through David's email folder, I can trace our relationship through our messages to one another beginning in late 2015, when we started working together. Until the onset of the pandemic in March 2020, we emailed frequently each week about the usual subjects for academic coworkers: administrative and curriculum details, student questions, asking for advice, job tips or suggestions, asking for help (usually me), and offers of assistance (mostly David). Not all our emails were about work. We were often just "touching base" or "catching up." David's earliest emails after moving to Rochester reveal his adventurous spirit. The remarkable photographs he sent of downtown Rochester murals and the abandoned remains of Rochester's subway were unexpected glimpses of his capacious curiosity and creative mind. After only one or two months in Rochester, David already had explored all manner of places I knew nothing about after living here for twenty years. David was a keen observer of the world, just as he was of human nature. His expert eye eventually led us to plans to collaborate on a "then and now" photographic series based on my collection of vintage postcards of Japan and other related twentieth-century tourist ephemera.

David's enterprising and creative spirit extended to his teaching. He was an enormously popular teacher, always willing to explore new territory through course design. During his six years at the University of Rochester, he created ten original, highly transdisciplinary courses in Japanese literature and Gender, Sexuality, and Women's studies, mobilizing popular culture and media spanning one thousand years. His subjects included women writers and detective fiction; the intersection of Japanese literature with gender, media, and fantasy; youth cultures and subcultures; self-presentation and body alterations, especially tattoos; the precarity of Japan's "lost decades;" and manifestations of Japan's AIDS crisis in the 1980s–1990s popular culture and media. Planning new courses activated David's innate sensibility for design and playful use of words. He was, hands down, the master of the artfully illustrated syllabus and eye-catching course title. Thanks to his influence, I abandoned subjecting students to the "naked" syllabus: dreary, unadorned pages lacking a single image that might capture in a glance (and in color!) the course's promise of discovery. David was also a master of gripping titles, but none topped "Hello Kitty Must Die," an introductory survey course on contemporary Japanese culture and a lasting testament to his quirky sense of humor.

Skimming through our email correspondence revives David's voice and the particular banter that characterized our relationship. How's the new semester? Borrowing a DVD? Belated thanks. Tattoo exhibit. Coffee or lunch? As the pandemic deepened in the fall 2020 semester, the subject turned to COVID protocols, extensions, canceled conferences, and "library journals we need to retain." Other topics looked forward to the future: book proposal drafts and presses, junior leave, promotion, and tenure. Correspondence slowed in the spring. Perhaps, like so many others, we were both overwhelmed by the circumstances of the ongoing pandemic. David's last email to me is characteristically thoughtful, kindly phrased, and generous in spirit. He apologizes for his delayed response and thanks me for asking after his mother. We planned to grab coffee and catch up with each other after his first vaccine shot, which was scheduled. Then in the next email, exactly one month later, I had to tell colleagues the sad news of David's passing. David's voice is gone. His name moves to the subject line as our engagement through email shifts to the third person. Even now, this shift brings back memories of how abruptly David's vibrant voice—as a friend, a valued teacher, and a promising colleague—was cut short.

As it turns out, his voice was interrupted but not entirely silenced. Rather, David's gift for communication turned an unexpected corner, an unforeseen detour. When David started working in our department, he took over one or two courses formerly taught by a recently retired colleague, coincidentally also a "David." In program faculty meetings, we started distinguishing David from his predecessor in curriculum discussions by referring to David as "the new David" or the "other David." This habit quickly faded. "New David" was more than new: he was sui generis.

The final class of University of Rochester students that David taught and mentored just graduated this spring. So many of them gratefully acknowledged how much they learned from him, warm tributes to his deep commitment to teaching, and his love of Japanese literature and culture. I will continue to hear from David's former students. They have been eagerly looking forward to this book. David's investment in students continues through the student awards for excellence in Japanese his family established in his memory at the University of Rochester and his alma mater, Washington University in St. Louis.

I have only mentioned a few of David's fondly remembered qualities as a friend, a colleague, and a teacher. I am still discovering his many dimensions. I knew about his flash fiction and his music, but his love for fashion, for example, was a revelation. (Nevertheless, if anyone had asked, I wouldn't hesitate to call him dapper.) David's legacy recalls the Greek proverb that "society grows great when old men plant trees in whose shade they may never sit." David left us too soon, but not before planting a forest.

Joanne Bernardi
Rochester, N.Y.
July 2024

EDITORS' NOTE

Japanese names are given consistently in Japanese order (family name first) except for individuals who publish in English using Western name order and any other specified exceptions. Macrons (diacritical marks) are used for Japanese romanization except for the following exceptions that are typically rendered in English without them: Anglicized words (e.g., kaiju, kimono); principal cities such as Tokyo, Kyoto, and Osaka, except when they appear as part of a longer Japanese language reference, as in citations for Japanese language publications; and names with long-established precedents for Anglicized variants or romanized renderings. We generally follow a variant of Hepburn style romanization, the most common form in use today that follows English phonology and uses hyphens sparingly. Cited material is an exception and is reproduced intact. With a few exceptions, Japanese words (e.g., specific terminology) used in English language sentences are italicized the first time they appear in each chapter (followed by their English translation) unless they have entered the English language, but not thereafter in order to keep the use of italics to a minimum. In-text references to titles of Japanese literary works and other publications are referred to by their original title the first time they are mentioned and by their English title (or translated English title) thereafter.

INTRODUCTION

Literary Dislocations: Rediscovery and Reorientation

This book takes as its aim the pursuit of stability in works of contemporary fiction by Japanese women. These works share the same historical backdrop—what I am calling the millennial turn—the years bracketing the twenty-first century (approximately 1990–2010). A thorough consideration of the literary production of the millennial turn sheds light on the ways in which authors—women authors, specifically—grapple with the social and affective challenges of life at a precarious moment in Japanese cultural history. To be sure, the millennial turn owes its characteristics to a cluster of events, perhaps most notably a recession that ushered in an era of crisis through which the Japanese have not yet passed.

To date, scholars have been particularly focused on exploring how the Tōhoku Earthquake, a triple disaster on March 11, 2011—an earthquake, a tsunami, and a nuclear accident in Fukushima—reshaped Japanese subjectivity. Azuma Hiroki (2011), for one, writes that the disaster "broke" the Japanese master narrative by bringing to the fore a number of social, philosophical, economic, and cultural anxieties that had lurked, until then, just below the surface. The disaster did not *create* a nation of "numb" individuals, he says, so much as it *created an opportunity* for a latent sense of unfeeling to set in. To this end, Azuma argues that the Japanese are experiencing a "slow death" (Azuma 2011).

This is an intriguing turn of phrase: cultural theorist Lauren Berlant has likewise deployed similar language in her own research. For Berlant (2007: 754), "slow death" indexes the ways that certain "populations" are susceptible to being "physical[ly worn] out" by the conditions of living, conditions that are persistent fixtures in the lives of those who circulate in constant states of flux and vulnerability. Lives of exhaustion and attenuation are often defined

DOI: 10.4324/9781003231806-1

by warped expressions of self-control and destructive ways of self-medicating, giving way to permanent states of being in which living implies dying, and agency gives way to more maintenance. Berlant's concept of slow death reveals the proximity of processes of "life building" to conditions of "the attrition of human life," reminding us that choices of living sometimes read like choices of dying.

If Azuma is correct that the contours of the post-Fukushima cultural climate were shaped in the decades preceding the crisis itself, then the millennial years take on special significance. In other words, the perpetual state of "slow death" in which the Japanese now find themselves is not a new phenomenon. While the March 11 Fukushima disaster deserves our attention, we would be remiss not to consider the effects that the recessionary era had on Japanese citizens. The recessionary years did much to alter the state of Japanese social life; Fukushima simply exacerbated a deteriorating condition by exposing the extent to which the Japanese populace remains suspended in crisis. As Azuma (2011) writes, the disaster *was supposed* to unite the Japanese. Instead, it exposed the extent to which everyone is on their own.

This sense of aloneness is codified in the contemporary slogan *ibasho ga nai* or, loosely translated, "no place (to call home)," which has gained currency in the 2000s. This phrase underscores the importance of *ba* (as in *iba*sho)—or "place"—to Japanese subjectivity, while also reminding us that many Japanese today feel "out of place, out of sorts, disconnected," "panicky and insecure" (Allison 2013: 14, 175). According to Mary Brinton (2011: 3), *ba* is a "social location," a "bounded collectivity to which individuals belong and from which they derive a sense of identity and security." Or, it is a place to which individuals have historically belonged. To this end, Brinton (2011: xvi) observes that "[t]he very idea of a secure *ba* has begun to vanish." Anne Allison (2013: 14) agrees that *ibasho ga nai* is part of a gloomy lexicon of terms and phrases in current usage that convey a pervasive sense of "precarity" that is endemic to contemporary Japan. The phrase also encapsulates the sense of homelessness that has been rampant in Japanese social life since the recession took hold. *The End of Transgression*, then, establishes a trajectory of disquiet between the millennial turn and the current state of affairs, and in doing so, expands our understanding of contemporary Japanese subjectivity.

My book's contention is that this "secure *ba*" began "vanishing" well before contemporary scholarly work on Japanese social life (Brinton 2011: 3). I argue that fiction from the millennial turn anticipates contemporary academic and popular interest in the erosion of the Japanese sense of place (*ba*). In contrast to Fukushima, the millennial turn is benchmarked not necessarily by physical or geological rupture (though there was that, too), but rather by a sense of affective dissonance. The recession in particular helped catalyze a mass revolt against staid institutions that had been embedded in Japanese social life since the end of the war. Many Japanese came to view academic credentialism, family-centric ways of living, and corporate loyalty as dubious, worn out, and outdated institutions that had no place in Japan shaped by socioeconomic stagnation and other manifestations of recessionary existence. Thus, the creative landscape of the time was determined by expressions of the rejection of tired ways of living. But this is only part of the story. The rejection of norms is complicated and contradictory, and in this book, I argue that in their desire to defy the status quo, the authors I focus on betray a quiet complicity with and preference for it.

I argue that fiction from the millennial turn is determined by the extra-textual sense of rupture and crisis that pervaded Japanese social life during the 1990s and early 2000s. Beginning with the late 1980s, the Japanese found themselves in a holding pattern, an enduring moment of "dithering, tottering, bargaining, [and] testing" (Berlant 2011: 97–98) that has continued to the present day. During such unstable times, the status quo—as suffocating and dislocating as it may be—can provide a warped sense of security, belonging, and place. The purpose of the fiction I analyze—two works each by authors Kanehara Hitomi (b. 1983), Sakurai Ami (who also works as a journalist under the alias Hayami Yukiko), and Kirino Natsuo (b. 1951)—is the search for this experience, referred to above as "stability." It is a convoluted and contradictory search that is obfuscated by what I will call "transgression," or behavior that mocks or challenges heteronormative and hegemonic culture.

From at least the early twentieth century, women writers have used the pen to confront cultural norms and dictates that have been detrimental to women's experiences. Prominent examples of transgressive literature come from the politically charged milieu of the 1960s and 1970s, a time—not unlike the millennial turn—of unrest and upheaval. This book begins with an examination of literary works of this period in which female characters embrace lives that are militant, contrary, and aggressively unfeminine. Julia Bullock (2010) shows that Japanese women writers during the 1960s addressed themes that anticipated the work of second-wave feminists in the United States, including attention to the politics of sex, sexuality, and the body. "The contributions of these writers of fiction to emerging feminist discourse," Bullock (2010: 5) writes, "helped to lay the theoretical groundwork for a more explicitly political 'women's lib' in the following decade. What they imagined first in the realm of literature [...] reemerged in later decades as more explicitly political articulations of feminist theoretical discourse." In concert with the burgeoning feminist interest in sex and sexuality, Japanese women writers created a new lexicon of female sexual desire and agency. Lesbianism, bestiality, interracial sex, interspecies sex, genderqueer sex, sadomasochism, incest, pederasty, extramarital sex, and recreational heterosexual sex are some of the myriad expressions of sexuality these authors employed. Never before had Japanese women written so openly, brazenly, and explicitly about the female body and the depths of its desires.

This fiction, like that of preceding generations, was shaped under the constraints of the "good wife, wise mother" (*ryōsai kenbo*) ideology, which was making a quiet resurgence amid the rapid economic growth of the postwar era. Although initially a product of the Meiji Period (1868–1912), the *ryōsai kenbo* doctrine constructed circumscribed lives out of female subjects, advancing a dialectic between the private (i.e., feminine) sphere and the public (masculine) domain of national social life. In this paradigm, articulations of social immobility were, for women, contingent on the traditionally gendered roles of wife on the one hand and mother on the other. The writers of this period transgressed "normative femininity through their literature, crafting female protagonists who were unapologetically bad wives and even worse mothers, frequently wanton, excessive, or selfish and brazenly cynical with regard to 'traditional' conceptions of love, marriage, and motherhood—when they did not opt out of this system entirely" (Bullock 2010: 2) There was a reactive quality to this literature—protagonists behaving badly in response to discourses that devalued such behavior as bad in the first place.

The mechanisms of transgression are not easily parsed. Transgression is not the complete transcendence of a norm, boundary, or limit, but rather the creation of new knots of confinement. That is, transgressive behavior can only be temporarily political. As Michel Foucault (1977: 34) writes, "Transgression incessantly crosses and recrosses a line which closes up behind it in a wave of extremely short duration, and thus it is made to return once more right to the horizon of the uncrossable." The contestation of limits leads eventually to the vivification of those limits. Transgression is therefore the constant negotiation between the status quo and actions that are meant to subvert the norm. Foucault's ideas are part of a rich genealogy of theoretical inquiry into the relationship between the will to transgress and how transgression is contained. This book offers a new contextualization for themes and motifs that have been historically important in Japanese women's fiction. When we read about literary characters behaving badly, we must be mindful of the amorphous nature of *bad*. In other words, transgression is historically situated. What may have been shocking or brazen in one historical moment could very well become commonplace or banal at a later point in time.

In calling this book *The End of Transgression*, I argue that women writers of the millennial turn were less interested in pushing boundaries and making "noise" than they were in finding moments of affective quietude for their characters. While Kirino, Sakurai, and Kanehara deploy protagonists who are unruly, they must negotiate the ways in which literary dissonance has become naturalized over the past several decades. Kōno Taeko (1926–2015) and her contemporaries from the 1960s and 1970s blazed trails with their full-frontal stories and novels, but by the 1990s those trails were well-worn and oft-traveled. Literary expressions of transgression no longer served subversion by the end of the century. Rather, I suggest, transgression had become an avenue of restoration and reaffirmation.

My goal is not to deny or contradict progressive readings of these texts. To be sure, fiction by Kirino and the others invites strong feminist readings. Rebecca Copeland (2018), for example, writes of the feminist implications of Kirino's 2004 novel *Gurotesuku* (2003; trans. *Grotesque*, 2007), along with *Riaru wārudo* (2003; trans. *Real World*, 2008). Elsewhere, Copeland (2004) notes how Kirino advances a proactive, woman-forward agenda in her fiction that challenges many of the social constraints placed on female citizens in Japanese society. Rachel DiNitto (2011), too, has addressed feminist-inflected aspects of Kanehara's breakout novella *Hebi ni piasu* (2004; trans. *Snakes and Earrings*, 2005) (the subject, along with her untranslated 2007 novel *Haidora* (Hydra), of Chapter 3). Sakurai Ami (whose 1996 *Inosento wārudo* [trans. *Innocent World*, 2004] and 1998 *Tōmorōzu songu* [untranslated, *Tomorrow's Song*] are the focus of Chapter 4) has yet to receive scholarly treatment in either Japanese or English letters, but her works invite provocative readings. Her female protagonists shirk familial duties while embracing an ethos of aggressive sexuality that flies in the face of tired discourses extolling supposed feminine refinement. I neither negate these interpretations nor challenge them, nor do I *ignore* the political implications of a given text. My aims are different.

This book seeks to complicate the affinity between transgression and subversion. My readings suggest that the six works of fiction under discussion here, though heavy on "bad behavior," are ultimately conservative in scope and aim. In a sense, my readings could also be called conservative or perhaps anomalous since the potential for feminist readings is in each case obvious and abundant. Yet I would argue, too, that my anomalous readings are grounded in an abnormal moment in Japanese social history. Chapter 2 of this study gives shape to the historical milieu from which the attendant works of fiction emerged. Emperor Hirohito's death in 1989 was the metaphorical beginning of a period of unrest that included the Great Hanshin Earthquake (*Hanshin Awaji Daishinsai*) on January 17, 1995; the domestic terrorism of Aum Shinrikyō on March 20 that same year; terrible acts of violence committed by a fourteen-year-old boy in 1997; and the economic recession. The context of this historical moment, I suggest, compromised the authors' relationship with transgression praxis. Although the recessionary climate nurtured the crescendo of dissenting and frustrated voices that targeted the failings of normative culture, this climate also fostered space for reflection and longing. The 1990s inaugurated an era of struggle, uncertainty, loss, and vacillation. I sense a sustained attempt to put an end to such instability in the works of fiction by Sakurai, Kirino, and Kanehara. My readings suggest that for these texts, survival takes precedence over other potential political ambitions. To paraphrase Anne McClintock (1995), norms become reified when they are least stable.

This is not to say that the present moment is the only time the Japanese have been stripped of sanctuary, safety, or security. In the 1930s, literary critic Kobayashi Hideo (1902–1983) lamented the loss of his spiritual home. More specifically, he famously confessed in "Literature of the Lost Home" (1933 [1995]: 49) that he envisioned himself as a mere apparition floating aimlessly down the streets of his hometown of Tokyo: "I do not easily recognize within myself or in the world around me people whose feet are planted firmly on the ground, or who have the features of social beings." Because of the pace at which Tokyo was changing and evolving, Kobayashi felt left behind and alienated, or in Seiji Lippit's (2002: 3) words, "dislocated." Kobayashi situates his argument vis-à-vis the state of Japanese literature, which is no longer recognizable to him. Western influence has rendered Japanese literature anything but Japanese, and his sense of being Japanese is under threat. He writes (1933 [1995]: 54), "At this juncture, it is indeed pointless to call out for the 'Japanese spirit' or 'Eastern spirit.' Look wherever we might, such things will not be found." Kobayashi argues that his sense of alienation causes him to identify more readily with foreign places and concepts than with more proximal locales. For example, having seen the film *Morocco* (1930), he states (1933 [1995]: 53): "The style elicits a sense of intimacy, so that we feel closer to the Moroccan desert we have never seen than to the landscape of [the Tokyo district of] Ginza before our eyes." Lippit (2002: 5) understands Kobayashi's concerns in terms of the latter's anxiety over "a pervasive feeling of cultural homelessness." Kobayashi, however, is not advocating a "return" to Japan, which would have been an argument in line with the nationalistic sentiments of the interwar years. Rather, he suggests that there is no longer a Japan to return to. He does not call for a restoration of so-called Japanese spirit so much as he mourns the death of Japan's "cultural singularity" (1933 [1995]: 54). "It is a fact that ours is a literature of the lost home," he says, "that we are a young people who have lost our youthful innocence" (1933 [1995]: 54). To him, what has been lost cannot be recovered.

Lippit's (2002: 5) phrase "literature of dislocation," used to describe Kobayashi's thoughts, is coeval with the cultural moment and literature at the core of my study. The literature that I will examine in the ensuing pages is thick with anxiety over displacement and dislocation. While I am invested in pinpointing an epicenter of affective rupture, and offering close readings that coalesce around it, I do not suggest that prior to the 1990s Japanese social life was idyllic. Far from it. In Chapter 1, I establish a historical lineage of disaffection from the 1960s to the millennial turn. My focus is on key literary works from the 1960s, such as those by the aforementioned Kōno Taeko, but I do not exclude works from the 1970s and 1980s—decades worthy of a study in their own right. In doing so, I argue that the recession was not the *cause* of rampant generational discontent; it made visible latent problems of, again, dislocation. In contrast to Kobayashi's engagement with "Japanese" versus "Western" discourse, this is not a *cultural* dislocation per se, though it is firmly grounded in literary characters' relationships with a particular moment of Japanese cultural history. The lens of loss and disjunction through which Kobayashi views the world anticipates contemporary ways of seeing.

There is an important difference, however. Where Kobayashi recognizes a temporal gap between how life is and how it used to be, the conditions of the millennial turn invite a myopic perspective. This is because, for contemporary citizens, there is no past, no "how things used to be." The term "lost generation" entered the public consciousness in 2007 to capture the experiences of those struggling to get by during the "lost" 1990s. In socioeconomic terms, these were citizens who were denied access to a stable income and other markers of middle-class life. "Since I was born, I've never experienced a time of prosperity," reflects author Kanehara Hitomi (Onishi 2004). Born in the early 1980s, Kanehara belonged to the first generation to grow up in a Japan nearly bled dry of its symbolic and cultural cores: gone were those facets of Japanese social life that had given order to the daily lives of so many Japanese for so long. For Japan's "lost generation," the past has never existed. The cultural framework of postwar Japan collapsed with the recession, and those who, like Kanehara, grew up in the late 1980s and early 1990s came of age in a post-postwar Japan that had little if any resemblance to the life experiences of their parents and grandparents. Kobayashi's lamentation for a time now past would be out of place among a populace whose defining framework can only be rooted in the unstable, untenable, and unfair present.

What, then, is the object of longing at the millennial moment? If the postwar nuclear family, for example, has never existed for this "lost generation," how do young Japanese know what to look for? In other words, what is life supposed to look like? I would argue that in the pages of this fiction there is a critical engagement with the *idea* of normativity. Characters establish families, pursue romantic relationships, and even approach marriage, but in each case something is off and abject. On the contours of these crooked unions, choreographed by crooked citizens, stirs the end of transgression. Central to these works of fiction is the seemingly paradoxical longing for confinement and containment provided by the status quo, for a time orchestrated by rule and regulation.

For this reason, literary characters are not necessarily nostalgic in their attachments, because nostalgia functions as a kind of "collective memory" that facilitates attachment to a shared past:

> Nostalgia is located in an experience of loss and calls for a politics of recovery and recuperation, and for a political agency adequate to that task. That agency could be the state. It could also be the individual. The political task of nostalgic memory, whether individual or collective, is to recover and preserve, make the past a part of the present.
>
> (Chakbrabarty 1998: 290)

Nostalgia requires the symbolic recovery/recuperation/preservation of the past in the name of the present. As such, the characters in the fiction I read can only orient themselves toward a future that is intended to replace the present. For them, the past has never existed. The question, then, is how to overcome the present to find a sense of normal.

My readings of these six works interrogate the ways in which female characters inevitably give up on what pop sociologist Miyadai Shinji (1998) calls "the endless everyday," or *owarinaki nichijō*. Miyadai maintains that from the 1980s young Japanese began to give up on any hope for a better tomorrow and, as a result, have turned to ways of living focused solely on the present. These young Japanese have stopped searching for meaning in their lives; in the wake of the Aum Shinrikyō gas attacks of 1995 (see Chapter 2), Miyadai claims that it is dangerous to do so. Instead, the emptiness of everyday life should be embraced. In his study, Miyadai teases out the dynamics of a kind of existential boredom that arises from the tedium of an everyday existence bled of its ideologies. He wonders how young Japanese can survive a historical moment in which they are at risk of being bored to death. "The only way to cope with [...] reality," Michael Marra (2010: 213–214) observes, paraphrasing Miyadai, is by embracing "a sense of lassitude," "skepticism," and "indifference."

Miyadai does not interrogate boredom at the level of epistemology. He does not ask what it *means* to be bored. Boredom is indeed endemic to the lived experiences of Japanese youth, who find themselves in a state of stasis due to "the endless everyday." At its core, boredom is about "emotional flatness and resigned indifference" rather than any "dramatic and sentimental nostalgia [for] happier times" (Haladyn and Gardiner 2017: 15). Here we see the grip of the present, which engenders "flatness" and "indifference." Kanehara, for one, is noted for using "detached" and "indifferent" language in *Snakes and Earrings* (Matsuura 2007: 19). She writes about unsettling themes—murder, masochistic sex, and self-harm—with a narrative voice that could be described as bored. Sakurai, too, presents sibling incest, rape, and prostitution with nonchalance. And Kirino writes about prostitution and violence with narrative voices that are apathetic at best and cynical at worst. It is no surprise that these respective voices, all rich in indifference, should emerge from a historical moment characterized by disenchantment with and ambivalence toward Japanese social life. The key to neutralizing the effects of "the endless everyday" is escaping the boredom it represents. In other words, boredom itself has become boring.

To this end, Miyadai asserts that those best equipped to weather the mundanity and stagnation of the present are sexually aware teenage girls. His claim is that the physical body is the solution to an everyday without end, and that teenage girls aware of their value as sexual commodities are ahead of the curve. He argues that the body is "the last controllable environment, the modifiable exterior. This is why there is no problem with the body being consumed by others" (qtd. in Iida 2002: 233). In a milieu in which nothing matters, Miyadai contends, the body is all that matters. The body is of crucial importance in the literature of Sakurai and her contemporaries. My close readings attend to the role of the body, especially the sexual body. In these texts, the body is the way out of the endless everyday. By opening it, infecting it, abusing it, seducing it, selling it, and modifying it, literary characters (who are often teenagers) are able to force their way into a new conceptualization of self. Theirs is a retreat into the body, probing their own scars, sensations, and desires to find access to an alternative temporal space. In contrast to Miyadai's theory, these characters come to find the present intolerable. Because there is no past to return to, and because the present is awful, there is only the future to provide refuge. Bodies come together to escape the harrowing conditions of the present.

The image of the family therefore looms large in this fiction. With the sole exception of Kirino's *Real World*, each text concludes with a heterosexual familial union—man, woman, and even child. These images nod toward the future. Today, the family is at the center of a variety of demographic shifts, including a rapidly aging population and declining birthrate, and the fall of guaranteed employment and the concomitant rise of wage labor. This constellation of changes and challenges—particularly the strain on socioeconomic guarantees—has compromised the integrity of the family. The recession stirred a discourse of ridicule directed at the family, which has been stripped of its middle-class comforts. Young Japanese have been hardest hit, finding secure employment difficult, if not impossible, to attain. Accordingly, these individuals have been vocal in their disenfranchisement

Kanehara, Kirino, and Sakurai take their discursive frustrations out on maternal figures in particular. Time and again, mothers are portrayed as tyrannical and menacing. Fathers, meanwhile, are either absent or comically ineffectual. As for the daughter, consider here Ueno Chizuko's (2009: 251) thoughts on the contemporary family dynamic and the daughter's place within it: "With no sympathy for her father or mother…the daughter becomes the most scathingly critical member of the family."

Modern and contemporary Japanese fiction has offered portraits of the disjointed family before. Author Enchi Fumiko (1905–1986) is noted for often excluding the father from her fiction (Mikals-Adachi 2001: 194). Yoshimoto Banana (b. 1964), too, gained fame for her 1988 novella *Kitchin* (trans. Kitchen, 1993), in which orphaned protagonist Mikage comes to live with a boy named Yūichi and his transgendered mother Eriko. In each case, the family does not look quite right. Yet for Enchi, as Eileen Mikals-Adachi (2001: 194) has demonstrated, the father is removed in order to "retain" his "purity," even while Enchi critiques the patriarchal system "he would normally represent." Enchi seeks to preserve the image of the father, "to protect him from charges that he could be less than perfect" (Mikals-Adachi 2001: 194). Banana, on the other hand, constructs a makeshift family for Mikage out of warmth and love, offering her a space where she fits right in. Amanda Seaman (2004: 61) explains: "Mikage [...] devot[es] herself to creating meals for her new roommates and crafting a role for herself as the mother figure in a home without one. Indeed, what begins as a place of friendly hospitality is quickly reimagined as a family home[.]" Both Enchi and Banana engage critically with issues of the family, love, and patriarchy, among others. They do so, however, without venom or carnage. Enchi's texts are autobiographical in nature (Mikals-Adachi 2001: 203), and her use of the absentee father is personal. Her texts are populated with "paternal phantoms" that serve as specters for her own lost father (Mikals-Adachi 2001: 203). In contrast, the lost father in *Kitchen* (before Eriko was his mother, she was Yūichi's father) does not seem so proximal for Banana. Nevertheless, through the figure of the transgendered individual, she offers us a portrait of the Japanese family in transition, choosing to emphasize the ways in which such shifts can have a positive impact.

In contrast, the authors studied in *The End of Transgression* take umbrage with the family and the ways in which its ineffectuality has affected Japanese youth, especially daughters. Kirino, Sakurai, and Kanehara want you to ***know*** that they are displeased. Their displeasure is historically rooted. Japan's legendary period of high economic growth (1955–1970) put into place many of the familial institutions against which young Japanese have since grown to despise. The salaryman doxa defined Japanese conceptions of masculinity (McLelland 2003; Dasgupta 2013), while the "professional housewife" (*sengyō shufu*) was heralded as his feminine counterpart. As in the prewar era, young boys and girls were tracked to reproduce the efforts of their parents, either as future contributors to Japan's capitalist production or supportive wives. In this paradigm, the salaryman's corporate duties superseded his domestic responsibilities. Indeed, *kaisha shugi*, or "companyism," complicated family dynamics, demanding allegiance to the corporate home and setting in motion mass social identification with a white-collar, middle-class lifestyle. The privileged status of economic success on a national level and affluence on a personal level tenuously held families together. But to what end? Sociocultural emphasis on class and prestige, combined with the rising importance of educational pedigree (*gakureki shakai*) turned young Japanese into trophies among middle-class families with visions of upward mobility. Children, especially sons, were taxed with carrying the burdens of parental labor, often by attending the best, most expensive schools; the father's capitalistic labors provided financial comforts while the mother's domestic labor was reflected in her child's academic success and advancement. In short, the best families were those that labored together, for the child's intellectual advancement reflected the efforts and affective investments of the household.

The failure of the economy in the following decades jeopardized the aspirations of many middle-class households. Corporate restructuring meant the end of white-collar job security and the hegemonic masculine ideal of the salaryman,[1] postwar visions of leisurely consumerism, and financial security. It meant, too, that families were stripped of their nuclei. They were, in Ueno's (2009: 259) words, reduced to a "chance collection of individual people." If families had labored and sacrificed in unison for the sake of upward mobility and national progress, what were they to do now that neither aspiration seemed feasible or, to young Japanese, worth the effort? "Once Japan's remarkable boom years came to an end, a new generation of men and women were wondering whether the sacrifices made by their parents, in both their professional and personal lives, were really worth it," writes Mark McLelland (2003). Prior to the recession, the common belief was that success in school almost guaranteed employment in a reputable firm and a lifetime of financial stability. This did not mean that families were perfect or even content. It meant that with financial stability came personal stability and the accumulation of wealth.

As the recession dragged on, however, some people became convinced that Japanese capitalistic impulses were to blame for the collapse of the economy, and by extension, the collapse of familial relations. In this way, millennial Japan was defined by a hollowing out of the family, leaving father, mother, and child to fend for themselves and to direct their attentions and goals elsewhere. Young Japanese, Ueno (2009: 259) writes, "are all too aware of how fragile the family is. [...] For them, family is not a secure shelter but rather an ongoing project." The sociologist Miyadai is not interested in the family or its potential. He would have it that young Japanese turned inward, toward themselves and toward each other. He would have it that the body was a means of suturing relations between individuals for the sake of navigating a historical moment lacking both a past and future.

My close readings complicate this assertion and suggest, again, that the aim of millennial fiction is not eulogistic. The resurrection of familial bonds is meant to portend healing, community, and *ba*—place. Because the family has been the object of scorn and ridicule, my argument is that Kirino and her contemporaries are attempting to restore the family as a site of promise and futurity. This is not a simple or saccharine endeavor, for literary characters are sometimes *forced* into familial bondage, as is the case in Kanehara's *Snakes and Earrings* and *Hydra*. Other characters are punished for resisting this same bondage (Kirino's *Real World*). Still others build familial relationships with whatever is at their disposal, even if that means sifting through issues of incest (Sakurai's *Innocent World*), murder (Kirino's *Grotesque*), and disease (Sakurai's *Tomorrow's Song*). These narrative developments suggest that, at least in some cases, hegemony is the lesser of two evils, and that weathering the conditions of millennial Japan is easier if you have someone by your side.

Each novel analyzed in this monograph puts on display the draw of hegemonic familial culture. The cluster of texts I examine work well together because they follow the same general format in which characters, in line with the prevailing discourses of the day, offer up to ridicule and mockery the state of the family. Yet they all figure its inevitability.

This is in contrast to the ways in which the family has been historically thematized in postwar Japanese literature. Yumiko Iida draws our attention to the dynamics of the "family novels" of the postwar. She (2002: 134) notes that "[t]he popularity of the family as a novelistic theme" during this period "was closely related to the breakdown of the traditional family system." Iida (2002: 134) goes on to explain that changes to the family, including "the collapse of the extended family into the nuclear family," as well as shifting gender roles within the household, found expression within literature. "Reflecting these changes, the 'family novels' no longer concerned themselves with oppression in the stable and traditionally sacred sanctuary of the family [as they had in prior eras], but moved on to an exploration of the territories of conflict, distrust, confusion, and despair" (Iida 2002: 134). This is a literature devoted to characters' trials in navigating the shifting topography of the family in a rapidly changing Japan. This is a literature whose characters are embedded firmly in the familial structure.

As an example, Iida (2002: 134) draws from the novels of literary critic Etō Jun (1932–1999). According to Iida, this author sees a direct correlation between the ebbs and flows of the modern world and the ups and downs of Japanese family life: "Etō interprets the process of modernization as a destruction of the relation between the mother and the male child" (Iida 2002: 134). And elsewhere: "Etō [...] diagnos[es] the fundamental change in family structures as the root cause of then current Japanese socio-political problems" (Iida 2002: 134). Iida finds that in Etō's writings, modernization comes at great cost to the traditional makeup of the family.

> Etō sees the essential problem of modern Japanese society as the intrusion of the other [...] that have caused the breakdown of the traditional family system symbolized by the sacrificing mother and the authoritative father, and the consequent loss of the stable cultural/familial environment in which children grow into mature adults"
>
> (Iida 2002: 136).

Etō's lamentation is directed at a vision of the Japanese family that, by the recession, became the subject of discourses of ruination. While prior generations of authors might have detailed the struggles to adjust to changes within family life, more recent iterations of these themes might disregard the family entirely or examine the lengths to which characters go to excise themselves from (transgress against) familial bonds.

Thus, a prominent motif in millennial-era fiction is familial strife and dysfunction. In *Grotesque*, for instance, Kirino indexes critically the ways in which mothers and fathers have failed their children, while in *Real World* she uses matricide as an event that is central to a story of young Japanese women retaliating against Japanese social life. Sakurai is even more explicit in her novels. In *Innocent World* and *Tomorrow's Song* incest, prostitution, and rape occur as a direct result of frayed familial bonds and parental ineptitude. In contrast to these authors, Kanehara excludes the family entirely. *Snakes and Earrings* and *Hydra* feature no parents or siblings (or friends for that matter), and instead show us what life is like for female protagonists with no attachments to the domestic sphere. However, as Norimitsu Onishi (2004) has remarked, in Kanehara's texts, the family (among other institutions) is "noticeable by [its] absence." In all of these works of fiction, we bear witness to characters falling victim to a social system that no longer works. Accordingly, we also watch as they attempt to leave this system behind by forging new bonds and connections; they attempt to put the family—whatever that is—back together.

Here, I reiterate my claim that transgression in these texts is temporary. In the pages to follow, I elucidate the ways in which characters step beyond familial bonds to challenge prevailing discourses of gender. More importantly, I show that transgression—in the form of incest, prostitution, illicit love affairs, body modification, self-starvation, and other corporeal acts—illuminates the extent to which these characters *need* those boundaries and limitations. In the context of the recession and the pervasive sense of displacement and "dislocation" (Lippit 2002: 2) that has resulted, transgression opens up a space for rediscovery and reorientation.

Note

1 Since the early Meiji Period (1868–1912), the Japanese masculine ideal has been characterized by the white-collared, capitalistic, and patriarchal salaryman. The turn to industrialization and modernization at the end of the nineteenth century created an environment in which capitalism and patriarchy thrived. It was not until the end of the Asia-Pacific, however, that the national push for economic prowess on the world stage thrust salaryman masculinity to the apex of Japanese conceptualizations of masculinity. While the Japanese social fabric has been and continues to be populated with other "types" of masculinities, "hegemonic" masculinity refers to the extent to which the salaryman possesses the socially, culturally, and politically ideal traits.

WORKS CITED

Allison, Ann. 2013. *Precarious Japan*. Durham: Duke University Press.
Azuma Hiroki. 2011. "Shinsai de bokutachi wa barabara ni natte shimatta" (The Disaster Broke Us Apart). *Shisōchizu beta* 2: 8–17.
Berlant, Lauren. 2007. "Slow Death (Sovereignty, Obesity, Lateral Agency)." *Critical Inquiry* 33(4): 754–780.
Berlant, Lauren. 2011. *Cruel Optimism*. Durham: Duke University Press.
Brinton, Mary. 2011. *Lost in Transition: Youth, Work, and Instability in Postindustrial Japan*. Cambridge: Cambridge University Press.

Bullock, Julia. 2010. *The Other Women's Lib: Gender and Body in Japanese Women's Fiction*. Honolulu, HI: University of Hawai'i Press.
Chakbrabarty, Dipesh. 1998. "Afterword: Revisiting the Tradition/Modernity Binary." In *Mirror of Modernity*, edited by Stephen Vlastos, 285–296. Berkeley, CA: University of California Press.
Copeland, Rebecca. 2018. "Lost in the Grottos: The Subversive Allure of Kirino Natsuo's Murder Mysteries." *Japanese Language and Literature* 52(1): 145–160.
Dasgupta, Romit. 2013. *Re-reading the Salaryman in Japan: Crafting Masculinities*. New York, NY: Routledge.
DiNitto, Rachel. 2011. "Between Literature and Subculture: Kanehara Hitomi, Media Commodification and the Desire for Agency in Post-bubble Japan" *Japan Forum* 23(4): 453–470.
Foucault, Michel. 1977. *Language, Counter-memory, Practice: Selected Essays and Interviews*. Edited by Donald F. Bouchard. Translated by Donald F. Bouchard and Sherry Simon. Ithaca, NY: Cornell University Press.
Haladyn, Julian Jason and Michael Gardiner. 2017. "Monotonous Splendour: An Introduction to Boredom Studies." In *Boredom Studies Reader: Frameworks and Perspectives*, edited by M. E. Gardiner & J. J. Haladyn, 3–17. Oxon and New York, NY: Routledge.
Iida, Yumiko. 2002. *Rethinking Identity in Modern Japan: Nationalism as Aesthetics*. New York, NY: Routledge.
Kobayashi Hideo. 1995 [1933]. *Literature of the Lost Home: Kobayashi Hideo—Literary Criticism, 1924–1939*. Translated by Paul Anderer. Stanford, CA: Stanford University Press.
Lippit, Seiji M. 2002. *Topographies of Japanese Modernism*. New York, NY: Columbia University Press.
Marra, Michael F. 2010. *Essays on Japan: Between Aesthetics and Literature*. Leiden and Boston, MA: Brill.
Matsuura Hisaki. 2007. *Kuronikuru (Chronicle)*. Tokyo: Tokyo Daigaku Shuppankai
McClintock, Anne. 1995. *Imperial Leather: Race, Gender and Sexuality in the Colonial Contest*. New York, NY: Routledge.
McLelland, Mark. 2003. "Review of *Men and Masculinities in Contemporary Japan: Dislocating the Salaryman Doxa*." *Intersections: Gender, History and Culture in the Asian Context* 9. Online at: http://intersections.anu.edu.au/issue9/mclelland_review.html [accessed 11 July 2018].
Mikals-Adachi, Eileen B. 2001. "Enchi Fumiko: Female Sexuality and the Absent Father." In *The Father-Daughter Plot: Japanese Literary Women and the Law of the Father*, edited by Rebecca L. Copeland and Esperanza Ramirez-Christensen, 194–214. Honolulu, HI: University of Hawaii Press.
Miyadai Shinji. 1998. *Owari naki nichijō o ikiro: Aum kanzen kokufuku manyuaru*. Tokyo: Chikuma shoten.
Onishi, Norimitsu. 2004. "The Saturday Profile: Just 20, She Captures Altered Japan in a Debut Novel." *The New York Times*, 27 March. Online at: http://www.nytimes.com/2004/03/27/world/the-saturday-profile-just-20-she-captures-altered-japan-in-a-debut-novel.html?mcubz=0&_r=0 [accessed 24 September 2017].
Seaman, Amanda. 2004. *Bodies of Evidence: Women, Society, and Detective Fiction in 1990s Japan*. Honolulu, HI: University of Hawai'i Press.
Ueno Chizuko. 2009. *The Modern Family in Japan: Its Rise and Fall*. Melbourne: Trans Pacific Press.

1

THE LEGACY OF TRANSGRESSION IN JAPANESE WOMEN'S FICTION

Liberation, Liberty, Lightning

Since at least the Meiji period (1868–1912), education has been considered key to Japanese national progress. The promulgation of the Imperial Rescript on Education (1890) served as a vector of imperial ideology that emphasized the importance of loyalty and obedience to the State. Amid this drive for universal education, the Ministry of Education championed *ryōsai kenbo*, a gendered discourse that espoused maternal and domestic ideals for women above all else. Women's desires and sensations were sublimated to a patriarchal agenda that demanded "good wives and wise mothers" (the literal meaning of *ryōsai kenbo*) be the linchpin in an emergent "family state" (*kazoku kokka*).[1] Under this regime, devotion to family echoed devotion to state (and by extension devotion to husband: devotion to emperor), setting in motion the virtual disappearance of women from Japanese social and political life (Itō 1982: 9). As the female body became a locus of ideological control and regulation, the narrowing of women's experiences simultaneously imbued the female body with transgressive power as both a manifestation of selfhood and an object of cultural surveillance. Transgression is "a deeply reflexive act of denial and affirmation" (Jenks 2003: 3). It reflects the perpetual struggle between the will of the individual and the conditions of her restraint. Where there is limitation, there is a will to freedom. And yet, to step beyond bounds, to challenge authority and law (indeed to transgress) is to reaffirm the conditions of contestation. This is the logic of transgression at work, the retaliation against technologies of dominance.

Almost as soon the paternalistic walls of the Meiji order were constructed, Japanese women writers began writing against them. With the heightened nationalism of the era, motherhood took on greater dimension, and the imperative to raise and nurture one's child was coded not as coercion but

DOI: 10.4324/9781003231806-2

as natural and expected. In this context, a woman who did not marry and did not have a child was seen as abnormal or aberrant—hardly a woman at all. Thus, as sociologist Ueno Chizuko (cited in Copeland 1992: 101) observes, "being a [Japanese] woman is virtually synonymous with being a mother. And there is a tendency to regard women who are not mothers as not women either." Women were expected to become dutiful wives and mothers at the expense of sexual desire, autonomy, self-actualization, and self-care. Authors responded by creating restless, contrary protagonists who questioned the order of things. Depictions of the body offered a way to push against normative traditions of female comportment and silence by cultivating a transgressive politics of opposition through themes of sex, sexuality, divorce, and violence, and even the act of writing itself.[2] These authors inaugurated a legacy of female transgression in modern Japanese literature.

As occupation-era reforms promoted greater equality for women, the residual influence of the Meiji-era *kazoku kokka* ideology evaded their efforts. While some women were able to take advantage of the new legislation, they found that life at home continued to reflect prewar ideals. To be good Japanese, women were expected to shoulder the burden of the domestic sphere, running the household as wives, and raising future subjects as mothers. The historic economic growth of the postwar era was, as Bullock (2010: 2) puts it, "underwritten by a strictly gendered division of labor that required women to take full responsibility for the domestic sphere so that their husbands could devote themselves to rebuilding the nation's economy through paid labor." On paper, women had greater options than ever before. Yet many women's lives failed to reflect these new promises. And yet, these social and economic changes did afford women greater creative expression, including access to education. Thus, the 1960s was a time marked by "discontent and oppression" for those caught between ideas of progress and the reality of stasis (Tanaka 1994: 344).

Women writers of this era shared "a profound sense of unease regarding what it meant to be a woman in Japanese society" (Bullock 2010: 2). To this end, women's literary enterprises were largely fixated on the abnormal and the contrary, themes that were oppositional to "the previously accepted norms for women's writing" (Jones 2003: 223). Women writers were searching for a "revised identity more befitting the new age. The quests on which these women embark range from self-discovery to outright rejection of social or cultural norms. The use of deviant modes of behavior seems intentional, however, and reflects a deliberate effort to defy norms or at least force readers to reconsider preconceived notions of femininity and womanhood" (Jones 2003: 224). What these authors wrote, and the explicitness with which they did, disrupted (and disturbed) the *bundan*,[3] a predominantly male and old-fashioned literary community, that was accustomed to particular conventions regarding gender, sex, and sexuality.

What follows is a brief reading of Kōno Taeko's 1961 "Yōji gari" (trans. "Toddler Hunting," 1991). The story is a meditation on the gendered implications of masochism. The historical moment of this text's production anticipated an evolving political excitement and aggressive feminist agency, affording the emergence of literature that spoke to, and even anticipated, the broader interests of progressive Japanese women in the 1960s and 1970s. Kōno and her contemporaries regularly challenged convention with stories of women behaving badly and, in doing so, contributed to a nascent feminist discourse. In this short story, as well as in others Kōno has written,[4] masochism functions as a discursive device to critique patriarchal ideology. Kōno's middle-aged protagonist, Akiko, disavows notions of marriage and motherhood, choosing instead to submit to the whims and desires of her sexually violent lover, Sasaki, though where his intentions end and hers begin is not always clear. Readers and critics at the time of publication were not accustomed to the idea of a masochistic woman. The term "masochism" itself was only gaining entry in popular vocabulary in the 1950s (Jones 2003: 430).

Although masochism was not a new motif in Japanese letters per se, Kōno's usage of it was novel. Previous literary endeavors into the realm of masochism tended to focus on men and their gleeful and self-induced demise. In the early twentieth century, Tanizaki Jun'ichirō (1886–1965) cut his teeth on stories of men yearning for punishment at the hands of beautiful women. His 1911 short story, "Shisei" (trans. "The Tattooer," 1963), culminates in the presumed destruction of the protagonist, Seikichi, who takes pleasure in his own fall. Subsequent works such as "Aoi hana" (1922; trans. "Aguri," 1963) and *Chijin no ai* (1924–25; trans. *Naomi*, 1986) feature versions of the Tanizaki hero and the woman who destroys him.

In "Toddler Hunting," Kōno inverts the paradigm and situates masochism within the history of structural violence against women. The story is one of explicit savagery. In one scene, Akiko requests that Sasaki beat her with a vinyl wash-rope. He obliges to an extreme degree and thrashes her until she is unconscious.

> As he reached for it and started doubling it up, Akiko was already begging him to use the jagged metal hooks on her - they'd make a clicking sound. It depended on what they used, but they both enjoyed the sound things made whipped against her skin. The more excited the noises made them, the more they would have to suppress their cries. That night, however, Sasaki had been especially resourceful with that length of rope, and Akiko's screams smothered out the thrashing sound
>
> (Kōno 1996: 63).

Their playtime is interrupted by a knock at the door and a curt reminder from the apartment manager to keep the noise down. It is a timely interruption because Akiko passes out and lies unconscious for nearly half an hour. Critics have often wondered why Kōno's protagonist yearns to be beaten—or worse—by men. A middle-aged woman eschewing the family unit and domesticity in favor of chains and whips betrays a number of concerns. A woman seeking a selfhood that does not revolve around motherhood unsettles the security of the family system. Moreover, her active and "perverse" sex life may pander to male fantasies of sexual domination, but it also parodies social insistence on female submissiveness and self-loathing.

What is more, in "Toddler Hunting" Kōno includes a famous scene in which a young boy is strung up and disemboweled. This scene takes the form of a dream sequence in which a disembodied woman's voice instructs the boy's father to commit these acts of violence against his child. One of the more troubling moments from the dream reads thus:

> The woman gives the order: the man cuts the cord around the child's hands. The boy drops down from the branch to the ground. Now the man pulls the purple rope until it is tight, and jerks the child's body about as if trying to get a kite to rise into the air. The little body at the end of the purple rope is smashed against the corrugated tin shack repeatedly. Every twitch on the rope brings forth pitiful, horrifying screams
>
> (Kōno 1996: 61).

Gretchen Jones has offered a nuanced interpretation of the sequence, noting, for instance, that the dream of the boy being beaten contradicts Akiko's pedophilic interest in little boys. Indeed, Akiko, who cannot have children due to illness, spends much of the text "hunting" little boys, intent on lavishing them with gifts and other affections. The dream complicates things. Furthermore, the boy's disembowelment reads like a transgression of gender: "There it is, the red blood trickling down over the child's buttocks, over his thighs. The blood is smeared over the surface of his flesh by yet more thrashes from the cane" (Kōno 1996: 61). As Jones (2000: 99) observes, in this moment of the dream the boy is feminized, and the presence of blood flowing in this manner reminds the reader of menstrual blood. In like mind, when the child's stomach splits open and his entrails spill out, Kōno evokes imagery similar to childbirth. "The child gets a few lashes on his belly, and suddenly, his stomach splits open. Intestines, an exquisitely colored rope of violet, slither out. The woman gives the order: the man cuts the cord around the child's hands. The boy drops down from the branch to the ground" (Kōno 1996: 61).

Kōno employs graphic imagery in challenging ways. Her scenes of masochism and violence remind us of the implicit violence with which women live every day, while her dream sequence asks us to think about the state of motherhood in Japan. Writes Jones (2000: 83): "The discourse of masochism, seemingly discordant with feminism, can function as a strategy that dismantles patriarchal notions of femininity as it subverts them. Kōno's masochistic aesthetic is thus an implicit commentary on gender, power, and modern Japan." Literary critics such as Jones have been interested in "Toddler Hunting" from a psychoanalytic perspective. Jones's interpretation of the story is inspired by the philosophies of Gilles Deleuze. And for good reason. Deleuze's study of masochism, which is based on his close reading of Leopold von Sacher-Masoch's *Venus in Furs* (1870), stands out as one of the most nuanced to date. A controversial novel from the late nineteenth century, *Venus in Furs* explores the complexities of the so-called perversion masochism. The text offers no substantial conclusions regarding the pursuit of pleasure through pain, telling readers that protagonist Severin is, in the end, asking for it. Since the text's publication, scholars, and clinicians have been captivated by Severin's devotion to the coldhearted and cruel Wanda. In his reading of the text, Deleuze argues that, in Jones' (2000: 84) words, "masochism is not merely a sexual urge gone awry, but rather [...] a stance adopted and maintained for a particular purpose." In other words, masochism is not just about sex. Masochism is, to him, a philosophy—"a new way of thinking and feeling and an entirely new language" (Deleuze and von Sacher-Masoch 1991: 16). In her study, Jones notes that Deleuze's interpretation of masochism affords ready application to women's fiction because it can be divorced from ideas of "perversion" and used to complicate the ways we think about institutions and ideologies governing the body. In women's texts, this is especially important because in liberating masochism from a strictly sexual context we can consider its narratological function. Masochism can be a "strategy" capable of inducing "textual pleasures" (Studlar 1994: 14; also qtd. in Jones 2000: 86).

Pleasure, of course, is central to Kōno's agenda. Akiko takes a kind of scopic pleasure in watching little boys. "She didn't know exactly when her attraction for them first surfaced, but with every passing year she found their company more intoxicating. Lately, her encounters with little boys had been intensely pleasurable" (Kōno 1996: 46–47). Early in the story, Akiko buys a shirt for the son of a coworker (she works for an opera production): "Akiko was thrilled: the shirt was a good fit and also a great success with the boy. But she couldn't resist one last shot at getting to watch him try to get himself out of it" (Kōno 1996: 52). This affection toward little boys is contrasted with an almost pathological hatred of little girls, girls who are at an age when they are vulnerable to the spell of gender differentiation.

> The more typical a girl this age, the less Akiko could bear to be near her. The pallid complexion; the rubbery flesh; the bluish shadow at the nape of the neck left by the bobbed haircut; the unnaturally high, insipid way the girl would talk; even the cut and color of her clothes. [...] She could hardly bear to look at a little girl, still less touch one
>
> (Kōno 1996: 46).

In this light, the joy Akiko takes in being beaten by Sasaki *could* be interpreted as a manifestation of self-loathing. "Akiko [...] appears to replicate traditional images of femininity while her desire to be dominated seems to indicate that she is complicit in her oppression" (Jones 2000: 106). Masochism is more complicated than this, however. Akiko, supposedly submissive in her relationship with Sasaki, "actively chooses to be beaten, and finds some degree of power in her ability to both make the choice and control it" (Jones 2000: 106). We see this agency prominently in the dream sequence, where the female voice commands the action, rendering the boy's feeble body powerless and feminized, where it, too, becomes the site of gendered violence.

Pain as a route to pleasure disturbs conventional notions of sex and sex roles, but even beyond the pain/pleasure register, masochism exposes a number of seemingly contradictory impulses and desires in other erotic binaries such as dominant/submissive, master/slave, and active/passive. Because women have historically been reduced to the latter category in each opposition, masochism offers an attractive rhetorical and textual device for Kōno. Violation is central to masochism. It fragments the body, breaking it down, waking it up. As Hal Foster (1996: 123) has written: "The violated body is often the evidentiary basis of important witnessings to truth, of necessary testimonials against power." Yet violated bodies have the potential to disrupt power structures and subvert binaries. In this sense, masochism can be read as a call for a moral moratorium in Kōno's work, a revolt against the rules governing women's uses of their own bodies in contemporary Japan.

Kōno's fiction, like that of her contemporaries, was a product of its time and, as Bullock (2010: 13) says of the work of one contemporary, Takahashi Takako (1932–2013), such writing "violated assumptions of feminine passivity, sexual innocence, maternal instinct, and marital bliss." This generation of women writers "resisted the gendered division of labor that underwrote the prosperity of the era. Their unconventional protagonists [...] forwarded a trenchant critique of the social and political order that had come to define a newly stabilized and prosperous Japanese society." The transgressive fiction of this era directly engaged the sociopolitical context and, in the process, "subvert[ed] expectations of normalcy by explicitly rejecting the culturally defined common sense of the 1960s" (Bullock 2010: 18).

In Foucault's bleak rendering, transgression is an exercise in *temporary* freedom; a flash of lightning that dissolves into darkness. He continues: "a limit could not exist if it were absolutely uncrossable and, reciprocally, transgression would be pointless if it merely crossed a limit composed of illusions and shadows." The force of Foucauldian transgression is always temporary because the boundaries of acceptability are always redrawn. It is not, however, "a victory over limits" (Foucault 1977: 35).

What do transgressive individuals ultimately desire, then? A space of limitation. Sexuality's rich transgressive possibilities, in other words, are paradoxically its limitations. Žižek (1991: lxi) contends that participation in the "unwritten obscene rules which regulate the 'inherent transgression'" is necessary for social cohesion. Members of a given community are *expected* to violate norms and customs. Following those norms and customs "to the letter" can lead to exclusion and ostracizing because "the transgressive rituals [...] actually keep [a] community together" (1991: lxi). Consider the interesting fact that Kōno and other writers of the time[5] shared a common language of textual transgression. Theirs was the kind of community of which Žižek writes—one in which the violation of norms was itself the norm.

This dynamic can be seen in Ueno Chizuko's criticism of the works of author Yoshimoto Banana (b. 1964). Banana "clearly avoids" sex in her novels, Ueno (1989) contends. Although sex is an important and complex part of daily life in Japan, Ueno states, Banana buries sexual innuendo in polite and even childish metaphors, focusing in her early popular novel, *Kitchin* (1988; trans. *Kitchen*, 1993), on the dinner table rather than the bedroom. In an odd inversion of sorts, by not writing sex into her novels, Banana is stepping out of bounds, at least according to this critic. In the novel, characters bond at the dinner table and ignore the bedroom. Ueno (1989) demands that in the novelistic realm food and fornication are one and the same. So why beat around the bush? Is Banana in the wrong, however, for choosing to eschew explicit references to sex? Ueno finds bodies eating where she expects to find them embracing. If transgression is an affront to expectation, then Banana's fondness for the "episodic refreshment" of eating is, at least for Ueno, truly transgressive (Berlant 2007: 780). This is how we arrive at "the end of transgression," through a process of naturalization that is inherent in the idea of transgression itself. Aberrant and taboo acts possess force to the extent they are and remain inappropriate. But Banana's novel illustrates the consequences of repeated literary engagement with transgression, particularly sexual transgression. The more certain motifs and themes surface in works of literature, the more such repetition compromises their transgressive efficacy.

What is lost when readers come to *expect* transgression? It is stripped of its power to violate, as what was once transgressive becomes expected. Hastings Donnan and Fiona Magowan (2009: 3) argue that "sex is a powerful mediator in transgressive contexts, since sexual encounters invoke uneasy tensions between consent, demand, resistance and reciprocity, in which elements of domination, vulnerability, risk and safety all play a part." Sex can be conceptualized as the locus of boundless impulse and possibility—as the primary manifestation of transgression. However, as Ann Sherif notes, the "rejection of heterosexual reproductive sex" is "far from a new topic in Japan" (Sherif 1999: 281). Sherif uses Ōe Kenzaburo's (b. (1935–2023)) 1964 novel *Kojinteki na taiken* (trans. *A Personal Matter*, 1969) as an example of "assertively nonreproductive sex." Drawing from Susan Napier's observations, Sherif demonstrates that Oē's novel "explores the liberating nature of 'what might be called deviant sex often involving pain and sacrifice.'" She explains that Ōe's use of sex "'is clearly linked to an almost utopian dream of connection and perfection,' or the sublime." She also mentions the novels of women writers from the 1960s as an example of a kind of transcendent sexuality in literature (1999: 281).

The transgressive novels of this cohort of women writers in the 1960s and 1970s helped to legitimate a discourse of sexual transgression in Japanese literature. In doing so, however, they also contributed to the naturalization and even expectation of sex as an avenue of political critique and inquiry (a process we could call "the mainstreaming of transgression"). Thus, by the time Banana was writing in the 1980s, the expectation was that she would use sex in a manner analogous to other women writers. This expectation is so great, in fact, that Ueno is let down by Banana's refusal to do so. In this light, I call attention to Georges Bataille's (1962: 140) warning: "If the taboo loses its force, if it is no longer believed in, transgression is impossible." For Ueno, it appears that what is taboo—what unnerves and unrests her—is the lack of a transgressive sexual politics in Banana's novel. Ueno's reaction demonstrates the extent to which transgression needs to be rethought. If transgression is the new normal, then what is truly transgressive is not resistance to the status quo but rather complicity with it.

As evinced by the close readings that begin in Chapter 3, we are in a cultural moment in which transgression has reached a saturation point. It would be shortsighted to suggest that there are no more limits to transgress. Following philosopher Jean Baudrillard, transgression as a *discursive* construct is what is under fire here, the effects of what he calls "liberation" rather than the futility of, in his words, "liberty." Liberation, he contends, is the *appearance* of sexual/political/artistic liberty, or freedom.

> The process of liberation is never innocent. It starts out from an ideology and an idealist movement in history. [...] There is an element of simplification and transparency, of the elimination of the dark continent, the dark side, the accursed share, and the coming of the reign of value: all these things are present in the Rousseauist concept of a happy destiny, a natural vocation, a "liberation"
>
> (Baudrillard 2001: 53).

Like Foucault, Baudrillard invokes the illumination of darkness. Although he does not conjure transgression, per se, Baudrillard's evocation of liberation seems dependent on similar dynamics. "Liberation" is achieved through the continual expression of agency against an established and ultimately antagonistic framework. Baudrillard (2001: 53) continues: "Liberty has succumbed to its perverse effect: liberation. In its accepted philosophical sense, liberty is an idea, and by fulfilling it, we have lost it." This is a condition of life without limits, in which limits themselves have to be reimagined. As Siobhan Holohan (2016: 81) observes: "There can be no transgression of norms, since these have long since been wiped out, and there is, as a consequence, no morality beyond the simulation of morality which is always hyper, overblown, and absurd."

Capitalism has coopted transgression as part of what Thomas Frank (1997) terms "the countercultural idea," which "holds that the paramount ailment of our society is conformity, a malady that has variously been described as over-organization, bureaucracy, homogeneity, hierarchy, logocentrism, technocracy." While Frank is not channeling Japanese society here, his words are apt. The antidote to homogeneity, in other words, is heterodoxy. Japanese women's fiction of this era was often predicated on the immediate, the instinctual, the liberated, and the libidinal. Transgression in Japanese texts is *normal*, expected, part of the experience of the literature itself. The repeated packaging of transgression as a consumer product ultimately compromises its legitimacy. Part of the story of transgression's end is here, at the site of processes of normalization and commodification. This is the topography of transgression mainstreamed: the repeated deployment of once disruptive images and themes that have lost their aims and urgency. Baudrillard's ideas of liberation hinge on the ways in which widely circulated spectacles of transgression are consumed by an eager public. In this formulation, transgression is an illusory pursuit that engages with an imaginary limit. Baudrillard would have it that this pursuit is ultimately nostalgic in scope. The chapters that follow claim that ostensibly transgressive acts disguise a quiet longing for a time now past, *a time of boundaries and limits.*

These claims are not made in a reckless fashion. Neither are they meant to suggest that all fiction from the millennial turn (see the Introduction) is animated by the inevitability of failure. My argument is specific to the six texts on which I focus. These literary works elucidate the contours of a distinct experience for members of Japan's subaltern. The texts I focus on are about the lived experiences of prostitutes, drug addicts, anorectics, bulimics, masochists—those individuals whose broken relationships with Japanese society are mediated by the body. As such, the characters in the texts I will analyze in *The End of Transgression* occupy abstract and abject positionalities. Their social vulnerability means they have nothing to leverage against hegemony and its dictates. By studying these individuals in these texts and contexts, we can come to a richer understanding of the ways in which Japanese women constitute their subjectivities and claim and reclaim expressions of agency at the level of the body.

Notes

1 *Kazoku kokka* was a term originating in the Meiji period that conceptualized the Japanese nation (*kokka*) as a family (*kazoku*). In this paradigm, the emperor was the symbolic father, and the citizenry his symbolic children.

2 If women historically constitute a subaltern group, they are denied voice. Writing disrupts patriarchal rhetoric and canonicity by offering women themselves the chance to gain authorial agency.

3 *Bundan* originally referred to a loosely defined literary group. Author Tsubouchi Shōyō (1859–1935) introduced the term in 1889 to describe the Ken'yūsha group, which, under the guidance of author Ozaki Kōyō (1868–1903), "controlled the literary page of the *Yomiuri [Newspaper]*, and even exercised a veto power over what was published by two major houses" (Keene 1999: 547). From this definition, we get a sense of the control that the *bundan* would develop over Japanese literary production in later years. "By the 1960s," Bullock (2010: 31) writes, "the term *bundan* had come to refer broadly to those with the 'power'[…] to determine the success and failure of the literary careers of aspiring authors." She goes on to call attention to how the *bundan* "restrict[ed] or shape[d] women's literary production" through unequal master-disciple relationships or the "selective […] reward[ing of] those who conformed to expectations of legibly 'feminine' writing" (2010: 31). Not all scholars agree on this view of the *bundan*, often because of different interpretations regarding the true meaning and implication of the term. Marvin Marcus (1993: 32), for example, notes the "amorphous" nature of the *bundan* as a category, but nevertheless considers it to be "virtually coterminous with the entire literate population of Japan." On the other hand, Irmela Hijiya-Kirschnereit (1996: 227) writes of "the rivalries and cliquish behavior" that underpin "the narrow world of the *bundan*." In short, *bundan* means different things to different people.

4 Bullock (2010: 83) demonstrates that in Kōno's 1969 piece, "Hone no niku" (trans. "Bone Meat," 1989), the protagonist internalizes the power imbalance of her relationship with a man. The protagonist is initially turned on by the sadomasochistic games she and the man would play at the dinner table, particularly the act of her being fed or starved at her lover's behest. Her lover's absence seems to bring the subtext of the game to the surface; for without him there to allow her to eat, she literally starves. And by the end, she sees herself as no better than the garbage he has left behind at her house.

5 Note, for example, Kurahashi Yumiko's (1935–2005) "Uchūjin" (1964; trans. "An Extraterrestrial," 1998), in which siblings discover a hermaphroditic alien in their beds and eventually escape into its "womb." In this story, the male narrator, K, wakes one morning to find an egg beside his bed. He and his sister, L, eventually break the egg open to discover a hermaphroditic alien whose genitalia appear almost in answer to their own sexual interests. The siblings initially take turns having sex with it, and then they have sex with the alien at the same time. The subtext of the story is K's secret desire to have sex with his sister, who is engaged to a man named S, and K's use of the alien's body as a substitute for that of his sister. One night K confesses his secret to L, who suggests that they escape into the alien's womb, where they have the freedom to consummate their incestuous desires, free from social persecution.

"The Extra Terrestrial" is just one of several works in which Kurahashi explores the possibilities of androgyny and hermaphroditism in a fantastic and indeed otherworldly setting. In this story, K and L explore their awareness of sexual differences through the alien's body, which develops breasts when K thinks about L's own breasts, as well as an erect penis when K expresses reverie about L's breasts. Atsuko Sakaki (1999: 168) has suggested that in Kurahashi's works, characters are sustained by their relationships with others and that her continual engagement with non-normative sexuality—such as incest and hermaphroditism in "The Extra Terrestrial," but also masturbation and partner swapping in other works—points to Kurahashi's intent to "question the romantic view of the self as an autonomous, substantive individual being."

WORKS CITED

Bataille, Georges. 1962 [1957]. *Eroticism: Death and Sensuality*. Translated by Mary Dalwood. San Francisco, CA: City Light Books.

Baudrillard, Jean. 2001. *Impossible Exchange*. Translated by Chris Turner. New York, NY: Verso.

Berlant, Lauren. 2007. "Slow Death (Sovereignty, Obesity, Lateral Agency)." *Critical Inquiry* 33(4): 754–780.

Bullock, Julia. 2010. *The Other Women's Lib: Gender and Body in Japanese Women's Fiction*. Honolulu, HI: University of Hawai'i Press.

Copeland, Rebecca. 1992. "Motherhood as Institution." *Japan Quarterly* 39(1): 101–110.

Deleuze, Gilles and Leopold von Sacher-Masoch. 1991. *Masochism: Coldness and Cruelty & Venus in Furs*. Translated by Jean McNeil and Aude Willm. New York, NY: Zone Books.

Donnan, Hastings and Fiona Magowan. 2009. "Sexual Transgression, Social Order and the Self." In *Transgressive Sex: Subversion and Control in Erotic Encounters*, edited by Hastings Donnan and Fiona Magowan, 1–24. New York, NY: Berghahn Books.

Foster, Hal. 1996. *The Return of the Real: Avant-garde at the End of the Century*. Cambridge: The MIT Press.

Foucault, Michel. 1977. *Language, Counter-memory, Practice: Selected Essays and Interviews*. Edited by Donald F. Bouchard. Translated by Donald F. Bouchard and Sherry Simon. Ithaca, NY: Cornell University Press.

Frank, Thomas. 1997. "Why Johnny Can't Dissent." In *Commodify Your Dissent: Salvos from the Baffler*, edited by Thomas Frank and Matt Weiland, 31–45. New York, NY and London: W.W. Norton & Company.

Hijiya-Kirschnereit, Irmela. 1996. *Rituals of Self-revelation: Shishōsetsu as Literary Genre and Socio-cultural Phenomenon*. Cambridge: Harvard University Press.

Holohan, Siobhan. 2016. "(A)moral Representation: The Hyper-sexual Construction of Amanda Knox." In *Transmedia Crime Stories: The Trial of Amanda Knox and Raffaele Sollecito in the Globalised Media Sphere*, edited by Lieve Gies, 69–85. New York, NY: Palgrave Macmillan.

Itō Mikiharu. 1982. *Kazoku kokkakan no jinruigaku*. Tokyo: Mineruva.

Jenks, Chris. 2003. *Transgression*. New York, NY: Routledge.

Jones, Gretchen. 2000. "Subversive Strategies: Masochism, Gender and Power in Kōno Taeko's 'Toddler Hunting.'" *East Asia* 16(4): 79–107.

Jones, Gretchen. 2003. "Sado-masochism." In *The Encyclopedia of Contemporary Japanese Culture*, edited by Sandra Buckley, 429–430. New York, NY: Routledge.

Keene, Donald. 1999. *Dawn to the West: Japanese Literature of the Modern Era*. New York, NY: Columbia University Press.

Kōno, Taeko. 1996 [1961]. "Toddler Hunting." In *"Toddler Hunting" and Other Stories*, translated by Lucy North, 45–68. New York, NY: New Directions Publishing Corporation.

Marcus, Marvin. 1993. *Paragons on the Ordinary: The Biographical Literature of Mori Ōgai*. Honolulu, HI: University of Hawai'i Press.

Sakaki, Atsuko. 1999. "(Re)Cannonizing Kurahashi Yumiko: Toward Alternative Perspectives for 'Modern' 'Japanese' 'Literature'" In *Ōe and Beyond: Fiction in Contemporary Japan*, edited by Stephen Snyder and Philip Gabriel, 153–176. Honolulu, HI: University of Hawai'i Press.

Sherif, Ann. 1999. "Japanese without Apology: Yoshimoto Banana and Healing." In *Ōe and Beyond: Fiction in Contemporary Japan*, edited by Stephen Snyder and Philip Gabriel, 278–302. Honolulu, HI: University of Hawai'i Press.

Studlar, Gaylyn. 1994. "Masochistic Performance and Female Subjectivity in 'Letter from an Unknown Woman.'" *Cinema Journal* 33(3): 35–57.
Tanaka, Kazuko. 1994. "The New Feminist Movement in Japan, 1970–1990." In *Japanese Women: New Feminist Perspectives on the Past, Present and Future*, edited by Kumiko Fujimura-Fanselowa and Atsuko Kameda, 343–352. New York, NY: The Feminist Press at SUNY.
Ueno Chizuko. 1989. "Middonaito kōru." *Asahi Shinbun*, 4 June 1989.
Žižek, Slavoj. 1991. *For They Know Not What They Do: Enjoyment as a Political Factor*. New York, NY: Verso.

2

CLASS, IDENTITY, AND RECESSION IN MILLENNIAL JAPAN

In Antonio Gramsci's (1975: 32–33) *Prison Notebooks*, he famously elaborates on the death of hegemony and the unforeseen consequences that can result, writing, "The crisis consists precisely in the fact that the old is dying and the new cannot be born; in this interregnum, morbid phenomena of the most varied kind come to pass." When dominant cultures lose their grip on the subjugated masses, he suggests, the latter will inevitably question the conditions of their own entrapment. The interregnum is a liminal space between a rejected ideology and an as-yet emergent counter-ideology, or rather, when "the great masses have become detached from traditional ideologies, they no longer believe what they previously used to believe." Gramsci's conceptualization of the interregnum deviates from and is more creative than the more standard and perhaps familiar definition as a gap between the deaths of successive sovereigns. During the interregnum, the state was accordingly vulnerable to the threat of chaos or dissent and needed to be protected, even by force, until the new order was in place. Gramsci (1975: 32) sees in this term the opportunity to address deeper social and cultural fissures that precipitate what he calls "cris[es] of authority" in which the masses lose faith in the competence of the ruling elite. Such crises catalyze rule by coercion or force, and the conditions of this authority are, in Gramsci's view, reflected in the conditions of modern life. What is old no longer works, but there is no viable replacement. And it is this hazy space that nurtures "morbid phenomena" (Gramsci 1975: 33).

Zygmunt Bauman (2000: vii) sees the present as a vacuous moment of stasis and sociocultural shillyshally. Something must change, he holds, referring to "the current *condition humana*." Echoing Gramsci, Bauman sees our present as "a time of 'interregnum'—when the old ways of doing things no longer work [… but] unlike our ancestors, we don't have a clear image of a

DOI: 10.4324/9781003231806-3

'destination' towards which we seem to be moving." This vision of the unending present has been spoken of by other scholars in the context of the collapse of modernity. There was a time when the present was fascinating when it held the optimistic promises of tomorrow. Relevant to this study are the observations of Japanese modernists such as Kon Wajirō (1888–1973) and Tosaka Jun (1900–1945), who saw in the fabric of the present "the full promise of modern life—including the hope for a better future" (Harootunian 2000: 95). Modernists probed the present to articulate a vision of the future that was always on the brink of becoming a reality. The current age that comes through in Bauman's words is also concerned with the present. It is a spectral present, idle. Although Bauman rejects labeling this impasse in "postmodern" terms—preferring instead what he calls "liquid modernity"[1]—he nevertheless identifies the breakdown of the old and the concomitant inaccessibility of the new. Liquid modernity affords continuity with the past; what is liquid spreads out, and adjusts. To this end, Bauman sees the interregnum as a temporary holding pattern. Rather than a permanent state of crisis in which the new "cannot be born," as in Gramsci's formulation, Bauman finds that the new *has yet* to be born.

In the case of Japan, when the current and sustained period of discontinuity will end is anyone's guess. This chapter establishes a context for my close readings that follow in subsequent chapters. What I call the millennial turn—roughly 1990 to 2010 (I also speak of "millennial Japan" in this light)—can be thought of as a cultural interregnum, a dead zone of sorts. Japanese social life remains very much in the grip of a crisis of progress that has altered the materiality of ordinary life. The aim here is not to delve into the minutia of Japan's long recession, about which other scholars have written at length.[2] I also do not intend to rehash at great length the political, economic, societal, and even natural disasters that converged on the Japanese beginning in the late 1980s. Much has been written on the volatility of Japan's "lost decade" (and, extending into the 2000s, the "lost decades") and the cultural forms and practices of millennial Japan. Rather, I sift through this volatility to trace the origins of the end of transgression in fiction from this era. Because the ultimate goal of this study is to illuminate a regressive shift in women's writings from the millennial turn, this chapter indexes key developments in the continuing attrition of Japanese cultural norms from the early 1990s. In response to those developments, this chapter shows, a conservative social impulse took hold across Japanese social life. If an interregnum is defined by the haze of liminality, the social incoherence that settled over the Japanese in the 1990s has yet to dissolve. The regressive trends in this literature paradoxically offer a way out of the impasse by directing literary characters back to a version of Japanese life before the cultural splintering that has, in the years since the recession, defined contemporary Japan. In other words, this chapter will show that the 1990s can be conceptualized as an interregnum, as the interval between the end of postwar affluence and a coherent sense of Japanese national identity and the beginning of an era of renewed interest in ways of living defined by pre-recession cultural hegemony.

The "lost" 1990s begin with the death of Emperor Hirohito in January 1989. The period of public mourning generated by Hirohito's death was an homage to the emperor and his legacy, as well as—in retrospect—a time of mourning for an era of cultural and economic prosperity. The crisis of capitalist progress that climaxed in the late 1980s and led to Japan's continuing recession coincided with the emperor's passing. Marilyn Ivy (2006: 195) calls attention to the ways in which "the recession … stops us by its forceful disclosure of the abnormal status of the Japanese nation-state." For Ivy, what is "abnormal" has to do with the primacy of the economy in postwar Japanese culture. The unique conditions of Japan's postwar recovery—namely the "U.S.-imposed constitution and [the] forever-symbolic emperor"—robbed the nation-state of important avenues of subjectivity formation (Ivy 2006: 195). As a result, "the economic miracle would…function as the stand-in for Japan" (Ivy 2006: 195). When the economic bubble burst in the early 1990s, following on the heels of the emperor's death, the perverse fantasy of postwar life fully disclosed itself. Japanese social life had, since the end of the war, been shaped by and for economic recovery followed by economic greatness. The result was a single-minded devotion on the part of citizens to "ever-proliferating consumer signifiers" (Ivy 2006: 195). This worked for a time, after which "a latent sense of every day desperation" set in among a populace that was suddenly without a defining frame (Ivy 2006: 196). The recession compounded the void left by Hirohito's empty chair. Certainly not *all* Japanese mourned his passing with intensity and passion. Younger generations in particular were not as effectively bound to his legacy as those who lived through the war and those who witnessed the emergence, decay, and death of a human Hirohito.

In "The Day the Emperor Spoke in a Human Voice" (1995), author Ōe Kenzaburō (b. 1935) captures the opacity of the emperor's existence for young, rural Japanese following the war. Ōe's first-person protagonist recalls gathering around a radio to listen to Hirohito deliver the news of the nation's defeat in his *gyokuon hōsō* (jewel voice broadcast), which was the first time most Japanese had ever heard the emperor's voice:

> After a dazed silence following the broadcast, the adults tried without confidence to decipher the Emperor's words: the war is over—Japan has been defeated—you must now endure your suffering and survive. Some had different interpretations, but were unable to assert them with any conviction. The radio's owner put the precious device away inside the house and saw his guests to the door; the people who had been standing in the garden went their separate ways, mostly in silence. But among the children,

> there were a few with the rebellious courage to imitate the Emperor's voice: bearing the unbearable, enduring the unendurable. The children lifted their voices in laughter and then fled the angry voices of the adults who emerged from the house to yell at them. In truth, they were running in fear of their own laughter. I was among them. But I didn't return home: I went down to the river, took off my clothes in the bamboo grove and submerged my body in the inlet
>
> (1995).

The children's innocence speaks to an affective dissonance that takes the form of playful mockery of a previously infallible figure, to the irritation of the town's adults, who are in the grips of ontological shock. This passage concludes with the narrator's trip to the local watering hole, which reads as a casual moment of renewal and cleansing, a starting over. If the contents of the emperor's four-minute broadcast represented the end of one chapter in Japanese history, his death similarly brought to a close much of what his legacy stood for.

If Ōe's grade-school narrator expresses consternation regarding the figure of the emperor, how far removed from him must later generations have felt? Those who came of age in the decades of postwar recovery knew the emperor only in his abstract symbolic role. Accordingly, they may not have felt emotionally invested in what he stood for and what his passing symbolized for Japanese cultural history. But they were certainly affected by the economic despair his death seemingly foreshadowed. In this light, author Kanehara Hitomi (cited in Onishi 2004), the subject of Chapter 3, has this to say regarding a worldview shaped by recession and stagnation: "Since I was born, I've never experienced a time of prosperity." Born in the early 1980s, Kanehara was of the first generation to grow up in a Japan bereft of its symbolic and cultural core. Gone were those facets of Japanese social life that had given order to the daily lives of so many Japanese for so long: even if, after the war, young Japanese did not identify with the emperor's symbolic position, they had certainly been enthralled in the culture of capitalism that came to structure postwar Japanese identity as much as—if not more than—Hirohito had in the prewar decades. Andrea Arai (2016: 40) reflects on this generational divide: "[Y]oung Japanese [...] have little connection with the twentieth-century past of their parents and grandparents. This is a source of serious concern to older generations. Those raised prior to recessionary times hardly recognize the young who inhabit them." This is a Japan eclipsed by the conditions and pressures of neo-liberalism (restructuring, privatization, and increased competition between citizens under the guise of free-market independence), which has rendered "unavailable and unrecognizable" a social landscape that, rightly or wrongly, had once seemed so full of promise (Arai 2016: 40).

Tomiko Yoda (2006a: 16) warns us not to see Japan's "lost decade" solely as a cultural and economic dead zone, and she further argues against reading the recession as the breakdown of something unique and uniquely flawed in Japanese subjectivity. There is a tendency to see Japan's economic collapse in myopic terms, divorced from the ebbs and flows of global markets and economic systems. What makes the Japanese experience distinct is not the failing of the economy but rather what this failure meant for the Japanese. The importance of the economy to postwar Japanese ignited a process in which, by the millennial turn, the economy was Japan, Japan was the economy, and participation in the hyper-consumerist culture of economic vitality was inherent to being Japanese.

Not that long ago, consumerism was aligned in the Japanese public consciousness with a cultural mindset antithetical to Japan. Harry Harootunian (2000: 49) has written at length on the consumeristic processes in modern Japan, drawing attention to Japanese intellectuals who, in the famed symposium of 1942 to "overcome modernity" (*kindai no chōkoku*), argued that "Americanism" was responsible for "the installation of a mass culture (especially consumption) in Japan and elsewhere after World War I." To these intellectuals, "Japanese culture was … collapsing into valueless mediocrity, shallowness, and triviality" under the weight of Americanism (Harootunian 2000: 49). This 1942 symposium was inspired by the notion among its attendees that modernity had eroded Japanese subjectivity. Japanese social and spiritual life had been compromised, and it was of paramount importance to "overcome" modernity and restore an authentic experience of Japanese consciousness; to "overcome" modernity was to overturn the rules of capitalism and imperialism that had been imposed by a Western world order.

There is a long legacy of "top down" consumer culture in Japan. The symposium's concern with the perverse underbelly of a foreign-imposed consumer culture was, according to Harootunian, a recasting of arguments from the late nineteenth century: "Americanism was simply a more recent manifestation and reminder of Meiji *bunmei kaika*—the period of 'civilization and enlightenment' of the 1870s and 1880s when the Japanese embarked upon importing the material and technological trappings of a modern life. Since that time, the image of Meiji had become a trope for superficiality …" (Harootunian 2000: 50). Maruyama Masao (1947: 128) has argued that the "philosophy of material culture" was among the first aspects of European culture imported to Japan. The same cultural climate that gave rise to the slogan "civilization and enlightenment" (*bunmei kaika*)—bringing with it the imperative to acquire a consumer-oriented lifestyle—also nurtured the seeds of war and imperial conquest (*fukoku kyōhei*) that would eventually lead, in 1945, to the destruction of Japanese life. We can thus graft the experiment of empire onto the Japanese experience of consumerism. Both processes reoriented Japanese daily life. Although the "overcoming modernity" symposium famously fell short of offering concrete solutions to any of the problems it attempted to address, it succeeded in conceptualizing "modernity" as a moment that had passed. War was the crest of "the 'modern thing'" that, in the years following the symposium, brought down Japan (Harootunian 2000: 35).

The symposium argued that the key to restoring a Japanese way of life was finding a way to move past all that modernity represented. The solution was to retreat into the past in search of a lost Japanese essence (Harootunian 2000: 94). The haphazard experience of modernity that typified Japanese social life from the Meiji period could be weathered by the purposeful construction of continuity with the past. But this "memory of a past time was the invention of the present" according to Harootunian. As evidence, he points to the belief among "thinkers" following the Meiji period that the encroachment of "civilization" on the Japanese way of life in the late nineteenth and early twentieth centuries precipitated a fragmentation of a unified national culture and consciousness. By the mid-century, the idea of an unspoiled past had become a repository of Japanese nationality that was immune from the potential complications of modernity; the past could be returned to or envisioned as a reminder of who and what the Japanese used to be.

But overcoming modernity was not possible. The ascent of the cultural position of consumerism alone betrays the extent to which the Japanese popular consciousness would ultimately be overwhelmed by the modern. Less than a generation separated the widespread notion that consumerism was a foreign-born imposition from materialist accumulation becoming an ingrained cultural imperative. From the 1950s through the early 1980s, consumption and accumulation were life's refrain for white-collar Japanese. The unprecedented and unexpected growth of the postwar economy gave rise to *shōhi kakumei*—"consumer revolution"—and it would be the defining economic ideology until the mid-1970s, when the period of high-economic growth ended.

Hiroko Takeda (2011: 822) argues that there were two cultural trends from the 1970s that emphasize the prominence of consumption. The first was an advertising campaign that appeared in department stores nationwide: *jibun, shinhakken*—"myself, a new discovery." Ueno Chizuko (1998: 189) reads the slogan optimistically, as an attempt on the part of the advertisers "to make people realize how human beings [...] could make the impossible possible." Ueno refers specifically to a Seibu Group advertisement in which a child is submerged in a swimming pool. Ironically, perhaps, the child has no clothes on. We see innocence here in the figure of the unclothed child whose exposed body seemingly has little to do with the consumption practices represented by the Seibu Group. I would tend to see this advertisement as an evocation of what we could call the "infantile capitalist," a future consumer whose body is a blank slate to be cloaked and adorned according to the rules of the new era of consumption, in which even children can participate. With these thoughts in mind, I follow Takeda's (2011: 822) understanding of the ad: "individual consumption patterns [are] an index representing identities."

The second trend Takeda references speaks to the same cultural space of the young consumer: the success of Tanaka Yasuo's (b. 1956) 1981 novel *Nantonaku, kurisutaru* (trans. *Somehow, Crystal*, 2019). Written while he was still a student at elite Hitotsubashi University, Tanaka's novel chronicles two weeks in the life of part-time model Yuri. It also contains an elaborate glossary of over 400 footnotes explaining the various brand names she sports and posh shopping districts she frequents, in order to help readers cultivate their own tastes and collective sense of style vis-à-vis her own. Even today the book invites controversy, both as a work of literature (because critics contend that it is not one) and as proof of the cultural primacy of capitalism and binge consumption. Despite its "complete critical dismissal," the text won several major literary awards on the strength of the glossary alone (Field 1989: 170). To this effect, one could assert that the novel is no more than a collection of nouns strung together by ill-formed and uninteresting sentences.

To some critics, this manifestation of emptiness reflected a larger cultural situation that Tomiko Yoda (2006a: 34) refers to as "Empty Japan"; consumer-based identities were the pinnacle of "a peculiar brand of modernity that developed in Japan." Yoda (2006a: 34) writes: "Many imagined that Japan, liberated from the telos of modernization that for long functioned as its structural and structuring lack, had become a posthistoric nation." We have already seen how the problem of history occupied the minds of thinkers of the 1940s who devoted their intellectual energies to finding ways of overcoming modernity. The cultural environment that nurtured the success of *Somehow, Crystal* was ostensibly evidence that modernity had indeed been overcome—all of history had been overcome, in fact. Whereas spiritual emptiness was of grave concern for prior generations, emptiness was, in the context of a materially affluent Japan, cause for celebration. The void left by history could be filled with consumer goods while at the same time extolled as proof of Japan's mastery of contemporary living.

In this way, the rise of consumer-based identity in Japan was matched by intellectual interest in postmodern discourse in the 1980s. If *Somehow, Crystal* was worth anything as a cultural text, its value was in giving shape to an economy of pastiche and superficiality. In the text, identities are constructed first and foremost from style, affording permeable memberships in a variety of substance-less clubs. Perhaps unsurprisingly, intellectuals took up the call for postmodernity in light of this celebration of the surface. Yumiko Iida (2002: 202) notes that "this relative lack of interiority [...] has made Japanese society appear to be, to many observers, the most 'advanced' among the industrialized nations, and particularly when it comes to discussion of things 'postmodern.'" *Somehow, Crystal* (about which I say more in Chapter 4) taps into the postmodern topography of Japan. Yet the text goes further, aligning spending power and the desire for material goods with Japanese identity. This is accomplished in the text through the role of Eurasian model Nao, who, in the eyes of protagonist Yuri, models to showcase her non-Japanese identity: "Modeling as a profession suits her. That's because if you model you don't need to worry about your identity." In contrast, Yuri works because she likes the money and "want[s] to 'live a life that somehow [feels] good.'" Here, then, as Norma Field's treatment of the book also reveals, Japaneseness and consumption go hand-in-hand. Specifically, brand-name goods speak to the experience of being Japanese. As the character Masataka explains: "I guess in the end you have to say that we have no resistance to brand names. Our generation. Maybe it's not just our generation, maybe it's all Japanese."

Brand-name savvy, for materialistic Japanese, is "a kind of linguistic island, separated from everyone else" (Jameson 1985: 5). Fredric Jameson identifies exclusivity, pluralism, and fragmentation as key components of this experience. He sees the appearance of pastiche—the hodgepodge manufacturing of lives according to individual styles—as important. Pastiche, Jameson (1998: 5) says, is parody without satire, irony, or humor: it is a "stylistic mask" lacking the political impulse of parody. This is the sartorial impulse driving *Somehow, Crystal*. These characters, after all, are little more than designer clothes. Furthermore, modeling—the profession of choice in this "somehow" world—brings together clothing and vacancy; the model herself is a clothes hanger, a mannequin, window dressing. Make no mistake, the text can be self-referential at times, but it lacks political and critical value, as academic intervention into the text has shown. In this way, it is emblematic of the ascent of pastiche in a Japanese cultural framework that reflects postmodern sentiments.

Perhaps unsurprisingly, the crash of the Japanese economy rendered postmodern discourse largely irrelevant among scholars who until this crisis enjoyed envisioning Japan as a postmodern playground. Karatani Kōjin suggested that by the early 1990s this discourse had run its course. While Karatani contributed to the rise of interest in the postmodern with the publication of his *Nihon kindai bungaku no kigen* (1980; trans. *Origins of Modern Japanese Literature*, 1993), he simultaneously argues that processes of deconstruction were not applicable to Japan, because Japan had never been "constructed" to begin with. More specifically, Karatani argues that Japan is representative of—to use Marilyn Ivy's words (1989: 40)—an "anti-constructed construction." According to Karatani (1989: 271), "the 'subject'" that is under threat in postmodern thought "has never existed in Japan." Karatani is not the only scholar to insist on the division between Japan and the rest of the world or to see in the present specters of the past.

The crisis of the 1990s created renewed interest in how things used to be—or at least how they were imagined to be. The collapse of the economy brought to the fore the dangers of what, in the prior decade, had been cause for intellectual celebration. As Yoda (2006a: 49) explains: "The return to modern...

struggles against the inertia generated by the fait accompli telos of global capitalism—the market and its self-regulating mechanism as the solution to all problems. [...] It is the terrifying prospect of disappearance [...] that calls for the apparition of the modern today." In other words, the world of *Somehow, Crystal*, a product of 1980s runaway consumerism, had lost its charm by the 1990s. Japan in the 1990s was not postmodern per se, but something else entirely, an entity betrayed by its own imperatives toward global prestige.

There was nothing fun, in fact, about the 1990s. While the recession stands out as *the* event that structured the decade and recalibrated the place of consumer capitalism within the Japanese social fabric, this was but one event that seemed to symbolize the gravity of national misdirection. Hirohito's death was the literal and figurative end of a particular era of Japanese life that gave way to nothing in particular. The 1990s was thus an interregnum-like period of stasis, liminality, and confusion for many Japanese that generated the need for serious national reflection. Even though it was the older generations who lost their symbolic father, those growing up in this time of uncertainty were characterized as "lost." Young people dominated headlines with antics and behaviors that seemed out of place and out of sorts.

High school girls were the subject of much fanfare through sensationalistic reports of "compensated dating" (*enjo kōsai*), transactional activities between (older) men and teenage girls predicated on the exchange of "time" for cash or designer goods. These reports were largely overblown, and data compiled on the subject inaccurate and misleading (Kinsella 2014: 29–30). Nonetheless, the media was eager to illuminate the supposedly seedy underbelly of Japanese society; readers, too, were invested in consuming titillating narratives of the moral ambivalence and turpitude of teenage girls. Sharon Kinsella's study *Schoolgirls, Money and Rebellion in Japan* analyzes the panic that arose in the wake of these reports, particularly from 1996 to 1998. Girls involved in compensated dating, she says, were offered up in the press as "materialistic, delinquent, militant, or vengeful," and their activities were regarded as a symptom of the moral decay of Japan's youth (Kinsella 2014: 20). Japanese society has long maligned women who demonstrate interest in material goods. Historically deemed "selfish," women who shop occupy a discursive space opposite of the self-sacrificing housewife of conservative family-oriented social ideology.

It is hard not to see this negative focus on the "materialism" of schoolgirls in light of the celebration of middle-class snobbery depicted in *Somehow, Crystal*. Consumerism was the driving force behind the so-called economic miracle of the 1970s, and the transition from necessity-driven consumption to lifestyle consumption was indeed cause for celebration as a demonstration of how far the Japanese had come. Women were afforded unusual space for financial agency, and those who participated in the consumer economy were referred to as members of the "Hanako tribe," or *Hanako-zoku*, a name derived from the fashion-forward magazine popular with trendy and upwardly mobile women.

In this way, the story of the affluent 1980s is one of easy money and far-reaching economic homogeneity among the rapidly expanding middle class, and even women were allowed to participate. In this climate, why not spend?

However, and of course, the new recessionary climate of the 1990s made the 1980s levels of spending far more difficult. The social imperative to accumulate goods and display wealth did not adjust with the times, and some women found that the street value of their bodies afforded participation in an otherwise exclusive domain of materialist privilege. Indeed, we might wonder that the "materialism" of schoolgirls was cause for concern because of the *avenues* through which they acquired goods rather than the acquisition of goods themselves. If selfishness was a trait of female degeneracy, lax sexual morals were even more so. In this way, *enjo kōsai* symbolized the primacy of consumerism in recessionary Japan while simultaneously positioning the female body as a site of nonreproductive sexual activity. This activity seemingly represented the broader repositioning of female subjectivity at the end of the millennium.

To Iida, compensated dating was an act of survival for those who participated. In an era of free-floating and empty signifiers, the performance of the teenage prostitute constituted what Iida (2002: 232) calls an "imagined identity"—membership in a subcultural tribe that offered a semblance of belonging. The recessionary turn stripped Japanese social life of the hegemony of its institutions. Academic credentialism, corporatism, and family life had been the cornerstones of the postwar experience, but the recession exposed fault lines in the flimsy infrastructure of this model of living. Corporate life—defined by long hours in exchange for financial security and company loyalty—lost its luster when citizens realized that devotion to one's company offered no guarantees. School, too, had long been a place of antagonism and pressure, but it was considered necessary to set oneself apart from others (*gakureki shakai*). Those with the best test scores got into the best schools, after which they were offered the best jobs. Prior to the recession, the common belief was that success in school almost guaranteed employment in a reputable firm and a lifetime of financial stability. Financial stability led to personal stability and the accumulation of wealth. However, as the recession dragged on, many became convinced that Japanese capitalistic impulses were to blame for the collapse of the economy and, by extension, the collapse of familial relations. In this context, compensated dating offered an escape and a means of oppositional identity-making for teenagers with nowhere else to turn.

This discourse of derailed teenage sexuality was part of a larger concern with adolescent femaleness in general as a signifier for the postmodern Japanese experience. The empty pursuit of capitalist accumulation at the core of the compensated dating experience was, to some, endemic of "empty" Japan. According to Brian Bergstrom, the grafting of the girl onto Japanese selfhood was "less about girls themselves [...] than about the apparent weakness or immaturity of the [...] Japanese national subject" (2011: 33). To be sure, contemporary "*shōjo* theory" (Bergstrom 2011: 33) unfolds at the confluence of subjectivity, capitalism, and sexuality. Bergstrom (2011: 34) demonstrates that girlhood (*shōjo* subjectivity) in Japanese social life is often equated to emptiness and lack: "lack of maturity, meaning, narrative, identity, history, value, productivity [...] you name it, *shōjo* lack it." *Shōjo* signify the rejection of norms, even "a strategy for escape" (Bergstrom 2011: 34). As a symptom of contemporary Japanese social life, the *shōjo* stands for indulgence and epistemological freedom. This is fine, cultural critic Ōtsuka Eiji writes, until this life mode becomes that by which Japanese identify. He contends (cited in Bergstrom 2011: 33):

> The Japanese are no longer producers. Our existence consists solely of the distribution and consumption of "things" brought to us from elsewhere, "things" with which we play. Nor are these "things" actually tangible, but are instead only signs without direct utility in life. None of what we typically purchase would, were we deprived of it, be a matter of life or death. These "things" are continually converted into signs without substance, signs such as information, stocks, or land. What name are we to give this life of ours today? The name is *shōjo*.

Ōtsuka describes a world circumscribed by accumulation and surfeit. It is a world ruled by the logic of the *shōjo* and her taste for nonconformity.

Compensated dating fit perfectly within the dynamics of this milieu. If young women sought out an "imagined identity," to quote from Iida above, then that identity was one hemmed in by lack. These were teenagers who exploited their positionality as nonentities. That is, *shōjo*, "detached from the productive economy of heterosexual reproduction" (Treat 1996: 364), have been conceptualized as occupying a liminal space that affords the emergence of a kind of marauding sexuality. This sexuality is neither defined by domesticity on the one hand nor maternity on the other. It is a sexuality that can be sold to the highest bidder simply because there is no reason not to. These were individuals who found an expression of agency through their bodies.[3] In so doing, they brought to the fore discussions of femaleness, sexuality, and subjectivity.

Unsurprisingly, Japan's economic crisis also became a crisis of Japanese masculinity. Two violent acts particularly stand out as defining moments in the reorientation of millennial masculinity. First, between 1988 and 1989, twenty-two-year-old Miyazaki Tsutomu committed a series of unsettling murders. Less than ten years later, fourteen-year-old Shōnen A (or "Young Man A"), as he was referred to in the press, attacked several young girls (killing one) and decapitated an elementary school student. Both events set in motion social reflections on the trajectory of Japanese male subjectivity.

Miyazaki's highly publicized arrest brought into focus a previously closeted discourse surrounding *otaku* superfans and manga/anime aficionados. The term *otaku* has gained cultural capital in Japan and beyond in recent years, but in the late 1980s *otaku* were widely considered to be awkward and perverse "database animals" (to use Azuma Hiroki's famous phrase) (2009) with intricate, unrivaled knowledge of the animation universe. Miyazaki was accused of being a sexual deviant who collected disturbing anime in which women and girls are violently murdered. Miyazaki's arrest inundated the public with details about the curious lifestyle of anime fans, and pictures of his bedroom—with floor-to-ceiling stacks of pornographic manga and anime—were widely circulated and consumed by a morbidly fascinated public. Miyazaki's arrest caused a moral panic among a population who interpreted the acts of this individual as representative of most self-identifying *otaku*. The term *otaku-zoku*, or *otaku* tribe, emerged as a way to classify young Japanese men who ostensibly felt more at home in the two-dimensional world of animation than in a world in which they were marginalized and, due to Miyazaki's crimes, looked down upon and even feared.

There is some affinity between the "tribal" mentality of young women engaging in compensated dating and that of *otaku*. The vacuous 1990s left many young people with few options for identity formation, and these two groups of Japanese, at least, found refuge through alternative means. It is not a coincidence that the emergence of a tribal mentality among young Japanese coincided with the dissolution of traditional badges of identification. Another source of similarity between these two groups is the panic that followed from media coverage. Kinsella (2014: 129) notes that "the sense that this unsociable otaku generation was multiplying and threatening to take over the whole of society was strong." She goes on to quote Otsuka Eiji, who proclaimed: "It might sound terrible, but there are over 100,000 people with the same past time as [Miyazaki Tsutomu]" (Kinsella 2014: 129). The underlying concerns over both groups were the polyvalent disappearance of Japan's youth, the erosion of any sense of moral or ethical wherewithal, and the physical dissolution of individuals into dysfunctional and self-centered tribes. This is indeed the story of millennial Japan—the search for a sense of place—*ba*.

Perhaps the best example of the individual's displacement is the second crisis of masculinity that occurred in the mid-1990s. When fourteen-year-old Shōnen A left the head of ten-year-old Hase Jun on the grounds of his junior high school (with a crudely written note stuffed in Hase's mouth), the nation reached the point of exasperation. "Let the games begin," the note read. This was the first of a series of notes that Shōnen A, calling himself Sakakibara Seitō, would send to media outlets ranting about the Japanese education system, which he blamed for reducing him to a specter of his former self. "I haven't forgotten [...] the revenge toward 'compulsory education' [...] which made me a person of transparent existence, nor the society which gave birth to 'compulsory education'" (qtd. in Ivy 2006: 205). Ivy (2006: 206) notes Shōnen A's warped conceptualization of human beings as fragile "things" that can be "broken" (*kowasu*) has been interpreted as an attempt to fill the "internal void" that haunted him so (Iida 2002: 206). Shōnen A's words struck a sympathetic chord with his peers, who also felt victimized by the educational system. Citing a reporter from the *Asahi Shinbun*, Shoko Yoneyama (2012: 4) reflects that given the state of educational life in Japan, "it was only a matter of time before somebody" committed a crime of such magnitude. Shōnen A's complaints about his "transient existence" also rang true to others in his age group (Yoneyama 2012: 4). It would not be an exaggeration, in fact, to suggest that Shōnen A's words resonated with many Japanese who were engaged in their own battles against erasure and displacement.

Beyond these recognizable concerns regarding school and subjectivity (not to speak of the magnitude of Shōnen A's crimes), there is much to be said about the agent behind them. That a fourteen-year-old boy would go to such extremes to act out his displeasure with a flawed social system certainly would have raised concerns about the well-being of Japan's young men. In line with the supposedly introverted, dysfunctional, and primarily male *otaku*, Shōnen A's actions manifest a crisis of masculinity in which Japanese males were unable to cope with emotional or psychological setbacks. The conditions of millennial Japan afforded some the chance to escape into distinct subcultural worlds where they did not have to engage with the systemic crises facing the nation, where they could slip away from "the work/production/masculinity nexus" (Dasgupta 2013: 159). Critics suggest that this is what *otaku* were able to do. However, Shōnen A failed in creating for himself a sustainable alternative world. Between the harmlessness of animation fans in general and the specific, harmful actions of Shōnen A, we can index the efforts some Japanese males took to construct alternative ways of living. One wonders if the source of Shōnen A's failure was his insistence in acting alone. In a time of isolation and displacement—a time during which other young Japanese were finding ways to connect with each other—Shōnen A was ever the loner.

It is somewhat ironic that given the extent to which recessionary Japan was reshaped by a neoliberal discourse of individuality and freedom, too much unwelcome freedom was detrimental. Returning for a moment to the discussion that begins this chapter, neoliberalism nurtures an interregnum: "[I]t thrives on the borders between the known and the unknown, the possible and the (yet) impossible" (Büscher 2013: 10; qtd in Arai 2016: 60). The Japanese were relatively late in their adoption of neoliberal policies, but the effects of global neoliberal capitalism infiltrated the Japanese economy by the 1980s and portended the collapse of "the Japanese style": ever resistant to the free market and the rise of self-determination and lifestyle. Anne Aronson (2015: 39) explains, "Neoliberalism offers a more extensive range of lifestyle choices and rewards those with individual ambitions. This increase in lifestyle possibilities as well as freedom comes at the expense of stability and security, cornerstones of the Japanese economic miracle." Remember that Tanaka Yasuo's *Somehow, Crystal* was a veritable celebration of lifestyle. Designer goods and wealth go hand-in-hand in the novel, as Yuri and Nao compete to see who the most successful embodiment of the new lifestyle era can be.

Although we tend to read *Somehow, Crystal* through a postmodern lens (advocating as it does superficiality, surface, and excess), the novel also subtly reflects the new importance of economic individuality that began taking root during the 1980s. This is not to say that ideologies of self-reliance were absent from the Japanese sociocultural landscape prior to this time. Modern Japanese history unfolded alongside such ideologies, in fact, packaged in the Meiji-era slogan *risshin shusse*, or public and personal advancement. As an ideal life mode, *risshin shusse* was tied closely to state ambitions: personal success means contributing to the betterment of Japanese society. As James Fujii (1993: 94) states, however, citing scholar Maeda Ai, by the early 1900s ambitions for material success gradually eroded the connection between self and state-inspired work ethic and sacrifice. As we have seen, 1980s Japan almost drips with self-indulgent material glamour. Neoliberalism inaugurated a number of sweeping structural changes to elevate the individual, often at the expense of his or her wellbeing.

In "The Temporality of No Hope," Hirokazu Miyazaki eloquently explains the tenuous place of the individual in Japanese neoliberal thought. Drawing attention to "the pervasive celebration by the government as well as by the media of the neoliberal ideal of 'strong individuals' (*tsuyoi kojin*) ready to take risks (*risuku*) while taking responsibilities for their own risk-taking action (*jiko sekinin*)," Miyazaki (2010: 239) says that intellectual concern in recent decades has focused on Japanese youth as the site of social anxiety-related "phenomena" such as young Japanese refusing to leave their homes and/or bedrooms (*hikikomori*); rampant disinterest in or inability to acquire full-time jobs or embrace strategies of upward mobility (NEET/Freeter); and the preference among some young people to eschew marriage and long-term romantic attachments in favor of depending financially on parents (known pejoratively as "parasite singles"). Here, again, we see the grouping of young Japanese into a variety of malformed segments, or reactive cliques, that emerged as a response to recession and the conditions of neoliberal life.

Scholars see these cliques or groups as a symptom of the loss of hope (Miyazaki 2010: 239). As the recession has dragged on, "hope"—or its absence—has emerged as a buzzword of the times. In 2004, the aforementioned Yamada published a study called *Kibō kakusa shakai: "makegumi" no zetsubōkan ga Nihon o hikisaku* (The Hope Disparity Society: The "Losers" Whose Despair is Tearing Japan Apart), in which he argues that hope is not unattainable per se, but rather available only to the socioeconomic elite. Those without financial security—that is, the majority of the population—are Japan's "losers" who are bringing the country down (*makegumi*). This discourse of losers and winners has become prominent in the past several decades.

Recessionary Japan splintered young Japanese from community, each other, and their own sense of selves. The recession encouraged the ascent of the individual but did not provide the individual with the affective resources necessary to succeed. In the following chapters, we will see the emergence of transgression as a claim to individuality. At the same time, transgression in these texts is a manifestation of resistance to Japanese hegemony, or what is left of it. Literary protagonists rebel against expectations, aware that the structures of society are crumbling. Yet we will also see the instability of transgression and the consequences of a kind of youthful myopia on the part of young Japanese who come gradually to the realization that, as individuals, they cannot navigate the vicissitudes of the recessionary landscape alone—that hegemony, in this context, constitutes the lesser of two evils. We will see the disappearance of the community as well as its re-emergence.

Given the symbolic and metaphoric importance of young Japanese as "yardsticks of peril," to use Arai's (2016: 89) words, the close readings that follow will graft social and cultural anxieties regarding the problem of the static present and unknown future onto depictions of teenagers and early-twentysomethings. Arai (2016: 2) conceptualizes recessionary Japan in terms of "the child problem," a discourse that emerged in the 1990s to describe the cost of recessionary life on Japanese citizens. The Shōnen A murder in particular, she writes, was capitalized on by the media and portrayed the villainous actions of a once "ordinary child" (Arai 2016: 4). While the reality of Shōnen A was never ordinary, in the sense of emotional and psychological stability, this hardly mattered. As Arai explains, "strangeness" was an apt interpretive lens through which to view recessionary Japan. Because the child stands for "the modern subjects' desire for certainty," while also representing the complexities and contradictions of contemporary Japanese society, a strange child is the embodiment of a strange temporal moment in Japanese cultural history (Arai 2016: 3–4). In addition, she writes, "In this recessionary time, the adult no longer represents a full or completed time of development. The representation of the adult as the instructor has disappeared" (Arai 2006: 141). It is as though adolescence is its own interregnum; there is nothing for adolescence to give way to. At the same time, the disappearance of adulthood as a representational goal is a recurrent motif, for the fiction analyzed in the pages that follow is almost entirely lacking in authority figures.

Elsewhere, Arai draws attention to what she sees as a mass cultural fascination surrounding popular representations of youth gone wild. She points to two examples specifically: San, the feral heroine of Miyazaki Hayao's 1997 film *Mononoke hime* (Princess Mononoke), and media portrayals of Shōnen A. Arai (2006: 216) situates both the unprecedented success of *Princess Mononoke* and the large-scale public fascination with grim news reports of Shōnen A's crimes within a cultural moment preoccupied with the "collapse of the classroom" (*gakkyū hōkai*) and the psychological unraveling of Japan's young people (codified in the slogan *kodomo ga hen da*, or in Arai's translation, "children are turning strange"). These divergent portrayals of wild children—San in the untamed sense, Shōnen A in the "repellent" sense (Arai 2006: 221)—"became the site of a newly intensified nexus of social anxiety" concerning the fate of Japanese young people on the eve of the millennium (Arai 2006: 216). Arai points out that social anxiety over the collapse of the classroom bled into anxieties over the collapse of the family, as seen in the uneasy portrayals of young people dividing themselves up into distinct tribes. In the wake of Shōnen A's arrest, a psychological discourse of blame emerged that fixated on the family as the locus of failure (Arai 2016: 50). Some psychologists initiated a campaign of "mother bashing" against Shōnen A's mother, who in their eyes had been too concerned with her son's education, ignoring the hegemonic importance of education in the lives of most middle-class Japanese. The social confusion caused by the Shōnen A murder inaugurated a moment of cultural reflection in which his actions (regardless of the state of his mental health, which was widely debated in public) "mirror[ed] the immanent problems of contemporary Japan: a fragmented, disembodied, and claustrophobic subjectivity, whose desperate attempts to recover have reached a point of violent explosion" (Iida 2002: 243).

The refrain in millennial Japan is one of collapse—not just financial, institutional, or educational but also personal. Time and again we hear stories of groups of people banding together in suspect circumstances, breaking off into distinct "tribes" (*zoku*) in a desperate effort to find a sense of community and continuity, or *ba*. This is the explanation for the unsuspected success the Aum Shinrikyō cult had in recruiting a number of young, upwardly mobile Japanese. The sarin attacks on Tokyo's subways on March 20, 1995, orchestrated by cult leader Asahara Shōkō, were carried out by former students from Tokyo University and Waseda University, a former cardiovascular surgeon and an engineer (Harootunian 2006: 102). Other Aum members included lawyers and doctors. In interviews with former Aum members, Robert Jay Lifton argues that the cult offered spiritually and emotionally crippled Japanese a sense of belonging and purpose. Citing the reflections of one former member, Lifton says that "at a time when the family and other institutions seemed to be breaking down," Aum was an attractive solution to the problem of contemporary life (Lifton 2000: 78). Aum Shinrikyō emerged as a surrogate institution for the emotionally vulnerable. In the aftermath of the attacks, which killed thirteen and injured thousands more, some cultural commentators recognized the need for serious reflection. In Lifton's (2000: 234) words: "Stressing the alienation of young people from the larger society and the absence of meaning in their lives, many commentators blamed the phenomena on the legacy of the emperor system, on the lockstep demands of the educational system, or on Japanese corporate practices that suppressed personal autonomy." Lifton draws attention to the fact that while there was unanimous condemnation of the terrorist attack, not a few Japanese identified with the sentiments driving the violence. This reaction mirrors the discourse surrounding the Shōnen A murders.

The year of the sarin attacks, 1995, was significant in other respects. In January, The Great Hanshin earthquake (*Hanshin Awaji Daishinsai*) destroyed the city of Kobe. The earthquake left 6,000 dead, 300,000 displaced, and caused between ten and twenty trillion yen in damage (Yoda 2006a: 20). Transportation came to a stop, water supplies were destroyed, and the city's bay-front area, an homage to "the city's economic success" by way of its "glittering futuristic buildings and a development plan supported by nearly all segments of the population," was left in ruins (Iida 2002: 237). While the disaster itself "exposed the precariousness of life in this highly urbanized nation," the fall of the bay-front area meant the symbolic fall of the city itself (Yoda 2006a: 20; see also Iida 2002: 237). In addition, the highly publicized failure of the government to adequately respond to the disaster, combined with "criticism for corruption and corner-cutting," exposed the fragility not only of the city and life in general but also of the whole of the social infrastructure (Koschmann 2006: 124). The year 1995 also marked the fiftieth anniversary of the end of the Pacific War. For many, the widespread destruction following the earthquake rekindled dormant images of war. Akira Mizuta Lippit (2005: 102), for example, suggests that these destructive "spectacles forced the nation to revisit the primal scene of postwar Japan." If Japan had been able to lay to rest much of what "postwar" had meant when Hirohito died, the earthquake brought it back to life.

Not everyone shared this anxious concern over the slow, spiritual death of the Japanese. Philosopher Karatani Kōjin writes of feeling "suffocated" by the effervescent 1980s (see Cassegard 2010: 42). He accordingly heaved a philosophical sigh of relief when the 1990s washed away everything that the Japanese seemingly had stood for. Karatani saw potential for vast social recalibration. In this sense, Cassegard (2010: 42) writes, "The end of the bubble-economy was not only a trauma, but also had a vitalizing effect." He points to Karatani's efforts to encourage political activism as well as a push for "the recovery of national self-esteem and economic and political might" (2010: 42). Cassegard (2010: 42) sees this latter development as one of two "competing ideas of 'recovery'" in the 1990s. The second, which is unimportant for our purposes but nevertheless crucial to an accurate portrayal of this "lost decade," was the "recovery" of a sense of political activism that had been largely absent from the Japanese popular consciousness since the 1960s and 1970s. Cassegard refers in part to the student movements of the late 1960s that criticized dominant systems of power in a newly affluent Japan. The critical consensus, however, is that these protests achieved little structural change, and that it would take something like the recession to expose faults in what Cassegard calls "the Japanese model" (2010: 42). He (2010: 42) thus explains: "Both conceptions of recovery are often articulated in a way which makes it clear that they are linked to a fundamental sense of discontent or frustration with 'the post-war system' of Japan as such." To critics such as Karatani, the fall of the Japanese system afforded the chance to build it anew.

This was the case for intellectuals and critics. But what of those Japanese whose ways of life were overturned by the events of the 1990s? Or those Japanese who could not theorize their way out of the darkness of the decade? Anne Allison's 2013 book *Precarious Japan* offers insight into the plight of ordinary Japanese. Allison discusses a pervasive sense of psychic homelessness felt by many emotionally displaced Japanese in the 2000s. She writes of Japan as a "relationless society" (*muen shakai*) and the affective harm that results from going at life alone. "[B]elonging to some unit beyond the singular self [...] is critical to the social condition," she writes. "And estrangement from this not only deadens the soul but evacuates everyday life" (2013: 168). *Precarious Japan* indexes the cost of trenchant loneliness and contextualizes the pain of living, or *ikizurasa*, in a Japan that seems depleted of its emotional resources (Allison 2013: 15). The oft-cited activist Amamiya Karin has given conceptual shape to this discourse of affective anguish. Many scholars, including Allison and Cassegard, see Amamiya as the central figure in a political movement to counteract further social erosion. In this way, Karatani's contention that the 1990s would afford renewed interest in politics was prescient. Amamiya may have popularized the notion of *ikizurasa*, but she is not the first or only Japanese to reflect on the pain of life. Author Kanehara Hitomi also has spoken openly about her generation's struggles with *ikizurasa* and "placelessness," *ikiba no nai* (Hosogai 2004: 94). Her early fiction is about young Japanese coming of age amid the cultural rubble of the lost decade. It is also about how young Japanese cope in a society that has, at least since the economy's collapse, denied people a way to move forward.

To this end, we might recall Kobayashi Hideo's eulogy for his own spiritual and cultural homelessness discussed in the Introduction. Frustrated by the spiritual cost of modernization in the 1930s, Kobayashi saw Tokyo as emblematic of the changing topography of Japanese subjectivity that effectively erased any link to the past. According to Seiji Lippit (2002: 4), Kobayashi felt that the clash between the innovation of the West and the familiarity of Japan left the latter unfamiliar and "unrecognizable." Modernity left citizens isolated, alone, and on unsure footing. Millennial Japan has much in common with Kobayashi's Japan. The preference among *otaku* for an alternative existence within visual media resonates with Kobayashi's concern with the abstract and the inauthentic. The Shōnen A murders similarly exude an aura of unbelievability. So, too, do we find that the primacy of consumer culture at the turn of the century—evident in the emergence of the compensated dating trend—speaks to the odd importance of superficiality. Competing *zoku* (tribes) offered people a chance to connect with others: *otaku*, teenage prostitutes, and even some Aum cult members found some sense of direction in their respective tribes. We will see in the close readings that follow a pervasive sense of unrest and anxiety among literary protagonists who have no tribe and, more importantly, no place to call home (*ibasho ga nai*). I argue throughout this study that the unrest and social instability endemic to the millennial turn necessitated a retreat to a social sphere that had more in common with life before the economic fall than after, a sphere that placed renewed importance on friends, family, and the warped stability provided by Japanese hegemony. In other words, if the Japanese could not move forward, moving backward was the only other option.

In bringing this chapter to a close, we might be reminded of Ivy's thoughts on the effects of the recession. She writes of "efforts to reestablish Japan-as-proper" in the shadow of the "unassimilated logic of recession" (2006: 196). Her focus is on the emergence of threads of neo-nationalistic sentiment as well as "intensifications and extensions of varieties of right-wing emperorisms and militarisms of the postwar period" that also took to task "consumerist hedonism" (Ivy 2006: 196). The discussions that follow in subsequent chapters are less vitriolic and political, but nevertheless coeval. Ivy (2006: 196) observes that the crisis of the 1990s was "perversely hopeful" among neo-nationalists, for the "recessionary moment" afforded the opportunity for "the restoration of economic, ethical, and national limits." The crux of *The End of Transgression* is an interrogation of the ways in which transgression itself is a means of restoring and reaffirming the status quo. In this light, this study tracks with Ivy's observations of the resurgence of a social desire to put things back to how they used to be. The goal here is to demonstrate a quiet longing for a time now past as evoked in a cadre of works of fiction.

Notes

1 "Liquid modernity" contrasts with "solid modernity" in Bauman's figuration. Bauman argues against a postmodern turn, instead insisting that what other scholars refer to as "postmodern" is in actuality the natural progression of the modern experience. In his view, there was no radical rupture between traditional modernity and that which followed. Accordingly, Bauman favors the terms solid and liquid modernity to illuminate the dynamics of change that characterize contemporary social life.

2 For example, see Harry Harootunian and Tomiko Yoda, eds. *Japan After Japan*, and Anne Allison, *Precarious Japan*.

3 These girls have not always been theorized in this light. The *shōjo*'s very liminality has been conceptualized not as a sexual space but rather its inverse. For example, John Treat (1996: 363) holds that "the shōjo's own sexual energy" is "directed [...] towards stuffed animals, pink notebooks, strawberry crepes[,] and Hello Kitty." He does not explain how sexual energy can be directed toward Hello Kitty. But he does not need to, for his reading of *shōjo* theory has at its core early twentieth-century readings of adolescence that focused on the more mundane aspects of an as yet burgeoning girl culture devoid of heterosexual eroticism. For those who subscribe to the asexual (or even homoerotic) discourse of *shōjo*, there is nothing necessarily novel about their existence save for the ways in which they are embedded in the Japanese economy as young capitalists.

WORKS CITED

Allison, Anne. 2013. *Precarious Japan*. Durham and London: Duke University Press.

Arai, Andrea G. 2006. "The 'Wild Child' of 1990s Japan." In *Japan After Japan: Social and Cultural Life from the Recessionary 1990s to the Present*, edited by Tomiko Yoda and H.D. Harootunian, 216–238. Durham: Duke University Press.

Arai, Andrea Gevurtz. 2016. *The Strange Child: Education and the Psychology of Patriotism in Recessionary Japan*. Stanford, CA: Stanford University Press.

Aronson, Anne Stephanie. 2015. *Career Women in Contemporary Japan: Pursuing Identities, Fashioning Lives*. New York, NY: Routledge.

Azuma Hiroki. 2009. *Otaku: Japan's Database Animals*. Translated by Jonathan E. Abel and Shion Kon. Minneapolis, MN: University of Minnesota Press.

Bauman, Zygmunt. 2000. *Liquid Modernity*. Malden, MA: Polity Press.

Bergstrom, Brian. 2011. "Girliness Next to Godliness: Lolita Fandom as Sacred Criminality in the Novels of Takemoto Novala," *Mechademia* 6: 21–37.

Büscher, Bram. 2013. *Transforming the Frontier: Peace Parks and the Politics of Neoliberal Conservation in South Africa*. Durham: Duke University Press.

Cassegard, Carl. 2010. "Japan's Lost Decade and Its Two Recoveries: On Sawaragi Noi, Japanese Neo-pop and Anti-war Activism." In *Perversion and Modern Japan: Psychoanalysis, Literature, Culture*, edited by Nina Cornyetz and J. Keith Vincent, 39–60. New York, NY: Routledge.

Dasgupta, Romit. 2013. *Re-reading the Salaryman in Japan: Crafting Masculinities*. New York, NY: Routledge.

Field, Norma. 1989. "*Somehow*: The Postmodern Atmosphere." In *Postmodernism and Japan*, edited by Masao Miyoshi and Harry Harootunian, 169–188. Durham: Duke University Press.

Fujii, James. 1993. *Complicit Fictions: The Subject in the Modern Japanese Prose Narrative*. Berkeley, CA: University of California Press.

Gramsci, Antonio. 1975. *Prison Notebooks Volume Two*. Edited and translated by Joseph A. Buttigieg. New York, NY: Columbia University Press.

Harootunian, Harry. 2000. *Overcome by Modernity: History, Culture, and Community in Interwar Japan*. Princeton, NJ: Princeton University Press.

Harootunian, Harry. 2006. "Japan's Long Postwar: The Trick of Memory and the Ruse of History." In *Japan After Japan: Social and Cultural Life from the Recessionary 1990s to the Present*, edited by Tomiko Yoda and H.D. Harootunian, 98–121. Durham: Duke University Press.

Hosogai, Sayaka. 2004. "Intabyū Kanehara Hitomi: ikizurasa o katachi ni." *Subaru*, March, 92–95.

Iida, Yumiko. 2002. *Rethinking Identity in Modern Japan: Nationalism as Aesthetics*. New York, NY: Routledge.

Ivy, Marilyn. 1989. "Critical Texts, Mass Artifacts: The Consumption of Knowledge in Postmodern Japan." In *Postmodernism and Japan*, edited by Masao Miyoshi and H.D. Haratoonian, 21–46. Durham: Duke University Press.

Ivy, Marilyn. 2006. "Revenge and Recapitulation in Recessionary Japan." In *Japan After Japan: Social and Cultural Life from the Recessionary 1990s to the Present*, edited by Tomiko Yoda and H.D. Harootunian, 195–215. Durham: Duke University Press.

Jameson, Fredric. 1985. "Postmodernism and Consumer Society." In *Postmodern Culture*, edited by Hal Foster, 111–125. London: Pluto Press.

Jameson, Fredric. 1998. *The Cultural Turn: Selected Writings on the Postmodern, 1983-1998*. London: Verso.

Karatani, Kōjin. 1989. "One Spirit, Two Nineteenth Centuries." In *Postmodernism and Japan*, edited by Masao Miyoshi and H.D. Harootunian, 259–272. Durham and London. Duke University Press.

Kinsella, Sharon. 2014. *Schoolgirls, Money and Rebellion in Japan.*
Koschmann, J. Victor. 2006. "National Subjectivity and the Use of Attonement in the Age of Recession." In *Japan After Japan: Social and Cultural Life from the Recessionary 1990s to the Present*, edited by Tomiko Yoda and H.D. Harootunian, 122–141. Durham: Duke University Press.
Lifton, Robert J. 2000. *Destroying the World to Save It: Aum, Apocalyptic Violence, and the New Global Terrorism.* New York, NY: Henry Holt and Company.
Lippit, Akira Mizuta. 2005. *Atomic Light (Shadow Optics).* Minneapolis, MN: University of Minnesota Press.
Lippit, Seiji M. 2002. *Topographies of Japanese Modernism.* New York, NY: Columbia University Press.
Maruyama, Masao. 1947. "Asō Yoshiteru 'Kindai Nihon tetsugakushi' o yomu." In *Maruyama Masao Senchū to sengo no aida*, 116–132. Tokyo: Misuzu Shobo.
Miyazaki, Hirokazu. 2010. "The Temporality of No Hope." In *Ethnographies of Neoliberalism*, edited by Carol J. Greenhouse, 238–250. Philadelphia, PA: University of Pennsylvania Press.
Ōe Kenzaburō. 1995. "The Day the Emperor Spoke in a Human Voice." *The New York Times*, 7 May 1995. Online at: http://www.nytimes.com/1995/05/07/magazine/the-day-the-emperor-spoke-in-a-human-voice.html?pagewanted=all&mcubz=0 [accessed 24 September 2017].
Onishi, Norimitsu. 2004. "The Saturday Profile: Just 20, She Captures Altered Japan in a Debut Novel." *The New York Times*, 27 March 2004. Online at: http://www.nytimes.com/2004/03/27/world/the-saturday-profile-just-20-she-captures-altered-japan-in-a-debut-novel.html?mcubz=0&_r=0 [accessed 24 September 2017].
Takeda, Hiroko. 2011. "Japan as a Consumer Culture." In *Encyclopedia of Consumer Culture*, edited by Dale Southerton, 821–823. Los Angeles, LA: Sage Publications.
Tanaka Yasuo. 1981. *Nantonaku, kurisutaru.* Tokyo: Shinchōsha. (trans. *Somehow, Crystal*, 2019).
Treat, John Whittier. 1996. *Writing Ground Zero: Japanese Literature and the Atomic Bomb.* Chicago, IL: University of Chicago Press.
Ueno, Chizuko. 1998. "Seibu Department Store and Image Marketing: Japanese Consumerism in the Post-war Period." In *Asian Department Stores*, edited by Kerrie L. MacPherson, 177–205. New York, NY: Routledge.
Yamada Yasuhiro. 2004. *Kibō kakusa shakai: "makegumi" no zetsubōkan ga Nihon o hikisaku* (The Hope Disparity Society: The "Losers" Whose Despair is Tearing Japan Apart).
Yoda, Tomiko. 2006a. "A Roadmap to Millennial Japan." In *Japan After Japan: Social and Cultural Life from the Recessionary 1990s to the Present*, edited by Tomiko Yoda and H.D. Harootunian, 16–53. Durham: Duke University Press.
Yoneyama, Shoko. 2012. *The Japanese High School: Silence and Resistance.* New York, NY: Routledge.

3

SKELETONS OF DESIRE

The Body in Kanehara Hitomi's *Snakes and Earrings* and *Hydra*

Millennial Japan was a nation in crisis, and this crisis manifested at the individual, physical level. The collapse, in the early 1990s, of Japan's "self-sustained and self-complacent space" (qtd. in Cassegard 2008) splintered Japanese youth from the postwar narratives of nation and sacrifice in which their parents and grandparents had found meaning, safety, and sanctuary. One outcome of this ontological crisis was renewed philosophical and intellectual interest in the physical body as the antidote to cultural meaninglessness. As noted previously, cultural critic Miyadai Shinji asserts that the body offered endless possibilities in the face of meaninglessness. His words tap into a lengthy discourse on the rise of the body in postwar Japanese letters. The Occupation-era cadre of male authors called *nikutai sakka* or "flesh writers," for example, wrote openly about the male body and the depths of its sensations, emotions, and affects (see Orbaugh 2007, Slaymaker 2004). Orbaugh and Slaymaker suggest that this was in response to the physicality of war and wartime censorship and paralleled a growing intellectual appreciation for the carnal (*nikutai*) rather than national body (*kokutai*).[1] "We now believe in nothing but our own bodies," wrote Tamura Taijirō (1911–1983) (1947: 62; qtd. in Slaymaker 2004: 3) in his 1947 "Nikutai no mon" (Gate of Flesh). These writers' anxieties over their own sense of displacement, emasculation, and vulnerability informed their protagonists, who often found in women a means of escaping the harrowing conditions of their present.

The question of how to live in the present when the present seems unlivable surfaced again at the end of the century. And intellectuals and authors, as in the work of the flesh writers, turned toward the body in search of meaning. In contrast to the postwar years and the age of economic ascent, Japan in the 1990s lacked familial, educational, and political stability. In addition,

DOI: 10.4324/9781003231806-4

economic stagnation, domestic terrorism, the devastation of the Great Hanshin Earthquake, and unfettered consumerism lent an apocalyptic air to an already tenuous sociocultural climate. To many critics, millennial Japan seemed vacuous, inhospitable, and on the brink of collapse. As a result, a number of public intellectuals were drawn to, but ultimately betrayed by, an untenable discourse of "the end." In response, Miyadai and his contemporaries reoriented themselves toward addressing the complexities of *living* in a Japan that had seemingly outlived itself. For Miyadai, at least, surviving the present was a matter of embracing the body. "By modifying one's own body, just by making a hole," he wrote, "one can be free [...]" (qtd. in Iida 2002: 233). Miyadai, consciously or otherwise, invoked Tamura's call for a purely sensorial engagement with the world. His work conceptualized the body as the locus of a new corporeal identity befitting a new Japan. To live by the body was to find reprieve from a nation in epistemological rupture; to create a new "self-sustained and self-complacent space" inside one's body and inside the bodies of others (Karatani qtd. in Cassegard 2008).

The fiction explored in this chapter responds to the conditions of millennial Japan by offering the body as an attractive, if unsustainable, antidote to the contemporary malaise. Kanehara Hitomi's novellas *Snakes and Earrings* and *Hydra* read like hyperbolic liberal fantasies, almost fulfilling Miyadai's prophesy that, after the nation (*kokutai*) has lost its leverage, only the body (*shintai*) remains. In the first text, nineteen-year-old protagonist Lui is presented as a casualty of neoliberal Japan who turns to her body and the bodies of men to craft a physical relationship with the present. To this end, body modification (including tattoos and piercings) and sadomasochistic sex become techniques through which Lui attempts to divorce herself from the broken-down social strictures governing Japanese social life. In *Hydra*, twenty-four-year-old Saki engages in an odd ritual of chewing her food and spitting it out, banking on the notion that manipulating her body's size and shape can make up for feeling out of control.

Beyond the domestic bounds of procreative sex and cultural imperatives of bodily integrity, these corporeal acts are meant to be transgressive alternatives to the hegemony of heteronormative Japanese culture, which continues to pressure women into becoming wives and mothers (*ryōsai kenbo*, see Chapter 1) and living dutifully *whole*. I argue that sexual-bodily transgression in these works proves unsustainable and only grants temporary autonomy to Kanehara's protagonists. The uncertainty of life ultimately eclipses the merit of transgression in these texts. In defiance of Miyadai's assertion that Japanese youth are preoccupied by the present, Lui and Saki demonstrate a sense of the uselessness in living for now by setting their sights on the undiscovered future.

Although Kanehara offers timely anti-narratives of Japanese social life, this chapter argues that she ends up participating in a discourse of reified female Japanese personhood. Along the way, she raises important questions about the feasibility of middle-class life and female agency. Her protagonists' refusal of the middle-class dream, or the inability to pursue it (manifest in their collective disavowal of education, employment, domesticity, and the body), is a crucial component of Kanehara's fiction discussed here. For only after realizing that their acts of transgression are no more than empty gestures do protagonists Lui and Saki turn, with mixed feelings, to that which they had sought to resist. Because these characters have nothing to leverage (education, for example, or material wealth), Lui and Saki are at the mercy of Japanese hegemonic culture. For these characters, there is something attractive, if disheartening, about repressing their own desires in light of the instability of living out of bounds.

In the fiction discussed here, the female body comes under fire: it is tattooed, pierced, scarred, and abused by male bodies. While *survival* may seem inconsistent with bodily degradation, Lui and Saki willfully submit to the whims, desires, and demands of emotionally unstable male characters, exercising a kind of codependent autonomy. In doing so, they reproduce narratives of female subordination and submissiveness. In a time of social unrest and uncertainty, the sublimation of female agency and transgression contributes to the reification of national stability and progress.

In the postwar era, many Japanese felt that effort and commitment to corporate ideology all but guaranteed access to a particular brand of class-specific Japanese identity. In this regard, to be middle-class was to be Japanese, and through the economic expansion of the 1950s and 1960s various politicians from Japan's diverse political spectrum promised, in Hashimoto Kenji's (2001) words, to "turn all citizens into middle class." This utopian promise, codified in ideas of upward mobility and meritocracy, excluded many working-class Japanese, but it succeeded in equating individual wealth with national wealth and marking as inferior anyone who failed to work hard enough to participate in a newly mythologized common national consciousness.

In this context, consider Murakami Ryū's (2000) novel *Kibō no kuni no ekusodasu* (*Exodus from the Land of Hope*), which follows a pack of teenagers who, in response to the ineffectuality of the Japanese government, flee to the northern island of Hokkaido to create their own self-governed state. Murakami's teenagers envision a kind of starting anew as an ideal solution to contemporary Japan's existential crisis, a lack of hope (*kibō*). *Exodus from the Land of Hope* offers insight into millennial age anxieties vis-à-vis the normative concept of citizenship that characterized Japan's postwar generation, and it contributes to an ongoing literary discourse lamenting "the pathological aspects of the present" (Vij 2015: 174). It is also just one of a number of millennial titles concerned with hope. Yamada Masahiro's 2004 study, *Kibō kakusa shakai: "makegumi" no zetsubōkan ga Nihon o hikisaku* (*The Hope Disparity Society: The "Losers" Whose Despair is Tearing Japan Apart*) argues that hope is not unattainable per se but rather available only to the socioeconomic elite. Those without financial security—that is, the majority of the population—are

Japan's "losers" who are bringing the country down (*makegumi*). According to Yamada, some of Japan's young people are comfortable with, or at least resigned to, the current state of affairs. These texts paint a morose, almost helpless portrait of millennial Japan and the citizens circulating within it. Murakami's novel, by way of conclusion, offers an untenable anarchic recommitment to politics, including the printing of new currency. It is politics not for the sake of change but for the safety of community. As Lauren Berlant (2011: 260) argues, the anarchist's goal is "to be in the political with others." As such, in Murakami's novel, political change is less important than the act of doing politics. In Yamada's work, too, we see "the precarious social deformations" that have resulted from a broken social and political system (Allison 2013: 43): temp workers who lack interest in marriage or family, and uneducated, jobless youth are seemingly making a bad situation worse. As in Murakami's novel, we see an acknowledgment of the problems at hand but no drive to fix them.

To many Japanese who came of age after the war, Japan's millennial youth were the root of the problem. They seemed "opportunistic, irresponsible, and hedonistic" and "morally degenerate, antisocial, and underachieving" (Yoda 2006a: 42). Media representations of Japanese young people were often fetishistic and helped to solidify these images in the public eye. For example, the rise of part-time labor was portrayed as a consequence of generational laziness rather than a byproduct of the failing economy. Furthermore, in criticizing Japan's highly structured but emotionally taxing education system, the youth were themselves criticized for turning their backs on Japan's "academic pedigree society" (*gakureki shakai*), "the foundation of Japan's economic prowess built up from the ashes of wartime defeat" (Allison 2013: 138). In short, the un(der)employed, un(der)educated, and unenthusiastic members of society were scapegoated by those who did not see Japan's problems for what they were.

Kanehara has been vocal about her generation's plight. Although Kanehara resists claims that she speaks *for* her generation (Neustatter 2005), in her fiction she attempts to give voice to a generation of citizens who have been denied the privilege of hope. Kanehara, who rose to fame with the unprecedented and unexpected success of her debut work, *Snakes and Earrings*, is invested in the marginalized voices of Japan's young underclass. Her texts are almost exclusively monopolized by the first-person perspective, which allows the author to readily conflate the textual and extra-textual. In interviews following her initial success, Kanehara insisted that her protagonists are stylized versions of herself. In encouraging a specific mode of reading, Kanehara (intentionally or not) draws upon the tradition of the self-referential *watakushi-shōsetsu/shi-shōsetsu*, or I-novel, which became a prominent literary movement in the early twentieth century. According to Tomi Suzuki (1996: 6), an I-novel depends on "the reader's expectations concerning, and belief in, the single identity of the protagonist, the narrator, and the author."

Kanehara is certainly not the only writer to play up the affinity between autobiography and fiction. Author Yoshimoto Banana gained attention for her novel *Tsugumi* (1989; trans. *Goodbye Tsugumi*, 2002), about an "ill-tempered and rude," "vulgar," "whining," "self-centered, spoiled, and terribly stubborn" woman who happily thumbs her nose at social convention. In a postscript to the novel, Banana claims that she and Tsugumi are one and the same: "By the way, I am Tsugumi. That terrible personality—I can only think that's me." (Yoshimoto, 1989: 236). Nobuko Awaya and David Phillips (1996: 252) argue that this is an "intentional" rhetorical flourish on Banana's part, affording her a space for social commentary. In addition, these scholars also suggest that Banana's identification with the unruly Tsugumi is meant to convey to readers that it is okay to "challenge accepted values and speak out without fear of ostracism" (Awaya and Phillips 1996: 254)—after all, Banana has turned out just fine.

Critics have responded to Kanehara's *Snakes and Earrings* in this manner, with the expectation that it is a "barely fictionalized self-portrait" of the author's experiences struggling to get by in millennial Japan (Driscoll 2007 182; see also *Bungei Shunjū* 2004: 319). While all of the authors discussed in *The End of Transgression* explore the sociocultural fissures that have come to define Japan's "lost decade," and do so from the first-person perspective, Kanehara is distinct for having grown up in the environment she describes. As a high school dropout, teenage runaway, and domestic violence survivor, but also as an award-winning author whose fiction supposedly reflects her own experiences, she offers a powerful and sobering glimpse into the lives of people like her.

With few exceptions, *Snakes and Earrings* has been the ongoing subject of critical analysis by scholars interested in Kanehara's fiction. Although published in 2003, the text remains her claim to fame despite an extensive oeuvre of novels and short story anthologies. *Snakes and Earrings*, a brief story of an uneducated, alcoholic teenager embracing sadomasochistic sexual practices and extreme forms of body modification, grabbed the attention of readers young and old. Many, such as author Murakami Ryū, felt that the text offered insight into the ways young Japanese cope with life in the new millennium (Saitō 2004: 71). The present chapter misses the opportunity to expand the body of secondary criticism on Kanehara's other fiction. It risks reiterating the importance of her early work at the expense of her more recent endeavors. However, the generational ennui, frustration, and displacement that defined her early years as an author continue to be relevant and important issues as the problems that gave rise to "the lost decade" remain unfixed. Many scholars have even begun treating the 2000s as an extension of the 1990s—a lost decade becomes lost decades. While the discourse of loss is pervasive, there is a subtle irony in referring to Kanehara's generation as "lost:" if Kanehara is to be believed, she did not have anything to lose in the first place.

Thus, *Snakes and Earrings* possesses a resounding quality in protagonist Lui's ambivalent refusal to stop struggling.

Hydra is an extension of the ideas offered in *Snakes and Earrings*. It is an even more sobering and indeed cynical glimpse into a life stripped of all but the will to survive. In many ways, it is the same story with the same conclusion. Like Lui in *Snakes and Earrings*, *Hydra's* Saki is young, hip, and desirable. Like Lui, she cultivates a discourse of misbehavior and transgression, doing what she wants, when she wants. However, also like Lui, she lacks an education and a means to live beyond bounds and on her own terms. In other words, for her, misbehavior is unsustainable. Saki therefore makes the same decisions Lui does when confronted with the uncertainty of living in uncertain times. In *Hydra*, as in *Snakes and Earrings*, Kanehara does not shy from the messiness of getting by. Taken together, these texts reveal a quiet and contradictory longing in Kanehara's writing—a longing for the warped stability that only convention can provide an antidote for generational hopelessness.

Concern with hopelessness and hope coincides with a broader intellectual interest in how "precarity" ("an ongoing mélange or collection of shattering events" (Berlant 2011: 10)) has given rise to ambivalent ideas about "the good life." A number of scholars have interrogated the social fantasies dictating what makes a life a good one. Ahmed (2006: 21), for example, writes: "For a life to count as a good life, it must return the debt of life by taking on the direction promised as a social good, which means imagining one's futurity in terms of reaching certain points along a life course." Thus "good" is equated less with personal growth and achievement than it is with forms of sociality (family, education, career, and so on) that are tied to a broader national agenda. In other words, a good life is a national life. Over the past several decades, ordinary Japanese have drifted further and further from the fractured state institutions that used to make a good life. In this sense, lives are no longer "good," so much as they are simply lives. Young Japanese, as Kanehara says above, have been excluded from the "good" of the good life; they do not know what this kind of life looks like. They must therefore invent it, or die trying.

Snakes and Earrings and *Hydra* emerge from this milieu. While the central characters in these texts participate in the discourse of hopelessness, indulging in recklessness and revolt in the process, they also seem tired of it all. Miyadai, Murakami, and their contemporaries may lament the current state of Japanese social life, but as male public intellectuals who grew up amid postwar affluence, they are divorced from the people they examine. Refracted through their own critical lenses, Kanehara's protagonists have a different, more immediate relationship with Japanese society. For this reason, her texts are not framed in terms of lamentation or eulogy but rather exhaustion. Her characters are tired of struggling and gravitate toward the dead promises of national life, entertaining no pretense that lives will become good in the process. *Snakes and Earrings* and *Hydra* read almost like instruction manuals for getting by in contemporary Japan. To get by is to return to the social order of Japanese nationalism.

While the term *ibasho* (place) would gain particular currency in the 2000s with the ascent of precarious labor, anxiety over "connectedness" emerged from the literature of the 1990s that grappled with the physical and emotional displacement of the lost decade. The infirmity of Japanese subjectivity in the last years of the millennium drove a textual need for recovery. The need for rebellion and transgression, a kind of will to "unfeeling," was derailed by a more urgent need for asylum. This situation manifests itself in Kanehara's texts vis-à-vis the absence of traditional locales of safety. These texts head toward a frontier void of friends or family, careerism, or education. There is a sense of powerlessness in these novellas, a desperation that unites protagonists Lui and Saki, both glumly aware that, having turned their backs on Japanese society, they must make difficult decisions in order to move forward.

And move forward they must, for Lui and Saki are at an impasse, bogged down by the numbing conditions of daily life that have stripped them both of aspirations for upward mobility and personal fulfillment. *Snakes and Earrings* and *Hydra* thus paint a morose picture of young Japanese women mired in personal chaos and boredom. Kanehara articulates the pressing concerns of young people who are ill-equipped to figure things out for themselves. For most characters analyzed here, getting by in millennial Japan usually means getting together. Accordingly, Kanehara's texts are appropriately invested in the longevity of romantic and familial attachments as the antidote to their meaningless present. In the process, Kanehara thematizes the problems such attachments engender, bringing characters together just to pull them apart. At the same time, she refuses to redeem her characters, who choose practicality and stability over something approaching love, which has no place in her Japan. Indeed, Kanehara sees love as a dangerous, naive concept that does more harm than good. It is not so much that love *hurts*—in the emotional sense—as it is an impractical pursuit, getting in the way of more immediate concerns. Kanehara makes this point clear by offering Lui and Saki the chance to love gentle, caring men, but ultimately leading them into the arms and beds of authoritative, cold types who have nothing to offer except financial stability and a place to sleep at night.

At the heart of these narratives is the precarious position of the individual, specifically, the single, uneducated woman. With nothing to leverage against the ruptures and instabilities of Japanese social life, she voluntarily confines herself to the world of potentially oppressive, violent men. In both texts, protagonists gradually lose faith in their own autonomy and make the deliberate choice to exchange their implied freedoms for enclosure. My readings of *Snakes and Earrings* and *Hydra* are contingent on how Lui and Saki attempt—but inevitably fail—to live beyond what Ahmed (2010: 59) calls "gendered scripts." Ahmed argues that women are presumed, encouraged, and pressured to orient themselves toward certain ways of living, namely, heterosexual romance, marriage, and motherhood. In Japan, women's lives have been governed by a stringent "script" of domesticity that espouses the virtues of being a "good wife" and "wise mother." This discourse (the previously mentioned *ryōsai kenbo*) has clung stubbornly to Japanese women's lives since the end of the nineteenth century, when it was championed by the Ministry of Education as the cornerstone of women's education (Ohinata 1995: 200). Today, in light of Japan's falling birthrate, childbearing and motherhood are once again important political slogans reminding women of the proper shape of femininity, citizenship, and morality. Terms such as "parasite single" have been used by the political right to pathologize those who choose not to marry (for example, Nakano and Wagamatsu 2004: 138).

At the same time, however, "state policies since the 1980s have also encouraged the trend toward self-realization (*jiko jitsugen*) and diverse lifestyles (*raifusutairu no tayōka*)" (Nakano and Wagamatsu 2004: 138). Women's fiction and women's magazines, too, regularly disavow the old orthodoxies in the name of freedom of expression and individuality (Nakano and Wagamatsu 2004: 138–139). The lives of Kanehara's protagonists reflect this moment. Lui and Saki trash expectations and obligations in a number of ways, including embracing liberal attitudes toward sex ("live sex acts") and disregarding "proper" feminine behavior. But they inevitably reorient themselves toward the domestic sphere, toward the very institutions that have historically threatened women's selfhood. Kanehara's texts articulate this disjunction and express concern over the fate of the individual who cannot afford to maintain the vision of autonomy popularized in contemporary media—they just do not have the means to do so.

This circularity is an important rhetorical mechanism in Kanehara's fiction that illuminates the unsettled state of gender politics in Japan, particularly for Japan's younger generations of women, who must make sense of the signs and contradictions that inform their lives. Kanehara's gender politics are predicated on how women survive within a system that is systemically flawed, in which "gendered scripts" remain hegemonic, yet promise very little for women. *Survival*, as literary critic Saitō Minako (2011) notes, is the common thread in Kanehara's writings. In the end, *Snakes and Earrings* and *Hydra* are about how Lui and Saki survive and negotiate a disappointing social topography by ironically burying themselves in potentially destructive relationships. To this end, the texts raise questions about the instability of agency, choice, and transgression in the face of impasse. These works are predicated on what I call a discourse of disappointment, a teleology lamenting the necessity for, and persistence of, a *gendered* means of sustaining; a kind of passive-aggressive acceptance of the status quo and women's place within it.

In 2003, Kanehara's Akutagawa Prize-winning *Snakes and Earrings* unsettled the literary establishment because of how it acknowledged and accepted the conditions of crisis that inform the lives of Japan's young people. The narrative ruffled feathers for its portrait of transgression: sex, alcohol, violence, sadomasochism, body modification, and immorality. Such themes were not in and of themselves striking, and neither was the media attention Kanehara received as Japanese literature's new bad girl. For example, Ishihara Shintarō's 1957 *Taiyō no kisetsu* (*Season of the Sun*), for which he received the Akutagawa Prize, shocked readers with its depictions of violence and sexuality and disavowal of traditional values. Ishihara was accordingly villainized in the press as a hedonist and iconoclast. It was almost routine, then, that Kanehara's exploration of millennial youth culture would have the same effect, as the most recent example of the new generation's transgression.

However, what was particularly striking about *Snakes and Earrings* was not sex or violence, or even sexual violence: these were themes regularly deployed by writers, as noted in the introduction, and prominent motifs in popular culture. It was, rather, the protagonist's supposed proximity to Kanehara herself (Driscoll 2007: 182), whose tumultuous early years reflected the conditions under which many young Japanese live. Kanehara dropped out of high school, lived on the streets, flirted with suicide and depression, and failed to find regular employment. In this way, Kanehara was one of the "precariat," a term popularized by activist Amamiya Karin to describe those trapped in low-wage, unstable ways of life. That Kanehara was able to escape such a way of life (thanks to her literary talent and supportive father, a professor and prominent translator) meant that there was such a way of life to escape. Kanehara did much to challenge the popular myths of social and financial homogeneity that remain entrenched in the Japanese psyche. *Snakes and Earrings* was thus considered an authentic depiction of a life on the fringes, and an acute snapshot of the physical and emotional toll it takes to live there. Critical engagement with the transgressive aspects of Kanehara's text meant there was little interest in how she considers the question of exhaustion. In what follows, I call attention to the subtle conservativism that emerges in her narrative and its advocacy of a life that is no longer marginal.

In Kanehara's own words, *Snakes and Earrings* captures the "pain of living" (Hosogai 2004: 94). The narrative focuses on the complexities and causes of this pain. Lui's pain is primarily emotional, originating from a sense of what the author describes as "placelessness" (*ikiba no nasa*) (Hosogai 2004: 94). Here, too, the importance of *ba* is evident (*ikiba*). At the beginning of the novella, Lui is at a dance club, a kind of "non-place" occupied by people circulating in anonymity (see Augé 1995). Club goers, "always, and never, at home," find comfort and disastrous familiarity in physical displacement, possessing a kind of generic autonomy to go where they please and when (Augé 1995: 109). It is a fitting start to a novella in which the central pillars of postwar life have fallen away. In other words, Lui does not seem to have anywhere else to go. She has gone to the club alone, and after meeting a man named Ama, whose commitment to body modification earns her admiration, she follows him home. She begins living with him almost immediately and decides to pursue her own interests in body modification, styling her body like his, down to her tattoo design and tongue piercing. After Ama is brutally murdered, Lui moves in with the man whom she assumes has killed him, and with whom she has been having a secret sexual relationship, the sadistic tattoo artist Shiba. Paradoxically, it is at that point that Lui begins to find a sense of stability and place, in concert with Shiba's dwindling sadistic tendencies and emergent interest in marriage. It is also then that she sheds the emotional turmoil that had haunted her throughout the novella, deciding that a domestic life with Shiba is exactly what she needs, if not necessarily what she wants.

The novella's investment, then, is in neutralizing the threat of what Mark Driscoll calls Japan's "at risk" youth—young people interested in casual sex, alcohol, and not much else. In Driscoll's (2007: 185) analysis, *Snakes and Earrings* offers a "quintessential advertisement for 'at risk' groups and behavior," and Lui is the torchbearer of a new vision of Japan as "a neoliberal utopia" in which young people can misbehave freely so long as nothing is demanded of them by the state and its institutions (Driscoll 2007: 184). In fact, none of the characters are contributing members of society: Ama earns a meager wage at a second-hand clothing store and Lui works sporadically as a "companion" when she is desperate for money (Kanehara 2006: 52). Only Shiba, the owner of his own body modification/sex shop, appears to have a tangential role in the Japanese economy. He has no customers, however. Even when Lui asks him to pierce her tongue and tattoo her back with images of a dragon and mythical kirin, representing Ama and Shiba respectively, he charges her "one fuck" per session instead of money (2006: 34). Moreover, there is little textual reference to the characters' friends or family, giving readers the impression that Lui, Ama, and Shiba are truly on their own, to do as they please. Thus, as Driscoll (2007: 184) observes, the text's representational "zero-future" is welcomed without cynicism or critique.

In this context, the characters' appreciation of body modification (an umbrella term that encompasses tattoos, piercings, and scarification) is an extension of the hedonistic and indulgent pulse of the text. Although not considered a subcultural or oppositional practice in Japan, body modification remains a fringe pursuit that contradicts "Confucian beliefs about filial piety and edicts against defiling the body inherited from [one's] parents" (DiNitto 2011: 462). Body modification in Japan is not often perceived as a means of "reclaiming" the body from authoritarian discourses, in contrast to its theoretical and social interpretations in the US (Pitts 2003: 7–8), but rather as a confrontational act against cultural imperatives for bodily integrity. DiNitto's observation on the influence of Confucianism on the body is but one part of the story. Note, too, that cosmetic procedures, oral contraception, and even organ transplantation are suspect practices that are presumed to disrupt one's body ecology. Indeed, the invasive nature of these procedures, in concert with the introduction of foreign substances into the body, mirror what it is like to get a tattoo or have one's body pierced. In short, the body—that is, the intact, unadulterated body—is of grave importance in Japanese social life.

In the Japan of *Snakes and Earrings*, there is nothing laying claim to the body, and acts of tattooing and body piercing are the logical consequence of lives that are almost completely "detach[ed] from mainstream Japan" and its injunctions against corporeal harm (DiNitto 2011: 462). With nothing to do, the characters turn to their own bodies and the bodies of each other, reflecting Kanehara's own thoughts about the meaninglessness of contemporary, post-bubble Japan: "There are many people who don't expect anything from society. That's precisely why they are looking inward or to the people closest to them" (Onishi 2004). The physical body is thus proffered as an object of consumption and source of commiseration with others, an acknowledgment of the triviality of the everyday. In this way, Kanehara's words speak to an "uneasy acceptance of a post-bubble economic reality" in which the body has emerged as a critical source of personal and public identity (Siniawer 2014: 166).

This is not to say that the body previously has not served this function. The "flesh writers" of the immediate postwar years reacted against the physical exhaustion and debilitation of war by writing the body as a way back to lost bodily and individual freedom. In the fiction of these male writers, the body and its desires were central to redressing the relationship between the fallen individual and the equally fallen state. Kanehara appears to see the body in this way, as the answer to the question of attenuation. Japanese youth today, in contrast to citizens ensnared in war, have not had their bodies taken away from them in a literal sense. Rather, their exhaustion and sense of entrapment come from stasis, and the fiction of millennial Japan is populated by characters who can only waffle.

For this reason, the idea of the autonomous subject is of great importance in *Snakes and Earrings*, and Lui's body becomes the platform on which she invests in the construction of a new sense of self that gives her the illusion of forward progress and change. Body projects such as tattoos and piercings appear to hinge on issues of sovereignty, offering the chance for invention and/or reinvention. The body's barriers can be challenged, broken, and its surface customized. When she first meets Ama, Lui is in awe of his split tongue and the various tattoo motifs decorating his body. She goes home with him less out of physical attraction than interest in his body and its defiance of typical norms. Later, she is equally impressed with Shiba's bricolage, and looks with envy at the homosocial bonds these two men have forged through the body modification process. In an era in which "loneliness has become [a] generic" experience (Allison 2013: 168), Lui is struck by the friendship Ama and Shiba have established. Body modification provides a space of cohesion and solidarity.

Lui is drawn to tattoos and piercings because, to her, body modification offers access to an exclusive domain governed by self-expression and autonomy.

Lui, recognizing the skin's importance in "mediat[ing] the dynamic relationship between the body and society" (Lee 2015: 54), sees in body modification an opportunity to become someone new, someone antithetical to the "Barbie-girl" (*gyaru* in the original text) label her friends have affixed to her (Kanehara 2006: 5). *Gyaru* as a cultural phenomenon emerged during the era of high economic growth, and in the popular consciousness it came to symbolize the hedonism, excess, selfishness, and materialism of Japanese consumer culture. Although Lui's dyed-blond hair, camisoles, and high fashion name (which she claims is short for Louis Vuitton) visually code her as a *gyaru*, she bristles at the term, denying any allegiance with the kinds of girls who are regularly criticized and caricatured in Japanese media. Lui is unable to claim affiliation with a different "tribe" or "clique," however, leaving her especially vulnerable to the emptiness of Japanese life. In other words, she is only able to identify herself by who she is not, a kind of affirmation of negative existence. Drawing from the work of the sociologist Miyadai Shinji, Tomiko Yoda (2006a: 37) reports that "the agents of subculture in [millennial Japan] were characteristically numb to the gaze of others outside of their specific 'tribes,' indifferent to the collective imagination beyond highly segmented and immediate social relations in which they resided." *Gyaru* were one such group—young people who gravitated toward each other not out of shared moral or ethical interests but rather as a "response to the seemingly endless flood of commercial signs that has suffused the realms of subjectivity and the social imaginary" (Iida 2002: 8). By removing herself from this subculture, Rui resists the commodification inherent to the identity of *gyaru*.

Beyond the scope of Miyadai's observations are people like Kanehara's Lui, whose dedication to body modification serves as a means of social cohesion. These kinds of permanent body marks are a rite of passage, a demonstration of sociality rather than—or at least in addition to—the individuality of being pierced or tattooed. For Lui, tattoos and piercings are not part of an anti-authoritarian agenda; they are a means of belonging and a source of identity-making. In this way, Lui's commitment to the pain of her tattoos and the tedium of widening the piercing in her tongue (hoping to eventually split her tongue down the middle like Ama's) underscores her need to belong somewhere. Her tattoo motifs of a dragon and a kirin represent the two men in her life. Her fear that, citing a Chinese legend, her tattoos will fly away and abandon her, speaks to Lui's anxiety about finding herself displaced and alone again, without a frame, without an *ikiba*. She thus asks Shiba not to give them eyes, rendering them blind, so they cannot leave her (Kanehara 2006: 69).

Accordingly, Lui's skin is a projection of her inner strife. In her more hopeless moments when she is overwhelmed by depressive thoughts, she rushes to stretch the hole in her tongue, causing herself intense pain: "On every day where I'd move up to a bigger stud, I found I couldn't even taste anything for the rest of the day. The constant pain also made me irritable and made me wish that everybody would just die" (Kanehara 2006: 80). The novella reaches its darkest point when Ama is murdered. Lui copes with his death by turning against her body, forcing the hole in her tongue even wider, binge drinking, and losing weight. She is especially distraught because Ama's sudden absence represents the collapse of the body modification community in which she invested herself: "Now there wasn't anyone to praise me for [my body modification]" (Kanehara 2006: 111).

It may be tempting to read Lui's actions through a lens of self-harm, in which breaking down the body is a cathartic response to psychological distress. For a life that is spiraling out of bounds, harming the body offers the illusion of control and order. Lui complains about the numbing effects of Japanese social life and finds that pain is the only sensation to which she has not become anesthetized. "There was nothing for me to believe and nothing for me to feel," Lui poignantly explains at one point. "In fact the only feeling with the power to kick me back to life was [...] acute pain" (Kanehara 2006: 91–92). Her attraction to Shiba is thus understandable. As a tattoo artist and "sadist," he is able to hurt her in a variety of ways, which is what she wants (Kanehara 2006: 34). Their sexual relationship, carried on behind Ama's back, is immediately violent and traumatizing:

> Shiba-san stubbed out his cigarette in the ashtray and stepped up toward the bed, undoing his belt as he walked. He stopped at the edge of the bed and pushed me down roughly with one hand, then brought his palm up against my neck. His fingers traced my veins and his grip tightened until his fingertips began to dig into my flesh. [...] The veins on his right arm bulged to the surface. My body was screaming out for air, and I began twitching. My face tightened and my throat felt like it would crack [...]
>
> (Kanehara 2006: 35–36)

Yet Lui finds pleasure here, climaxing from the pain. This first sexual experience sets the tone for the progression of her physical relationship with Shiba, who, as the text develops, becomes increasingly violent. "I felt as if his fingers were getting rougher each and every time we had sex," she reflects later. "[I]f he continued like this, then one day he would probably kill me" (2006: 89–90).

The relationship between self-harm and masochism can be misleading because although both practices involve physical violence, and certainly pain, their aims are different. Self-harm is a solitary process in which emotional and psychological anguish are brought to the surface and exorcised through deliberate acts of violence against one's body. In contrast, masochism is intersubjective, requiring the participation and cooperation of others; it depends on visibly harming the body to explore hidden dimensions of pleasure; it requires that the masochist retain a sense of agency. Although Lui is uneasy about Shiba's sadistic tendencies, she repeatedly sneaks away to see him, claiming that she is a "masochist" (Kanehara 2006: 13). She craves his violence, and even needs it. Throughout the novella, Ama is coded in a boyish, feminine way, performing poorly in bed, goofing off, and "arous[ing] a hint of maternal instinct" inside Lui, who is not shy about her disdain for children (Kanehara 2006: 18, 43). Lui's crisis of subjectivity precludes her from enjoying a relationship with a man who cannot make her suffer or feel alive. Shiba, then, as the more traditionally masculine man—employed (the owner of a tattoo shop), sexually aggressive, and physically violent—wins out, claiming Lui as his own.

The desensitized, numb subject is, to Frederick Jameson, symptomatic of the psychological fallout of late-capitalism, in which citizens have become fragmented edifices of their former selves. He writes: "The liberation, in contemporary society, from the older anomie of the centered subject may also mean […] a liberation from […] feeling as well, since there is no longer a self to do the feeling" (Jameson 1991: 15). Jameson is not necessarily eulogistic here, finding the loss of feeling to be the natural result of the ascendance of commodity culture, in which people relate better to objects and images than they do to each other. The skin, the surface, circulates in a "carnival of signs" (Tseëlon 1995: 124), a blank—or empty—flesh canvas ready to be inscribed. Accordingly, following philosopher Jean Baudrillard (1998: 30), the body is "the finest consumer object."

Because of their increasing visibility, even in Japan, body modification practices can be seen as a sartorial strategy, like fashion or jewelry—signs that, echoing Baudrillard, gain meaning only in relation to other signs. Lui, as an example, laments that her tattoos have lost their meaning once Ama is murdered. Tattoos can be a kind of visceral fashion. In his analysis of *Snakes and Earrings,* Driscoll (2007: 183) situates body modification within a rhetoric of "cutting-edge fashion" and other commodified expressions of consumer capitalism in Japan. Lui's friend Maki is of this mindset, commenting: "I think tattoos can be cute. Like a little butterfly or rose or something like that" (Kanehara 2006: 19). Margo DeMello's (1994: 75) contention that "many [women] […] only wear obviously 'female' tattoos so that their femininity (or heterosexuality) is not at risk" is affirmed here. Through this lens, the decorated, (re)fashioned body is an extension of other corporeal practices such as fashion, but also dieting, cosmetic surgery, and other techniques of self-augmentation, self-stylization, and femininity.

The permanence of tattoos is antithetical to the efficiency with which fashion cycles replace themselves, however. Tattoos as an aesthetic practice may fall in and out of style, of course, but the ink itself is stuck in the skin, anchoring the body to a particular historical moment. Furthermore, and more importantly, Lui's interest in body modification is more than skin deep and more than a retaliation against social decorum. Maki is dismayed to learn that Lui is not interested in, as Lui herself says, "the cutesy stuff," but rather "dragons, tribal patterns, [and] ukiyoe woodblock prints" (Kanehara 2006: 20). Designs, in other words, benefitted a male tattoo aficionado. Ama and Shiba are similarly shocked that someone *like her* would want to align herself with men *like them* and caution her that such motifs are an affront to her femininity (Kanehara 2006: 34, 67). Lui's goal is to gain entry into the exclusive world occupied by Ama and Shiba, and rather than seeing tattoos as an opportunity to challenge gender conventions, she constructs herself as an object of voyeuristic fascination for men who are unaccustomed to women who are so heavily invested in body art. For body art to function properly, the body itself must be revealed, and Lui's foray into this world depends on granting Shiba access to her body; with little income, she would otherwise be denied entry. Staying with him means a permanent place in his world. In this way, her attraction to heavily tattooed men, and her desire to become like them, speaks to the persistent allure of the commodity/body object as the solution to a life void of deep and meaningful connection.

At the same time, the progression of the novella depends on Lui's acceptance of her own superficiality, which comes, ironically, after Ama's disappearance and then death. He fails to come home, and several days later the police discover his body mutilated and sexually defaced, which Lui describes in gruesome detail:

> A weblike pattern was carved into his chest [...], and he had cigarette burns all over his body. All his nails had been pulled off, and something that looked like an incense stick was sticking out of the tip of his penis. His short hair had been torn out in places, and his scalp was all ripped and bloody.
> (Kanehara 2006: 104)

Here Shiba's true sadistic side emerges, and his actions once again cause Lui a great deal of pain. "I'd never experienced so much pain and despair as I did at that moment right then," she laments (Kanehara 2006: 104). In a text dedicated to hurt—the pain of living, the pain of body modification—emotional pain is the only kind that proves to be too much for Lui because it cuts to the heart. Her earlier investment in physical pain carried no emotional consequences and depended on finding elusive expressions of pleasure, either delayed sexual gratification or the anticipation of a completed tattoo. Convinced that she was but another numb, apathetic teenager, Lui is suddenly overwhelmed by grief because, in spite of herself, she had been "falling in love" with Ama (Kanehara 2006: 107). Almost immediately, she is confronted with the ramifications of a life dedicated to the surface. Because she did not know Ama's last name, she could not report him missing; in fact, she "knew nothing about him. Until [his death], I'd thought all I needed to know about Ama was what I saw with my own eyes. But now I realized I was blind because that's all I was looking for" (Kanehara 2006: 102). Here, Lui aligns herself with the blind creatures decorating her back; she is stuck groping her way through a "boring existence" just as they are stuck in her skin, lacking the vision to flee (2006: 108). She thus decides to abandon her myopic relationship with the world by investing in a relationship with Shiba and follows his lead by telling him about herself and her background (2006: 111–112), topics never broached in her relationship with Ama. She also has him ink in the eyes to her dragon and kirin in order "to give them the gift of life" so they can "do whatever they want" (2006: 118). Lui experiences a moment of recognition or anagnorisis here, discovering in her willingness to shed her attachment to her tattoos that "everything would be all right" (2006: 118). She continues this line of reasoning, describing the hole in her tongue that is nearly wide enough to finally split as "a useless, empty hole" (Kanehara 2006: 119).

Lui's devaluation of her body project coincides with an unexpected commitment to Shiba. Lui recognizes the brand of incense sticking out of Ama's penis as a rare import available only at Shiba's tattoo shop, where she is spending more time as his attendant since Ama's death. Rather than alerting the authorities, she rushes out to buy a different brand for his shop. Lui also tells Shiba that she "like[s] long hair on guys," and convinces him to grow his hair out, which will cover a distinct tattoo on his head and help him evade arrest (2006: 116). That night, Lui says: "I [...] got into bed with him and lay next to him until he fell asleep, all the time replaying sickening scenes of him strangling Ama as he raped him. [...] If Shiba-san was really the murderer, he must have choked Ama so much harder than he ever choked me" (2006: 117). As DiNitto (2011: 464) points out, in the original text, Kanehara uses the verb *okasu* (rape) to describe the ways that Shiba sexually violates both Ama and Lui (see also Kanehara 2004: 122). Here, Lui sees Ama's death as the logical conclusion of Shiba's sadism—perhaps glimpsing into her own future. Nevertheless, moments later Lui shakes these thoughts from her mind, concluding that Shiba "wouldn't be able to carry on violating me like he had" (Kanehara 2006: 118). The source of her confidence is elusive. It is as though Lui is convinced Shiba has expended all of his sadistic energy on Ama. If this is indeed the case, the timing is perfect, for Lui claims that Ama's death liberates her from her need for physical pain, as though her heartache (emotional pain she has no control over) jars her back to life. In this scenario, Lui and Shiba would no longer be the masochist and sadist they initially claimed to be, having found a sort of twisted equilibrium through Ama's death. Consider that her statement above focuses on Shiba's agency in his use of violence rather than on her own ability to negotiate the possible instabilities of their relationship.

DiNitto sees these developments in a more optimistic light than I do. She argues convincingly that the text's reversal is difficult to comprehend in light of the ways that Lui seems to initially represent generational opposition to state institutions such as marriage. DiNitto (2011: 463) observes that Lui "rejects the lifestyle of mainstream society by marking herself [...] through piercings and tattoos" even though in other respects she conforms to gender expectations for Japanese women. Lui does not have a steady income, for instance, and mostly lives off of Ama's meager income. Once he is dead, Lui moves in with Shiba and, according to DiNitto (2011: 464), "accepts love and marriage." The night Ama dies, Shiba asks Lui to marry him. He is nonchalant in his proposal and Lui briefly dismisses him. Nevertheless, he gives her a handmade ring before "pop[ping] over to the store" (Kanehara 2006: 91). In actuality, he goes out and murders Ama, who never comes home that night. (In all fairness to Shiba, he does go to the store afterward.) Once Lui accepts Ama's death, she accepts Shiba's offer. DiNitto (2011: 455, 464) demonstrates that Lui's turn to domesticity occurs in conjunction with other lifestyle changes, such as meeting Ama's father (at his funeral) and telling Shiba her real name. In a text that is devoted to superficiality, including an emphasis on first names and aliases, these developments are important. At the end, then, Lui is different, and not unlike a snake that has shed its skin, she emerges from the shadows and squints into the morning sunshine that is pouring optimistically in through the window (Kanehara 2006: 120).

Nevertheless, Lui seems to hint that everything may not be so simple, that loose ends might not be so neatly tied. She keeps her eyes on Shiba as he gets out of bed, for example, as though not entirely confident that he is done hurting her (Kanehara 2006: 120). She wonders, too, about stretching her tongue to a double-zero (00) gauge, the largest it can be stretched before it can be split in two (Kanehara 2006: 120). Her comments leave the text open-ended. Will she continue her body modification project? Will Shiba kill her? Or will he devote himself to her? Shiba has had marriage on the mind for some time. He suggests marriage after they have sex for the first time: "If you break up with Ama, you become my girl, right? [....] But if we did get together, [...] it would be with marriage in mind" (Kanehara 2006a: 40). After another sex session, Shiba turns to Lui and says, "I just kind of want to get married" (Kanehara 2006a: 90). Lui finds the remark vague and hardly heartfelt—is his remark even meant for her? Shiba then offers her a handmade ring to wear. It is not a traditional wedding ring, but rather a full-finger ring that makes moving her finger difficult. Lui wears it on her index finger. We see here traditional signs of domesticity that are slightly off-center: a vague marriage proposal, a handmade ring worn on the index finger, a cautious acceptance of Shiba's offer for practical rather than romantic reasons.

There is a tendency to look for resistance in this novella—how Lui does or does not conform to social orthodoxies. DiNitto (2011: 463) notes that Lui "resists the cultural stereotype of 'cuteness'" with her "Barbie-girl" look. Body modification naturally breeds discussion of resistance as well, particularly for women.

Lui embraces these resistant modes of living initially because it makes sense to her to do so. When she gives them up to embrace a life narrative seemingly antithetical to her previous ambitions, it also makes sense to her to do so. "Resistance" is attractive in the short term, but eventually Lui has to make strategic decisions regarding her future well-being, even if that means putting herself in harm's way. *Snakes and Earrings*, then, may "teas[e] the established norms of domesticity and sexual exchange," but it does not completely abandon them (Nadeau 1995: 215). Rather, it reaffirms them and reminds readers of their importance.

Yumiko Iida (2002: 8–9) argues that the lack of faith in state institutions from the 1990s has made "the formation of individual identity" a daunting task for Japan's youth. That is, pathological superficiality—the common charge against Japan's post-bubble youth—has only amplified the isolation and ennui of this generation, giving rise to a quiet resurgence of nationalistic discourse as the "defining frame" for the pursuit of identity (Iida 2002: 243). In this light, the domestic realm is attractive for Lui, who claims to have little attachment to the world around her, including few friends and only a passing reference to her family. Most importantly, the domestic realm offers a semblance of identity and a sense of "belonging to society in a deep and normal way" (Berlant and Warner 1998: 554). In spite of herself, this may have been what Lui wanted all along—something or someone to cling to in order to stay afloat in an increasingly impossible world.

This is the same personal struggle that *Hydra's* protagonist, Saki, faces. Her world becomes increasingly impossible and she, like Lui, is forced to navigate issues of control and consent in order to survive. She is searching for a place to call home, for an *ibasho*. And as in *Snakes and Earrings*, the body is central here. Saki takes up a body modification "project" in a different sense, however. Saki, a fashion (editorial) model by trade, devotes herself to a harmful ritual of corporeal neglect, in which she chews her food and spits it out. She grows thinner as the novel progresses. In addition, Saki is romantically involved with a deranged fashion photographer named Niizaki, who has a morbid interest in documenting with his camera her dwindling physique. The text asks us to think about the politics of the gaze: who is looking, who is looked at. We are invited to theorize the nature of fashion, the dynamics of photography, and the place of the (female) body as the visual object of inquiry in both disciplines. To draw on both fashion and fashion photography, as Kanehara does, is to emphasize a gendered visual discourse that affords us the opportunity to see millennial Japan, and the subject position of young Japanese like Saki (and indeed Kanehara herself) in new ways.

Saki is representative of a new breed of Japanese citizen, one of the cool, edgy, and vulnerable types called *shin-shin-jinrui* or *dai san jinrui* ("new, new human" or "the third race") who emerged during the tumult of millennial Japan. When the novel begins, Saki has gone to a house party in the trendy

Tokyo district of Aoyama. There she meets other urban youth who also occupy the margins of Japanese social life: cosmetologists, bartenders, writers, singers, and fellow models. In the context of the recession, when white-collar labor lost its luster and charm, these represent cool and offbeat professions. But they are precarious and outside of the domain of normative employment practices. Once the economic stagnation and widespread unemployment of the recession gave way to neoliberal restructuring many young Japanese began questioning the lifestyle choices of prior generations. It was not so much that these citizens could not find work (though this was often the case); rather, they rejected the blind faith prior generations had in a corporate system that, in retrospect, let everybody down. In this sense, Kanehara may be commenting on the degree to which young Japanese are not interested in the employment tracks of the immediate postwar generation. This party, then, is a gathering of those who have embraced life on the fringes, including the risks that accompany the realities of wage labor.

As contrary as these individuals might be, however, they are not unique in their thirst for rebellion. The term *shin-jinrui*, or "new human"/"second race," emerged in 1980s social discourse to describe a generation of young people—born in the 1960s and 1970s—who were seen by their elders as egotistical, selfish, and individualistic. This was a cadre of individuals for whom corporate loyalty, academic pedigree, and familial duty (the pillars of the immediate postwar generation) meant little. In the context of the surprising success of the bubble economy, their self-interest was seemingly valid and precipitated the mass rejection of old ways of thinking.

However, the end of the bubble economy necessitated the end of this discourse and brought about the rise of "the third race," who came of age in the shadow of the recession and its discontents. Kanehara, who was born in 1983, has been vocal in interviews about the plight of her generation (known colloquially as the "lost generation"), including a kind of generational numbness and, as the recession drags on even today, a pervasive sense of hopelessness. *Hydra* emerges from this milieu, and the text is populated with characters, like Saki, who do not know the prosperity of the past, who know only ennui and frustration, disappointment and displacement. These are people who have indeed rejected a popular consciousness and philosophy that, to them, precipitated social, cultural, and economic ruination.

As a model, Saki is familiar with the spotlight. At the height of her career, Saki was featured in two high-profile magazines, *Delilah* and *SS*. For the latter, she received a fair degree of notoriety and fanfare. Runway models by nature wear blank expressions or sneers, presenting themselves as bare canvases that are adorned and decorated by the couture of the moment. These kinds of models are the embodied hangers from which clothes are suspended—objects in the truest sense. In Eileen Chang's words: "The sloping shoulders, narrow waist, and flat chest of the ideal beauty, who [is] to be both petite and slender,

[…] disappear[s] under the weight of these layers upon layers of clothing. She herself […] cease[s] to exist, save as a frame upon which clothing [can] be hung" (2005: 66). In editorial fashion, too, the model is distanced from the viewer, appears synthetic, unreal, and unattainable. In contrast to the runway model, whose sashay down the catwalk is captivating and fierce, the editorial model is frozen in time, confined to the frame of the page. In sum, fashion produces the model object and the object model.

Fashion modeling occupies a space at the confluence of capitalism and class, gender and body, and technology and modernity. Through the vicissitudes of Saki's tumultuous relationship with her own body, Kanehara explores the emotional and physical costs of personal sovereignty. Quelling the body—its desires, its passions, its needs—is, for Saki, the only way to stay afloat in a world that is impossible for those without social capital. "I had the eyes of a dead fish," she reflects at one point, staring at herself in the mirror. "Just the way [Niizaki] likes me." Fashion is "capitalism's favorite child," according to Tansy Hoskins (2014: 24), offering a continual churn of novelty, innovation, production, and impermanence for those who can afford to participate. The model—the hanger—is similarly impermanent, as disposable and interchangeable as the clothes she showcases. She is but a body, a blank canvas to be decorated and adorned with the beautiful whimsicality of "the murderous, meaningless caprices of fashion" (Karl Marx, *Capital*, 1867, qtd. in Leslie 2018).[2]

Bourgeois, urban women tend to be the primary targets of and circulators within fashion systems. Dictating this association of fashion with women, or specifically with femininity, is a lengthy legacy of Cartesian ontology that equates women with the body and men with the detached head.[3] From the 1920s through the present, fashion has been synonymous with the female body—with adornment, with artifice: to be feminine is to be fashionable.[4] Furthermore, the ideological heritage of fashion articulates the latter as a marker of difference across socioeconomic, ethnic, cultural, national, and gendered lines. Fashion emerged at the precipice of modernity (experimentation and revolution) and modernization (industrialization and urbanization). Modernity has been associated with a legacy of self-fashioning—of renewal, temporality, and change. So, too, has fashion. "Fashion is indifferent […] She ignores what she no longer loves, she only appears fickle because she is so loyal—loyal to her own desire to please" (*Vogue Paris* 1930: 59; cited in Parkins 2012: 2). Here, in the words of an anonymous writer for *Vogue Paris* from 1930, fashion is equated not only as a woman but as a "fickle" modern woman at that.

But there is something postmodern about the contexts underwriting *Hydra*. A generation after the war, the modernist paradigm began fracturing in Japan, leading "to a process of departure from homogenic culture with people seeking new frames of reference" (Bartal 2015: 138) at the level of the individual. What occurred from the 1970s was the emergence of distinct "tribes" (or *zoku* in Japanese) of individuals "each uniting around unique aesthetics that differentiate[d] them from one another" (138). Following Jean Baudrillard, affective desire eclipsed material needs here, and fashion afforded the fashioning and refashioning of identity. Japanese society during this historical moment was materially rich, and (again following Baudrillard) individuals gravitated toward particular fashion styles for the purpose of formulating social meaning. This is especially the case in post-bubble, recessionary Japan: from the collapse of the postwar vision of collectivist thought emerged the scarred and wounded individual who turned to fashion as a marker of individuality. "Consumers use [...] various styles and brands as tools to form identity, becoming 'fashion victims'" (138).

In this milieu, fashion models become icons of individuality and difference, totemic expressions of a new world order that, in contemporary Japan, has come to be defined by precarity. As spokeswomen for the capriciousness and whimsy of the fashion system, fashion models represent the changeability of identity and, in the process, underscore the centrality of the body. As mutable as the logic of identity is, then, as easily as identity is acquired, it is just as easily lost. This is Saki's dilemma. In the face of losing her job, she is at risk of losing her identity and, accordingly, her sense of place, or *ba* in Japanese. According to Mary Brinton (2011: 3), *ba* is a "social location," a "bounded collectivity to which individuals belong and from which they derive a sense of identity and security." To this end, Brinton (2011: xvi) observes that the "very idea of a secure *ba* [and stable identity] has begun to vanish." Anne Allison (2013: 14) agrees, arguing that the phrase *ibasho ga nai*—"no place to call home"—is part of a gloomy lexicon of terms in current usage that get at a pervasive sense of precarity that is endemic to contemporary Japan and contemporary senses of self. Thus, Saki clings to photographer Niizaki as a means of clinging to what sense of self she has left.

Saki therefore indulges in rituals of self-harm as a means of maintaining his interest. Although Saki has had issues with food since her teenage years, under Niizaki's gaze these issues calcify into routine. As with many disorders, she is *compelled* toward a certain relationship with what she eats. She speaks of the "mechanical" (*kikai teki*) nature with which she frequents the supermarket and the convenience store, the routine of filling up her basket with foodstuffs, and the ritual of chewing and spitting (82). Routine and ritual provide structure, organization, and a sense of purpose—a solution to floundering and restlessness and chaos.

> While my bentō warmed in the microwave, I hid all the candy in my desk drawer. If Niizaki were to suddenly show up, I didn't want him to find anything. I took the lid off my warmed bentō and set it nearby; then I pried apart my wooden chopsticks and took a bite of hamburger and rice. As my jaw bobbed up and down, saliva infused itself with the rice and hamburger,

> churning my mouth's contents into mush. I grabbed the plastic bentō lid and spit it all out. Repeat, repeat, repeat. Like a machine, I chewed and spit. Even when my jaw started hurting, or when I ran out of saliva, or when my mouth got dry, I put food in, I spit food out.
>
> (36)

In her analysis of Kanehara's writings, Rio Otomo writes that "Kanehara thrives on talking about the body and its uncontrollability" (2009: 131). It is true that any number of Kanehara's works are concerned with the ways in which the body resists governance. Saki's is not an out-of-control body, however. Hers is a regimented, *disciplined* body. This is a body that is only out of control in its orderliness.

Chewing and spitting is a messy, chaotic practice that calls into question issues of female containment and controllability. In Cartesian discourse, the female body has long been conceptualized as leaky, fussy, and uncontrollable, as Elizabeth Grosz, Julia Kristeva, and others have commented. In this paradigm, female embodiment is a liability, and the body itself something to be contained, and mopped up. Consider, then, Saki's disruptive encounter with her own sense of disembodiment:

> I stuck my finger down my throat and began heaving so hard that I felt like my stomach was going to come up. I washed the saliva from my hands and went to sit near the bed. I piled all of the food onto the end table. [...] No matter what, I couldn't make a mess. I nervously wiped my hands and mouth with a tissue while I chewed and chewed. The more I chewed, the more I had to spit. Three pieces of tofu sushi, three bites of a sandwich, one hamburger bentō box, one fish and soy sauce bentō, one *maku-no-uchi* bentō,[5] two boiled eggs, four croissants, eight slices of raisin bread, one bag of cookies, four roll cakes, ten *senbei* rice crackers, one box of chocolates. I ate and ate, but I couldn't make a dent in it all.

This is Saki's attempt to contain herself. She does not want to make a mess. Yet the practice of self-harm in which she engages is not conducive to tidiness. Note how her list of foods begins small and balloons. As such, Saki's body is suspended in an act of transgression, testing the boundaries of feminine comportment and bodily submission.

The disciplined body calls to mind Foucauldian philosophies of the processes through which the body comes to heel. These are largely hidden processes of normalization and self-regulation. "There is no need for arms," Foucault writes, "physical violence, material constraints. Just a gaze. An inspecting gaze, a gaze which each individual under its weight will end by interiorizing to the point that he is his own overseer, each individual thus exercising this surveillance over, and against himself" (1977: 155). In the above passage, we witness the dynamics of the gaze play out. On the one hand, Saki's ritual is calculated, and precise. On the other hand, it is hidden, private. Saki worries about being exposed, about the dangers of Niizaki's gaze. As orderly as her ritual is, chewing and spitting is not an orderly activity. It is messy, chaotic, and antithetical to the order that Saki's body is meant to represent; she is simply supposed to exist in a perpetual state of disappearing, the labor of the body in distress perpetually hidden. Being *seen* would be an affront to the illusion of order.

The irony is that Saki depends on Niizaki's gaze in a different sense. His photographic frame provides her with an *ibasho*, a sense of place. Roland Barthes theorized in *Camera Lucida: Reflections on Photography*, that the camera freezes in time a particular person in a particular place (1981: 14). Barthes insists that the photograph "gives a little truth, on condition that it parcels out the body" (103). The truth that Niizaki's camera makes permanent is the dominance of the gaze and, concurrently, Saki's positionality as the object of it. This reality becomes clear when Saki meets another man, a garage band singer named Matsuki. He is immediately taken with her. They banter, flirt, and eventually sleep together. Matsuki represents all that Niizaki is not: gentle, caring, nurturing. Saki leaves Niizaki and moves in with Matsuki. He cooks for her, even, toward the end of the novel, proposes to her. He tells her that he loves her. Saki eats with him and puts on a kilogram of weight. But Matsuki is not the answer to the Niizaki problem because Matsuki's affection does not make up for his lack of social capital. He explains to her that, in order to make a name for themselves, his band will embark on a national tour. This revelation makes Saki uneasy. She runs to the bathroom to vomit and check the scale. Then, in the next significant scene, she has gone back to Niizaki. He picks up his camera and she grimaces: "I wish that camera would burn his eyes out," she thinks (147). His camera clicks. The novel ends shortly after.

The novel challenges readers to reconcile Saki's choice to leave the nurturing Matsuki in favor of the icy Niizaki. As I have suggested, the novel as a whole is concerned with Saki's attempt to find a place to belong, and the lengths to which she must go to secure this space. The answer, I suggest, is found in the domestic realm. Niizaki commands a specifically middle-class experience. Although a great majority of Japanese identify as middle class, Saki's life experiences preclude her from participation in this identity mode. This identity, Anne McClintock notes, is codified "with clear affiliations, distinct boundaries and separate values—organized around the presiding domestic values of monogamy, thrift, order, accumulation, classification, quantification and regulation—the values of liberal rationality through which the disunited middling classes fashion [...] the appearance of a unified class identity" (167–168). The trope of middle-class Japaneseness, in fact, depends on the positionality of the laboring female body, who is tasked to, one, provide for her male breadwinner and, two, raise dutifully the next generation of middle-class labor.

The extent to which women are central to the ideals of Japanese domesticity is important in the context of *Hydra* because all that Saki ostensibly represents is antithetical to the tidy confines of the Japanese household. If domesticity is in part constituted by boundaries and monogamy, Saki disavows this. For one, she begins a relationship with another man, Matsuki, the singer. In the process, conjugal boundaries are broken. Although Saki claims that Niizaki is sleeping with other women, notably a rival model who looks like Saki, this is largely speculation. The reader witnesses only Saki trespass the principles of monogamous attachment.

Moreover, Saki's devotion to consumption (and its complexities) forestalls other kinds of attachment. Throughout the novel, she is perpetually terrified of gaining weight and potentially jeopardizing what is left of her modeling career. For her, acts of consumption are solitary endeavors that carry with them high stakes indeed. Of course, the unhealthy relationship she develops with eating mirrors other unhealthy relationships. Most clearly, her relationship with Niizaki is in disarray, which is embedded in Saki's physicality. We see, too, that her relationship with Matsuki falls prey to the same dysfunction, for it cannot sustain Saki's imperative to self-destruct. Burdened by a private history of denial, Saki cannot sustain the kind of subjectivity required of an emotionally or physically healthy romantic partner. She *needs* the controlling Niizaki because she needs help punishing herself.

Saki is thus acutely aware of the bonds that tie her to Niizaki. These are ties that bind almost literally; for late in the novel, she wonders what it would be like to have "bound feet" (125). As Otomo has pointed out in her analysis of the novel, Saki's conceptualization of her own body as one that is bound and tied is driven by the internalization of Niizaki's photographic gaze. She strives to become "a doll-like girl who lives in the liminal moment where life is 'fading away from the body'" (Otomo 2009: 131). Saki does whatever Niizaki asks: she literally "will become whatever he desires" (Kanehara 2007: 33). He desires a body that is void of affect, and this is what she gives him. Saki is tired of struggling, and this exhaustion has to do with the material and symbolic value of herself as a person; the reconciliation of this struggle depends on a conservative national history that reduces the female body to an empty vessel. Against this national history is a counter-narrative and feminist politics that protects women's subjectivity against a harmful reductionist rhetoric. It is not so much that Matsuki represents this counter narrative as much as he stands for something oppositional. He offers Saki reprieve from the burden of living as an object.

But it is a risky offer. Saki decides to go back to Niizaki after Matsuki tells her that he is going on a national tour, as we have seen. This revelation makes her feel alone, vulnerable, and useless. Who is she without a man by her side? In Niizaki's viewfinder, she may be reducing herself to nothing, but at least she is somebody. Here is where transgression ends. Saki belongs to a class of citizens who cannot afford (financially, socially) to transgress. Feeling defensive and fettered, exposed and vulnerable, she goes back to Niizaki. Feeling anxious about her value to herself, she realizes she has no identity on/of her own. She is of negative value, in fact.

In this way, Kanehara is ostensibly mocking the positionality of women in contemporary Japan. This is familiar terrain for Kanehara. In her 2006 novel, *Ōtofikushon* (trans. *Autofiction*, 2006b), protagonist Rin states unapologetically (2007: 16):

> The desire to be wanted by a man. The desire to get a man. Most females go into hysterics if either of these can't be fulfilled or the fulfillment of either of these desires is unbalanced. Their pussies get all irritable, restless. What is hysteria, after all? It's a disease of the pussy.

In the original Japanese, Kanehara uses the term *mesu*, which translator David James Karashima accurately renders as "female." This is important because the term is animalistic, as though Kanehara is intimating some kind of feminine biological drive to be wanted. In the passage quoted here, she juxtaposes *mesu* with the more human and civilized *otoko* (man) when discussing men. Her words echo those of Jane Ussher, who notes that heteronormative and heterosexual ways of life "act constantly to remind women that they [are] worthless without a man" (1997: 352). Ussher writes: "Historically, the systematic undermining of the self-respect of women has worked effectively to render many women impotent and overly dependent on the attention and esteem of a man" (352). Ussher calls this a "fantasy of femininity," wherein "'man' is powerful and controlling and woman [...] is passive and resistant." In this fantasy, "women are encouraged to transform themselves into the object of masculine desire" (352). For Kanehara, this is indeed a "fantasy," because readers only get part of it.

That is, Ussher's "fantasy of femininity" is entwined with other fantasies—of masculinity, of capitalism, of family. Female passivity reaches its zenith in the model of the postwar housewife (*shufu*). This "kitchen princess" presides over a home bursting with the latest modernist appliances (Bardsley 2014: 42). She is a hallmark of a Japanese way of life, the core of an intimate scenario replete with breadwinner husband and dutiful children. This vision of a private, intimate culture has no place in Kanehara's fictional world. There are no families in the world of *Hydra*. There are no children, no wives, and no husbands. As close as Kanehara comes to enacting this postwar vision is when Matsuki proposes to Saki. But it is a perverted scene because Saki sticks her finger—but not, we are told, her ring finger—down her throat to gag. And in the next scene she has gone back to Niizaki. The reader comes to recognize that Saki is incapable of enacting the role of wife. Further, she is incapable of accepting even the idea of the domestic enclave where "the family" dwells.

In Kanehara's fictional world, the family as such exists as a nostalgia-based fantasy that is usurped by the cruel reality of fractured subjectivities. She recognizes that contemporary Japan, especially for the underclasses, is an inhospitable place for the concept of family and its identifications. Kanehara's Japan is void of traditional notions of home, family, and community. In *Hydra*, the very idea of the sacred family is made to seem ridiculous, impractical, a relic of bygone days that are unintelligible to Kanehara's new brand of citizen—the "third race." In fact, the family, in this world, is made to seem dangerous. Participation requires personhood—something that Saki is unable or unwilling to offer. Saki would rather exist on a plane of virtual nonexistence than offer herself up as someone who can, or at least does, participate in a discourse of fully formed citizenship.

Kanehara's crooked citizen does not ascribe to normative values. Neither does this crooked citizen circulate confidently in the public sphere. In *The Queen of America Goes to Washington*, cultural theorist Lauren Berlant argues that during the Reagan era of conservative ascendency in the United States, "a familial politics of the national future came to define the urgencies of the present. Now everywhere … intimate things flash in people's faces: pornography, abortion, sexuality, and reproduction; marriage, personal morality, and family values" (1) She suggests that these intimate things constitute an instruction manual of sorts for how American citizens should act and what America itself should stand for. Stories of "citizen-victims," or those traumatized by daily life in the United States, permeate "the political public sphere, putting on [a] display a mass experience of economic insecurity .. class conflict, and sexual unease" (1). Berlant calls this a "coupling of suffering and citizenship," and it resembles what is going on in Kanehara's fictional world. Saki stands out as the ultimate citizen-victim, her experience of Japanese subjecthood is defined by betrayal, pathology, and pain. Saki has been betrayed by the state, for one. Her professional ambitions are circumscribed by her failure to live up to the national ideals of proper female citizenship; she is neither wife nor mother, daughter (where is her family?), or student. Her dedication to modeling has left her vulnerable to life beyond a normative script. Furthermore, this life she has carved out has, in turn, left her vulnerable to the whims and desires of those with social capital. This includes Niizaki, whose fascination with her body has fed a pathological struggle with her subjectivity. All of this points to a personal narrative of pain and struggle.

Saki feels exposed and vulnerable, like so many of Japan's precarious individuals who have lost access to the Japanese dream. She feels anxious about her value to herself and to others. These feelings provoke within her a sense of unease about who she is. Her identity as such is constituted by who and what she is not. Her eating disorder marks her as an individual who is perpetually lacking. She, of course, has the opportunity to reinvent herself and build herself up as an iconic member of the nation. She *could* marry and therefore return to an order of things deemed normal, an order of what is felt to be a general everyday intimacy that is part of a supposed Japanese way of life. Her disavowal of this way of life, and the conditions under which she does so, reminds us of the cost of joining this world of iconicity. She would rather suffer in a life of half-subjectivity than give herself over to a man who demands only a living, breathing, feeling partner.

This narrative of traumatized identity radically rearticulates the cost of maintaining the fantasy of the Japanese dream. "It would be all too easy to ridicule the Dream, and to dismiss it as motivating false consciousness of national/capitalist culture," Berlant instructs (4).

> The fantasy of the [...] Dream is an important one to learn from. A popular form of political optimism, it fuses private fortune with that of the nation: it promises that if you invest your energies in work and family-making, the nation will secure the broader social and economic conditions in which your labor can gain value and your life can be lived with dignity. It is a story that addresses the fear of being stuck or reduced to a type, a redemptive story pinning its hope on class mobility
>
> (4)

Here, to be Japanese depends on "inhabit[ing] a secure space liberated from identities and structures that seem to constrain what a person can do in history" (4). Saki is unable to inhabit such a space. Or maybe she is unwilling, for the cost is simply too much. The novel, thus, is populated by individuals struggling to create for themselves the closest approximation of the dream. At the beginning of *Hydra*, we meet a group of these individuals who have resisted cultural hegemony and who are therefore paying the price. Yet they have each other and are able to commiserate and bond over their collective struggle to avoid normative public life. Being intimate in this way requires a degree of emotional intelligence that Saki lacks. And so, she must circulate alone in a world permeated by nostalgia for a particular way of life that seems like a relic of the past.

What we learn from Kanehara, then, is a lesson in survival. Her characters circulate in a haze of personal vulnerability, and we see the extent to which they must go to get by. We see the way characters of the subaltern develop tactics for survival within Japanese culture: shacking up with domineering men, undergoing intense forms of body modification, resisting the draw of counter-hegemonic ways of life—these means of living legitimate lives that Kanehara's protagonists live. Survival, for these characters, happens because they have no other option; they do not have the social capital to thrive beyond the reach of ordinary culture. Try as they might to resist, it seems resistance is ultimately futile. In this way, participation in Japanese social life is an annulment of sorts, a negation of agency, freedom, and will.

These are bleak lessons that Kanehara imparts. But they are important because they illuminate the limits of transgression for particular groups of individuals who are stuck between disavowing the promises—false, perhaps—of Japanese social life and finding room to start again with a better vision of life in mind. In these narratives, the body is initially offered as a means to attain safety and freedom from the anxieties of national life. Yet we come to see that the materiality of the body provides no guarantees and, in fact, offers very little when all is said and done. The Japan that emerges here is one that is abstracted, where suffering seemingly resists antidote. The performance of survival in this Japan speaks volumes about the cost of negotiating everyday life in a way that creates a transgressive counterculture. But this counterculture is unsustainable. Giving up on transgression is, for Kanehara, the easiest way to secure for her characters a sense of place, which is what everyone ultimately wants.

Notes

1 Postwar cultural productions, especially those created by men, often emphasized bodily carnality and physical liberation vis-à-vis the individual body, known as *nikutai*. The rise of the body during this time was in direct response to wartime propaganda that emphasized the cultural, ethnic, and racial uniqueness of the national polity (*kokutai*). This emphasis on *kokutai* was rejected in the postwar period by authors, for example, who responded to such rhetoric by penning literature that was underwritten by attention to the carnal body. By and large, male authors wrote of male protagonists finding a new sexual freedom and liberation in the bodies of women. In the shadow of the Allied Occupation, many female authors, in contrast, wrote of the continued subjugation of women in a supposedly different—“liberated,” “democratized”—Japan.

2 Scholars disagree on the meaning or meaninglessness of fashion. For some, it is “rarefied and elite,” while others see its whimsy and changeability as “fast and throwaway” (Arnold 2009: 20). For those who find academic worth in the study of fashion, it is a rich interdisciplinary field that “reflects its connection to historical, social, political, and economic contexts, [...] as well as to more specific issues including gender, sexuality, ethnicity, and class” (20).

3 Major Japanese philosophers tend to balk at the ontological dualism of the body and the mind. For example, Nishida Kitarō’s thoughts on the subject in 1936 bring Maurice Merleau-Ponty to mind when he writes:

> The life of our self, possessing the historical body and engaging in acting-intuition, is itself self-contradictory. Historical life itself is self-contradictory. We cannot say that the knower is known. Our self-awareness is self-contradictory. Our body is a thing as well. Things are that which are seen. But while being what is at work[,] our body is also what sees. [...] *But even the thinking self does not exist apart from our historical body.* (emphasis added)

Yuasa Yasuo, too, argues that mind and body are an integrated whole. In advancing this theory, Yuasa’s goal is to propose an inherent East Asian philosophy of embodiment in response to an entrenched Western paradigm of thought.

4 In “Fashion, or The Enchanting Spectacle of the Code,” Jean Baudrillard (2020) theorizes that “fashion has only to do with the feminine, and not with women” (633).

5 This is a type of bentō that typically consists of rice, fish, meat, pickles, eggs, and vegetables.

WORKS CITED

Ahmed, Sarah. 2006. *Queer Phenomenology: Orientations, Objects, Others*. Durham: Duke University Press.
Ahmed, Sarah. 2010. *The Promise of Happiness*. Durham: Duke University Press.
Allison, Anne. 2013. *Precarious Japan*. Durham: Duke University Press.
Arnold, Rebecca. 2009. *Fashion: A Very Short Introduction*. Oxford: Oxford University Press.
Augé, Marc. 1995. *Non-Places: Introduction to an Anthropology of Supermodernity*. Translated by John Howe. New York, NY: Verso.
Awaya, Nobuko and David Phillips. 1996. "Popular Reading: The Literary World of the Japanese Working Woman." In *Re-Imaging Japanese Women*, edited by Anne E. Imamura, 244–270. Berkeley, CA: University of California Press.
Bardsley, Jan. 2014. *Women and Democracy in Cold War Japan*. London: Bloomsbury.
Bartal, Ory. 2015. *Postmodern Advertising in Japan: Seduction, Visual Culture, and the Tokyo Art Directors Club*. Hanover, New Hampshire: Dartmouth College Press.
Barthes, Roland. 1981. *Camera Lucida: Reflections on Photography*. New York, NY: Hill and Wang.
Baudrillard, Jean. 1998. *The Consumer Society: Myths and Structures*. London: Sage.
Baudrillard, Jean. 2020 [2017]. "Fashion, or the Enchanting Spectacle of the Code." In *Fashion Theory: A Reader*, 2nd ed., edited by Malcom Bernard, 624–636. London: Routledge.
Berlant, Lauren. *The Queen of America Goes to Washington*.
Berlant, Lauren. 2011. *Cruel Optimism*. Durham: Duke University Press.
Berlant, Lauren and Michael Warner. 1998. "Sex in Public." *Critical Inquiry* 24(2): 547–566.
Brinton, Mary C. 2011. *Lost in Transition: Youth, Work, and Instability in Postindustrial Japan*. Cambridge: Cambridge University Press.
Cassegard, Carl. 2008. "From Withdrawal to Resistance: The Rhetoric of Exit in Yoshimoto Takaaki and Karatani Kōjin." *The Asia Pacific Journal* 6(3). Online at: http://apjjf.org/-Carl-Cassegard/2684/article.html [accessed 20 November 2017].
DeMello, Margo. 1994. "The Carnivalesque Body: Women and Tattoos." In *Pierced Hearts and True Love: A Century of Drawings for Tattoos*, edited by Don Ed Hardy, 72–79. New York, NY: The Drawing Center/Hardy Marks Publications.
DiNitto, Rachel. 2011. "Between Literature and Subculture: Kanehara Hitomi, Media Commodification and the Desire for Agency in Post-bubble Japan." *Japan Forum* 23(4): 453–470.
Driscoll, Mark. 2007. "Debt and Denunciation in Post-bubble Japan: On the Two Freeters." *Cultural Critique* 65: 164–187.
Foucault, Michel. 1977. *Language, Counter-memory, Practice: Selected Essays and Interviews*. Edited by Donald F. Bouchard. Translated by Donald F. Bouchard and Sherry Simon. Ithaca, NY: Cornell University Press.
Hashimoto Kenji. 2001. *Kaikyūshakai Nippon*. Tokyo: Aoki Shōten.
Hoskins, Tansy E. 2014. *Stitched Up: The Anti-Capitalist Book of Fashion*. London: Pluto Press.
Hosogai Sayaka. 2004. "Intabyū Kanehara Hitomi: ikizurasa o katachi ni." *Subaru*, March, 92–95.
Iida, Yumiko. 2002. *Rethinking Identity in Modern Japan: Nationalism as Aesthetics*. New York, NY: Routledge.
Jameson, Frederic. 1991. *Postmodernism, Or, the Cultural Logic of Late Capitalism*. Durham: Duke University Press.
Kanehara Hitomi. 2004. *Hebi ni piasu* (trans. *Snakes and Earrings*). Tokyo: Shūeisha.

Kanehara Hitomi. 2006a. *Snakes and Earrings*. Translated by David James Karashima. New York, NY: Plume.

Kanehara Hitomi. 2006b [2007]. *Autofiction* (trans. Ōtofikushon). London: Vintage.

Kanehara Hitomi. 2007. *Haidora (Hydra)*. Tokyo: Shinchōsha.

Lee, Mireille M. 2015. *Body Dress and Identity in Ancient Greece*. Cambridge: Cambridge University Press.

Leslie, Esther. 2018. "'The murderous, meaningless caprices of fashion': Marx on capital, clothing and fashion." *Culture Matters*, 4 May. Online at: https://www.culturematters.org.uk/index.php/culture/clothing-fashion/item/2809-the-murderous-meaningless-caprices-of-fashion-marx-on-capital-clothing-and-fashion [accessed 30 May 2023].

Murakami Ryū. 2000. *Kibō no kuni no ekusodasu (Exodus from the Land of Hope)*. Tokyo: Bungei Shunjū.

Nadeau, Chantal. 1995. "Girls on a Wired Screen: Cavani's Cinema and Lesbian S/M." In *Sexy Bodies: The Strange Carnalities of Feminism*, edited by Elizabeth Grosz and Elspeth Probyn, 211–230. New York, NY: Routledge.

Nakano, Lynne and Moeko Wagamatsu. 2004. "Mothers and Their Unmarried Daughters: An Intimate Look at Generational Change." In *Japan's Changing Generations: Are Young People Creating a New Society?*, edited by Gordon Matthews and Bruce White, 137–154. New York, NY: Routledge Curzon.

Neustatter, Angela. 2005. "With a Rebel Yell." *The Guardian*, 29 May 2005. Online at: http://www.theguardian.com/books/2005/may/30/japan.fiction [accessed 15 March 2021].

Nishida Kitarō. 1936. *Nishida Kitarō zenshū* (The Collected Works of Nishida Kitarō), 19 vols. Tokyo: Iwanami Shoten, 1953–1955. Vol. 8: 360.

Ohinata, Masami. 1995. "The Mystique of Motherhood: A Key to Understanding Social Change and Family Problems in Japan." In *Japanese Women: New Feminist Perspectives on the Past, Present, and Future*, edited by Kumiko Fujimura-Fanselow and Atsuko Kameda, 199–212. New York, NY: Feminist Press at CUNY.

Onishi, Norimitsu. 2004. "The Saturday Profile: Just 20, She Captures Altered Japan in a Debut Novel." *The New York Times*, 27 March 2004. Online at: http://www.nytimes.com/2004/03/27/world/the-saturday-profile-just-20-she-captures-altered-japan-in-a-debut-novel.html?mcubz=0&_r=0 [accessed 24 September 2017].

Orbaugh, Sharalyn. 2007. *Japanese Fiction of the Allied Occupation: Vision, Embodiment, Identity*. Boston, MA: Brill.

Otomo, Rio. 2009. "A Girl with Her Writing Machine." In *Girl Reading Girl in Japan*, edited by Tomoko Aoyama and Barbara Hartley, 130–141. New York, NY: Routledge.

Parkins, Ilya. 2012. *Poiret, Dior and Schiaparelli: Fashion, Femininity and Modernity*. London: Berg Publishers.

Pitts, Victoria. 2003. *In the Flesh: The Cultural Politics of Body Modification*. New York, NY: Palgrave Macmillan.

Saitō, Juri. 2004. "Akutagawa-shō wa wakai josei no jidai" (Young women rule the Akutagawa Prize). *AERA*. 26 January, 71.

Saitō Minako. 2011. "Jakusha no shishô." *Asahi Shinbun*. 31 August.

Siniawer, Eiko Maruko. 2014. "'Affluence of the Heart': Wastefulness and the Search for Meaning in Millennial Japan." *The Journal of Asian Studies* 73(1): 165–186.

Slaymaker, Douglas. 2004. *The Body in Postwar Japanese Fiction*. New York, NY: Routledge.

Suzuki, Tomi. 1996. *Narrating the Self: Fictions of Japanese Modernity*. Stanford: Stanford University Press.

Tseëlon, Efrat. 1995. *The Masque of Femininity: The Presentation of Woman in Everyday Life*. London: Sage.

Ussher, Jane M. 1997. *Fantasies of Femininity: Reframing the Boundaries of Sex*. New Brunswick, NJ: Rutgers University Press.

Vij, Ritu. 2015. "Cinematic Narratives of Precarity: Gender and Affect in Contemporary Japan." In *Visions of Precarity in Japanese Popular Culture and Literature*, edited by Kristina Iwata-Weickgenannt and Roman Rosenbaum, 169–186. New York, NY: Routledge.

Yamada Masahiro. 2004. *Kibō kakusa shakai: "makegumi" no zetsubōkan ga Nihon o hikisaku (The Hope Disparity Society: The "Losers" Whose Despair is Tearing Japan Apart)*. Tokyo: Chikuma Shobō.

Yoda, Tomiko. 2006a. "A Roadmap to Millennial Japan." In *Japan After Japan: Social and Cultural Life from the Recessionary 1990s to the Present*, edited by Tomiko Yoda and H.D. Harootunian, 16–53. Durham: Duke University Press.

Yoshimoto Banana. 1989. *Tsugumi*. Tokyo: Chūō Kōronsha.

4

GENDER AND BODY, PAST AND PRESENT

Sakurai Ami's *Innocent World* and *Tomorrow's Song*

The body as an egress to survival is the leitmotif of Sakurai Ami's writings. Her countless novels are primarily concerned with the ways in which young Japanese (fail to) relate to one another in an increasingly "relationless society" (*muen shakai*). Sakurai's works are dominated by young Japanese women, often teenagers, who are unable to relate to those around them. These are women who have fully embraced the ethos of transgression. They have turned their backs on school, family, and stable employment while turning toward an explicit lexicon of the body, including prostitution and casual sex. In this way, her oeuvre is a sustained critique of Japanese social life since the recession vis-à-vis the body. Like the other authors examined in *The End of Transgression*, Sakurai demonstrates an acute interest in the rise of the body amid the fall of the social pillars of postwar Japan.

This chapter offers close readings of two representative works, *Inosento wārudo* (*Innocent World* (1996; trans. 2004)) and *Tōmorōzu songu* (1998; Tomorrow's Song, untranslated). Both texts concern seventeen-year-old protagonists who turn to the body as the solution to their problems. Both novels address the lengths to which these female characters go to embrace transgression. For protagonist Ami in *Innocent World*, "compensated dating" (*enjo kōsai*) is her method of choice. Meanwhile, Akari, the protagonist of *Tomorrow's Song*, looks to drugs, partying, and casual sex. But these expressions of transgression are unsustainable and, ultimately, undesirable. What protagonists Ami and Akari desire is the antithesis of transgression: a defining frame, a sense of stability, and a place to rest. Together, these novellas contribute to the emergent discourse of *ibasho*, or place. In a milieu in which few young Japanese have a sense of "place" (*ibasho ga nai*—no place to call home),

DOI: 10.4324/9781003231806-5

these female protagonists go to lengths to secure for themselves that which their contemporaries lack. In doing so, they give up on rebellion and its insecurities.

Innocent World's protagonist, Ami, is modeled on the author, at least in name. Told from the first-person perspective, the novella is a fictionalized account of the life of a high school senior engaged in teenage prostitution, more politely termed "compensated dating." Sharon Kinsella (2014: 56) reports that Sakurai encouraged readers to conflate her with her fictional counterpart. As discussed below, the text is inspired by the emergence of a "moral panic" surrounding high school prostitution in the 1990s. Protagonist Ami realizes that offering her body to men is a lucrative endeavor and more worthwhile than school. She grows to hate nearly all men but finds solace in the bodies of her mentally challenged half-brother and estranged biological father. In the postscript to the narrative, in the form of a letter addressed to her friend, Ami makes an oblique reference to a sociologist named Miyadai (Sakurai 2004: 123). This is Miyadai Shinji, who made a name for himself in the early 1990s with his research on underage prostitution. The text's pseudo-real-life elements bring together the textual and extra-textual. In this way, Sakurai aims to write as both insider and outsider.

Sakurai, who is also a journalist, is specifically interested in writing for Japan's young people. She has a lot to say on the subject, having published numerous works with titles such as *Sekusharu* (*Sexual*, 2003), *Good Luck Marriage* (title in English, 2008), and *Shiawase na koi no hajimekata* (*How to Love Happily*, 2011), to name a few. Sakurai's texts do not draw much, if any, critical attention, and reader reviews tend to hover around neutral to slightly negative. But Sakurai also addresses social issues. In the aftermath of the March 11, 2011, triple disaster, she published *Fukushima Day* (2012), a novel told from the perspective of a man living in Tokyo whose family was in Fukushima when the disaster hit. Later in this chapter, I examine her *Tomorrow's Song*, a novel that delves into some of the ramifications of HIV. Because HIV is rarely discussed in Japan, *Tomorrow's Song* provides a view of how one writer addresses HIV in a creative context. As in *Innocent World*, it is about how young Japanese women push back against the hopelessness of today and the generational sense of placelessness.

While the term *ibasho* (place), in the form of the phrase *ibasho ga nai*, gained particular currency in the 2000s with the ascent of precarious labor, anxiety over "connectedness" emerged from literature of the 1990s that grappled with the physical and emotional displacement of the lost decade. "I never had any place to stay," seventeen-year-old Tamaizumi Ami laments at the end of *Innocent World* (Sakurai 2004: 123). Japanese youth were particularly susceptible to metaphoric, if not literal, permutations of homelessness, coming of age in the aftermath of the recession and the promises of Japan Inc., now broken, that had given direction, guidance, and inspiration to their mothers and fathers. *Innocent World* attends to the fallen status of Japanese youth "as the obligatory token of futurity" (Edelman 2004: 12), paying particular attention to the ways the family unit has failed Ami and her friends. The failure of the Japanese family has been thematized in literary works consistently since the 1960s, when the "traditional family system" began to crumble amidst the postwar changes that ushered in the nuclear family (Iida 2002: 134). As Yumiko Iida (2002: 134) explains, the "family novels" of the 1960s focused on "the territories of conflict, distrust, confusion[,] and despair" that haunted male protagonists who were forced to adapt to the shifting gender roles at the heart of the changing family unit. Male subjectivity and stability, often bound to the figure of the "traditional" mother and wife, were threatened by women who found autonomy in previously forbidden expressions of romance, desire, and sexuality.

In the literature of the 1990s, reflecting Ueno Chizuko's (2009: xxi) observations on the disintegration of the modern (nuclear) family during this same period, the family is in ruins, and its parts (father, mother, child) are nearly free-floating. Miyabe Miyuki (b. 1960), for example, interprets the destruction of the Japanese family through estranged relationships and indifference. In her texts, characters are constantly under threat and in harm's way. Miyabe's *Kasha* (1992; trans. *All She Was Worth*, 1996) focuses on murder and identity-theft, tracing the motivations of a killer who wants only to start over. To escape debt, Shinjō Kyōko kills and assumes the identity of Sekine Shōko, a woman with no family ties. Before she dies, Sekine wants to buy her parents a grave plot. It is at the cemetery that Shinjō decides to target Sekine, a woman who is betrayed by her desire to buy her parents a final resting place. Miyabe sees the consequences of isolation and family-less-ness as harbingers of moral turpitude and desperation.

Other authors, such as Kanehara Hitomi (discussed in Chapter 3), respond to the fractured family by excluding it altogether.

Innocent World does not shy from criticism and cynicism, taking aim at the household in all of its dysfunction. Sakurai's characters do not kill each other, in the manner of Miyabe, but they are desperate, adrift in a sea of listlessness and hopelessness. In Sakurai's novella, all of the characters are defective, maladjusted, and fractured. Groping at each other in symbolic darkness, these characters seek in others what they cannot find within, yearning to feel whole and complete. Protagonist Ami's solution to the problems of the family and her own sense of vacancy is to invest in the DNA of her mentally challenged half-brother, Takuya, and the child they will have together. Through incestuous sexual relations, brother and sister create a space to call their own beyond the reach of moral judgment and traditional, but ultimately worthless, familial bonds.

Corresponding with the changing status of the family and the ascent of the commodified female body in the last decade of the millennium, *Innocent World* contributes to the critique of "supposedly 'sacred' private realms" of Japanese culture (Iida 2002: 229). According to Iida (2002: 229), "conventional belief in the family" was bound to the figure of the morally upright and implicitly pure female body, and the commercialization and commodification of women's bodies compromised the integrity of the family unit and the "myths of the mother" that long occupied the minds of Japanese men. *Innocent World* tracks the cultural and economic value of high school girls who find unprecedented wealth in selling their bodies. Catty, defiant, and middle-class, Ami is singularly concerned with using her body for financial gain and youthful rebellion.

The founder of an escort service called Telephux (a portmanteau of "telephone" and "fucks"), Ami fits the stereotypical image of the mass-produced and -circulated sexy schoolgirl. "We were all bored and starved for money and stimulation," she says in reference to how Telephux got started. "We wanted some deal that was a little more engaging than flipping burgers at McDonald's at less than a thousand yen an hour. Something that totally mocked our parents and our school" (Sakurai 2004: 10). This nonchalance regarding parental and academic authority allows compensated dating to be seen as a kind of resistance through the female body. Kinsella (2014: 175, 177) notes that when "casual prostitution" is divorced from the "erotic labor" of the poor and helpless, the selling of sex can be and has been theorized and represented as a liberating and defying practice. She has also shown that the confluence of schoolgirls, money, and sex that codified the myth of compensated dating depended on a "cycle of content" in which this act occupied the minds of primarily male academics, journalists, artists, novelists, and filmmakers, whose interests were largely fetishistic rather than factual (2014: 20, 32). Kinsella shows that in 1996—the year *Innocent World* was published and two years before *Tomorrow's Song*—news outlets, extrapolating data from surveys taken by girls themselves, invited the public to consider the fact that 175,000 schoolgirls may have been "launching their careers as prostitutes." "A collective sexual fantasy" is how Kinsella describes this data that was "transmitted to entire households" through TV broadcasts and radio reports. However, as she also demonstrates in her field research, these girls were simply assuming the role they were accused of being: these girls essentially "performed" for and were "performed" by men who eagerly consumed titillating narratives about juvenile sex for sale.

In this way, *Innocent World* is part of the compensated dating "cycle of content" and circulates the contrived, rebellious, and overly sexual image of the Japanese schoolgirl that is consumed with fervor in Japan and elsewhere (Kinsella 2014: 30–33). On the other hand, the text extends itself beyond male-created images of compensated daters by offering a female protagonist navigating the uncertain world of middle-class sex for sale. The novel begins as an anthem of disaffected cool—teenagers determined to upset and contradict the adult world in which they begrudgingly circulate. The innocence of the title, then, responds to a time now past, a time ruined by those who have brought Japan to its current state. Ami's oppositional stance is diametrically opposed to stalled middle-class mobility and the perceived threat of innocence lost. Young people, numb to the myths of meritocracy and self-sacrifice, turned away from education, the promises of which were increasingly empty in millennial Japan, but they did not know where to turn instead (Allison 2013: 120). To Mark McLelland (2003), the generation that followed the end of the boom year was comprised of young people "wondering whether the sacrifices made by their parents, in both their professional and personal lives, were really worth it." Reflecting the overarching theme of this chapter, for some, the body was the new locus of professional and personal experiences.

Ami's contention that selling her body makes more sense than studying for college is made clear at the beginning of the text. The novella opens onto a quiet scene in Shibuya Central Library, where Ami is attempting to study. But the "viscous quiet that coated" the library is interrupted by the sound of Ami's pager, which earns her disapproving looks from the students around her (Sakurai 2004: 1). Ami checks her pager—an indication that she has a client on the books—and clicks her tongue, packing up her belongings and storming out. "My plan had been to breeze through [an] article [for class] today—so much for that," she explains. "My study schedule for all my classes [was] about to get *screwed*, again" (2004: 1). As a member of the middle class, Ami does not *need* the 80,000 yen (approximately $1000) she will receive from this particular client, a facet of the text that mirrors real-life accounts of compensated dating. Kinsella (2014: 177) argues that "the privileged socioeconomic status of schoolgirls" has long reflected "idealized attributes of virginity and cleanliness" that were compromised in the 1990s. Middle-class girls engaging in a form of sexual behavior that is more typical of "lower-class female lifestyles" illuminated a deliberate flitting of socioeconomic boundaries that compromised propriety and class-consciousness (Kinsella 2014: 177). At the same time, the ease with which Ami and her friends acquire cash underscores the difficulty faced by traditional financial tracts. Ami's investment in the monetary value of her body suggests an ironic twist in the economic landscape and the fallibility of once dependable white-collar labor: the resilience of the commodified female body amidst economic recession outpaced the earning potential of the Japanese salarymen.

From the 1960s through the 1980s, the salaryman and his "professional" housewife (*sengyō shufu*) were the archetypical, if ambiguous, figures of appropriate citizenship. Modernity, affluence, predictability, and stability were the cornerstones of this class-specific—"appropriate"—family, for postwar white-collar Japan, was defined by the complementary images of the hard worker, benefiting from lifetime employment and financial stability, and the dutiful wife, whose household contained the latest expressions of material wealth and who was responsible for raising the next generation of productive sons and daughters.

In this sense, husband and wife performed scripted roles in the family, which had important implications for the fate of the nation as a whole. In 1963, Prime Minster Ikeda Hayato (qtd. in Iida 2002: 119) famously spoke on the affinity between private identity and public policy, declaring that "creating people is the foundation of the creation of a nation." Iida (2002: 119) demonstrates that Ikeda's comments—part of "the new conservative ideology" of the 1960s—intended to reify the standing of the family in light of rapid industrial and capital change.

This period in Japanese history saw the emergence of the "family novels" noted at the beginning of this section. As the Japanese economy gained steam and international envy throughout the 1960s, middle-class families faced the stresses of maintaining the economic and moral integrity of the nation. Fathers stayed away longer to meet the demands of the growing economy, becoming estranged from their wives and children in the process. Unflattering monikers such as *sodai gomi* (oversized garbage), a colloquialism for a useless husband, or *nureochiba* (wet fallen leaves) followed him home and underscored the nature of the "'fatherless' society of the 1960s" (Iida 2002: 137). As already noted, however, many Japanese were concerned less with the disappearance of the father than with the changing role of the mother. Expected to stay the same while the rest of the nation progressed, the mother emerged as the site of social and cultural anxieties about the nation's future. Author Etō Jun's 1993 *Seijuku to sōshitsu: haha no hōkai* (*Maturity and Loss: Collapse of the Mother*) focuses on the "shame" protagonist Shintarō and his mother feel toward the absentee father/husband. Shintarō's mother reveals the exhaustion of trying to please a man who is never there. The author posits that the "fantasy" of upward mobility in contemporary Japan—in sharp contrast to the fixed social structure of the Tokugawa period (1600–1868)—has misled many Japanese who assume that access to education is a direct link to prosperity. Shintarō's mother thus concludes that her son's academic achievements will lead him to abandon her, just as her husband has done; in Etō's words: "Her achievement, which is embodied by the future of her son, results in her abandonment by her son, leaving her alone in the old world" (Etō 1993). The image here is one of isolation and national progress at the expense of the family, while the loss of the father meant renewed importance of, and stresses on, bonds between mother and child.

In Sakurai's world, the absentee and incompetent father figure takes on special significance. Ami and Takuya have different fathers. Their mother, after giving birth to Takuya, blamed her husband's bad DNA for his disability. Vowing not to make the same mistake twice, she sought out an anonymous sperm donor—"Donor No. 307"—to fertilize her second child, Ami. Ami discovers this information accidentally but is not surprised: "All sorts of peculiar doubts I'd had from my earliest days finally made sense. My father's looks and personality were never mine at all. Ever the pale A student no matter how old he gets, my father is one of those introverted research types, with raptorial eyes as expressionless as a Jurassic-era dinosaur" (Sakurai 2004: 30). She goes on to recount a memory from early childhood in which her father, that is, Takuya's father, attempts to abandon her at Disneyland, a place of childish innocence. "The first time I felt like he didn't like me was back when I was five years old," she explains. "From that day on I never trusted my father, nor any other adult. No matter how kind they were, you never knew, their gaze could turn distant and cruel like my father's did that day" (2004: 31–32). Takuya's father is a ghostly figure, rarely given a voice in the text but haunting its fringes and eyeing his surrogate daughter with spite. "Not a drop of his own blood ran through me. I was the daughter of a man he'd never met. My father had no obligation to love me at all," Ami reflects (2004: 32).

At the same time, Takuya is a living reminder of the father's own genetic failures. Jennifer Robertson has examined the historical importance of blood ties in the development of modern Japan and in maintaining the purity of the family. She notes that "until 1985, paternal 'blood,' or patrilineality, was the *de jure* condition of nationality and citizenship" (Robertson 2005: 345, n. 6). Ami's warped family tree is thus symptomatic of a microscopic rupture in the sanctity of the family that cannot be fixed by economic or social revision. In a rewriting of Etō's observations on the dynamics of abandonment in the contemporary Japanese family, *Innocent World* demands that it is the adults who abandon their children, leaving them to stitch together lives that fail to measure up to those achieved by prior generations. "Blood ties are knotty and irrational," explains Ami's friend Masaki. "I've often thought about how I'd rather live in a world that doesn't rely at all on family ties" (Sakurai 2004: 72). Ami concurs, commenting, "My family's been broken from the start. We tried taping it back together, but it was already beyond repair" (2004: 72).

The most terrifying figure in the text is the mother, the single genetic link between siblings. Seeking "revenge" against her husband, she keeps a number of men on the side, one of whom had sex with Ami through Telephux (2004: 75–76). Ami is not as concerned with her mother's sexual morals as she is with the way she treats Takuya, who sees their mother "as though she were some poisonous snake" or mythical *yamamba*-like figure who "swallow[s] children down in one gulp" (2004: 21). Ami writes:

> She played the perfect guardian, but we could see straight through the deception. As the eldest daughter of the manager of a regional bank, an accomplished woman with a degree from a respected women's university, life on the losing side had no meaning to her. The fact that her own eldest son wasn't qualified even to participate in the rat race seemed to her the shady scheme of some being bent on mocking her.
>
> (2004: 21)

Karen Nakamura's (2013: 35) observation that "mental illness is a disease of modernity" configures the successes of the mother as the roots of her own failure. While Ami's mother blames her husband for Takuya's disability, she continues to see her son as a burden to middle-class life and is unable to enjoy fully the luxuries of her own social ascension. In one moment in the text, Takuya's destruction of the already fragile home life is made explicit. Father, mother, and children go to the department store, where Takuya ends up breaking glass sculptures in the fine art section. Back at home, the mother responds by knocking Takuya to the ground and sending him to the hospital with a concussion. "It was the precise moment all of her obligatory affection as his guardian was inverted and she turned into his most brutal aggressor" (Sakurai 2004: 23).

The annoying, frustrating handicapped child has been thematized consistently by Ōe Kenzaburō. In his works, fathers grapple with the moral and ethical complexities of raising mentally and/or physically abnormal sons. Protagonist K, in *Atarashii hito yo mezameyo* (1986; trans. *Rouse Up O Young Men of the New Age*, 2002), reacts vehemently to the birth of his deformed son: "For five weeks or so, following my son's abnormal birth, I had longed for his death, in other words to destroy him. My longing [....] was merely my egotistical desire to protect a future for myself and my wife" (Ōe 2002: 90). Ōe confronts this tension time and again. Sometimes ambivalence gives way to compassion and optimism, as in *Kojin-teki na taiken* (1964; trans. *A Personal Matter*, 1968); sometimes ambivalence gives way to remorse and anguish. In either case, monstrosity confronts unwitting and unwilling fathers who end up changed at the end. In *Rouse Up O Young Men of the New Age*, K reflects: "Since then, pushing away the calamity that has continued to assail us as a family, we have survived. And my son has made it past his nineteenth birthday. Even so, no powerful detergent has allowed me to wash out of my life those disgraceful five weeks, nor do I expect to succeed at this as long as I live" (Ōe 2002: 90–91).

This same bond is not reproduced in *Innocent World*, for the mother does not question her hatred of her handicapped son. He is an embarrassment who is "always making a mess of [their] lives" and throwing into jeopardy all of her middle-class successes (Sakurai 2004: 22).

The mother, the beneficiary of financial stability and the promises of the postwar period, including access to education, represents all that is antithetical to her children's existence. If Takuya is physically and mentally unable to pursue a life of material wealth and mobility, Ami spitefully resists that same pursuit. Prostitution is initially a vector of resistance for Ami, who is able to turn her back on academics and traditional means of employment while taking advantage of her status as a desirable sexual commodity. In contrast to others of her generation who fall through the cracks after finding themselves in dead-end life tracks, Ami's willingness to sell her body provides her with an alternative means of getting by. At the end of the narrative, after she has dropped out of school and left home to share an apartment with Takuya and to give birth to his child, an exclusive contract with a wealthy client provides her with a sense of financial freedom and the means to start anew. No longer subject to the perverse whims of anonymous johns or the harsh treatment of her parents, Ami carves out a marginal space for herself and her brother to inhabit, to create a new family. This is the point of the text: the search for solidarity, union, and family in an increasingly divisive Japan. Aware that her family is in disarray, that she has no place to call home, Ami goes to lengths to create a new family with Takuya. Only Takuya—whose cognitive defects are symbolic of the "defective" nature of everyone in the text (2004: 13)—can offer Ami the communion she desires. Forever a child, Takuya's innocence is preserved, and through him, Ami can experience a purer, uncorrupted existence.

Takuya is therefore the antidote to Ami's fractal existence. She contends that prostitution is no different than masturbation (2004: 9), but admits that it is a draining, harmful process that intensifies her sense of isolation and self-contempt. Echoing sentiments expressed by other literary characters analyzed in *The End of Transgression*, Ami feels "empty" inside and finds no fulfillment in the present (2004: 26). She copes with sexual encounters with her Telephux clients by detaching emotionally:

> [The client] leaned towards me, grabbed me by my shoulders, and pushed me flat onto the bed. I avoided his gaze and stared vacantly at the ceiling. This was the moment when the guy became the faceless man of my masturbatory fantasies and I became a drifting sexual entity unmoored from the name 'Ami.' I'd float through the locked window and peep in on the obscene goings-on.
>
> (2004: 18)

Commodified, meaningless sex drains her of life and splits her subjectivity in two. And the split-off "other" Ami is displeased with what she sees. "You're hopelessly conceited, aren't you, bitch. [...] Splitting yourself to protect your pride and nurse it," she admonishes herself (2004: 18). This self "othering" is a defense mechanism that protects Ami from psychological trauma. Adrienne Hurley (2011: 35), in her study of youth violence in Japan and the US, calls attention to the term "Orpha," a coping mechanism through which victims of sexual violence emotionally distance themselves from ongoing trauma. Ami embraces this mechanism of purposeful fragmentation in order to survive her sexual encounters, demonstrating that prostitution is not simply the defiant act she initially claimed it to be. As she encounters more men, Ami finds that her emotional self—the self that watches from outside the window when she is with clients—has gone missing. She is but a shell, a body only. Thus, Ami feels that "[t]hrough anonymous sex, men were slowly depleting my store of some valuable element. What remained with me was more or less the sadness of a spent space probe drifting forever in the vacuum beyond" (Sakurai 2004: 40).

It is sex that has ruined Ami, but it is also sex that will repair her. After being with men who break her in half, Ami needs the body of her half-brother—with whom she has been having sex since middle school—to suture herself whole. She confides in him one night: "Takuya, I get lonely and want to cry when you're not with me. We're like two little trees growing from the same roots. That's why when we split, my heart aches and starts bleeding" (Sakurai 2004: 50). Ami is initially convinced that she is Takuya's lifeline, his guardian/sister/lover/savior. She comes to understand, however, that things are much more dynamic and symbiotic. "I didn't really think of him as someone of the opposite sex," she says. "My feelings for him were more 'unitary,' I guess. It was about loving the boy in myself—uniting with the other half of a single androgynous being" (Sakurai 2004: 9).

The incest theme makes explicit the need for wholeness. The androgyne—in possession of both male and female sex organs, masculine and feminine attributes—stands for the illusive prelapsarian figure of unity and innocence. Ami is aware that their sexual relationship would be seen as "terribly abnormal" by "the world" (Sakurai 2004: 5), but she finds comfort in Takuya's obliviousness to social and moral decorum. She therefore instructs him to keep everything a secret. The mother eventually catches on and has Takuya sent to live with relatives in Yokohama, exclaiming: "I don't know which of you is the worse devil, but you will not turn this house into a den of monsters. This is a home for human beings" (Sakurai 2004: 9). Ami's incestuous fantasy (and it can be her fantasy alone because to Takuya it seems natural and normal) is thus at odds with the specter of the normal Japanese family. The mixing of gender identities at the heart of her fantasy makes hazy the gendered divisions of the household and offers a means of fleeing from the trappings of home life altogether.

This pull toward androgyny through incestuous sexual relationships, and its simultaneous implications for escape, echoes Kurahashi Yumiko's "Uchūjin" (1964; trans. "An Extraterrestrial," 1998), in which siblings discover a hermaphroditic alien in their beds and eventually escape into its "womb." The male narrator K wakes one morning to find an egg beside his bed. He and his sister L eventually break the egg open to discover a hermaphroditic alien whose genitalia appear almost in answer to their own sexual desires. Their parents show no interest in the alien, which upsets K: "Perhaps grown-ups of Mom's age did not find extraterrestrials particularly exotic. Still, she could at least have tried to take a look at it. Her eyes looked exactly like those of a beheaded hen. When she saw anything amoral or absurd, her eyes took on that look. That is why I sometimes feel like slaughtering women over forty years old" (Kurahashi 2015: 14). In this story, in contrast to Sakurai's, the father assists the mother in enforcing rule and order. Siblings keep the alien as their own, initially taking turns having sex with it, after which they have sex with the alien at the same time. The subtext to the story is K's secret desire to have sex with his sister, who is engaged, and K's use of the alien's body as a substitute for that of his sister. One night, K confesses his secret to L, who suggests that they escape into the alien's womb, where they have the freedom to consummate their incestuous desires free from social persecution. Atsuko Sakaki (1999: 168) has suggested that in Kurahashi's works, characters are sustained by their relationships with others and that the author's continual engagement with nonnormative sexuality—such as incest and hermaphroditism in "An Extraterrestrial" but also masturbation and partner-swapping in other works—points to Kurahashi's intent to "question the romantic view of the self as an autonomous, substantive individual being."

"An Extraterrestrial" and *Innocent World* diverge in their respective treatment of incest. Against the backdrop of a fantastic and otherworldly setting, and within the safety of the androgynous alien's being, K and L are able to pursue illusive wholeness beyond the strictures of the incest taboo. Ami and Takuya, in contrast, are confronted with the ramifications of trying to love in socially corrupt ways. While K and L's parents dismiss the extraterrestrial as childish gibberish, Ami's parents are fully cognizant of the threatening nature of sibling incest. Anthropologist Claude Levi-Strauss (1969: 12, 24) has famously claimed: "The incest prohibition is at once on the threshold of culture, in culture, and in one sense [...] culture itself. [...] It is the fundamental step because of which, by which, but above all in which, the transition from nature to culture is accomplished." The destructive nature of incest is reproduced in *Innocent World*, for the mother sees the sibling bond as an affront to the order of her household. This is all the more apparent in her treatment of Takuya. Because of his disability, he is unable to comprehend the complexities of social-sexual behavior and expectation. Ami observes: "The idea that Takuya, unfettered by sexual morals, would grow to reproductive manhood must have been the symbol of all disasters for my mother" (Sakurai 2004: 8). Soon, Ami finds herself pregnant with Takuya's child and wrestles with the implications of carrying the fetus to term: "Abortion was the only way out. Unless I wanted the baby of my own half-brother. Incest, immoral, social trash [...] Words like those kept spinning around in my head" (2004: 62). In Kurahashi's story, incest is subtle, controlled, and nuanced. Sakurai's depictions are messy, chaotic, and confrontational.

While incest has been addressed consistently in Japanese literature, it is often buried under other plotlines or cloaked in delicately rich, sanguine prose. Rarely is the topic broached so openly and contextualized so brazenly as the undoing of the Japanese family. Sakurai's goal, however, is not to trash the family but rather to theorize a replacement, a means to survive the present. Indeed, the urgency of sibling, rather than parent-child, relations casts incestuous bonds as the consequence of shared experiences rather than romantic attraction.

Under duress and the oppression of the mother, siblings find refuge and sympathy in each other's bodies. Their "complicity" gives "Takuya a greater sheen of life than he'd ever had before" and transforms the inhospitable, angry world of millennial Japan into "a truly kind place" (Sakurai 2004: 8, 51). In this configuration, Ami controls the dynamics of their relationship, since only she is psychologically capable of finding horror or revulsion in the incestuous bond they share. Incestuous relationships are unstable in this regard—one party's erotic attraction may slip into disgust or guilt. Ami is thus able to preserve their relationship in its current state while directing it to its logical conclusion: a child. In the process, they lay the foundation for a new, improper family defined by the innocence of childhood, complete with child.

The decay of the family in millennial Japan necessitated the construction of new bonds and ties. In other texts discussed in *The End of Transgression*, characters turn inward—to friends and lovers—to make up for the lack of familial and genetic ties. Sakurai's text stands out for its literal take on this inward turn, for Ami's body, and specifically her womb, becomes the foundation for a new experience of Japanese family life. "My family never even existed," she says. "It was just a group that functioned like a family under limited conditions and with premises. If the premises and conditions disappeared, the entire thing would have disappeared too like foam. Wasn't it because no one else would accept us unconditionally that Takuya and I started wanting each other?" (Sakurai 2004: 72).

The text makes explicit the rewriting of the family by bringing Ami's biological father into the incestuous matrix. After discovering the truth about her birth, Ami first seeks out the doctor who administered in vitro fertilization to her mother and then moves onto the sperm donor himself. The doctor speaks confidently of saving Ami from her brother's fate and successfully breaking the "chain of genetic disease" (Sakurai 2004: 57). Tracking down No. 307 proves more difficult. Ami posts a message on an Internet bulletin board requesting information on the sperm donation process and asks her donor to come forward. To her surprise, the donor contacts her and they arrange to meet. Ami, pretending to be someone else sent on Ami's behalf, immediately demands 50,000 yen for sex. Although he is hesitant, No. 307 acquiesces but admits that he has been suffering from erectile dysfunction for the past two years, ever since his girlfriend had a miscarriage and then committed suicide. "From then on, I couldn't even masturbate, let alone sleep with women. Probably due to a sense of guilt about enjoying sexual pleasure. [...] I felt I was fundamentally abnormal and without any human worth" (Sakurai 2004: 105). No. 307's confession echoes the text's main themes of sexuality, connection, and deformation.

Furthermore, his own inability to get an erection underscores the sense of failed masculinity in the text. All of the men Ami encounters are defective in some way. However, just as Ami is able to comfort Takuya with her body, she is able to coax No. 307 into erotic ecstasy. Their sex, like what she experiences with Takuya, is out of this world, turning Ami into "a lithe, magical, unknown beast from outer space consisting only of sensory organs" (Sakurai 2004: 109). Broken bodies—physically and emotionally—are healed, at least momentarily while in the thralls of climax, and Ami's womb becomes the setting for a twisted family reunion. She elaborates:

> The movement of his hips got more aggressive until he was like a demon teasing me, penetrating me all the way up into my heart. The two life forms were coated in mucus, moving rhythmically, enshrouded in fever. They transformed from genitalia into spirits seeking fusion, mutually, intensely. Let him come and coat my inside with sperm, let it mix with Takuya's seed inside my uterus. Let all be one, cells, genes, blood.
>
> (Sakurai 2004: 110)

Here, Ami's ambitions become a means for leaving social decorum and genetics behind. But only for the short term. After having sex, father and daughter part ways. And Ami is convinced that No. 307—whose name is Takamori Kazuya—knows that she is his daughter. She is also convinced that she will never see him again and that he will disappear back into the sea of men, resuming the identity of a faceless, nameless number. If her relationship with Takuya allows the incest taboo to be transcended, with No. 307 it is reaffirmed and restored.

Nevertheless, embracing incest offers these characters a chance to reestablish gender roles. Both Takuya and No. 307 demonstrate masculine vigor by inseminating Ami, who, in turn, successfully, though cautiously, assumes the roles of mother and daughter. She comes to the aid of her distraught father and coaches him to his own expression of male sexual prowess while nurturing the fetus inside her and offering Takuya reprieve from their destructive home life. These dual roles, codified in meaningful rather than anonymous sexual contact, give Ami purpose, structure, and wholeness. In contrast, the public sex in which she engages represents the vacuous nature of her existence.

The text begins as a meditation on the shedding of traditional norms and desire to live for the moment that was rampant among Japan's youth at the end of the century. Telephux brings together older men and younger girls in a celebration of carnality, commodification, and anonymity. In this environment, Ami stands out as the voice of reason, offering intimate details on the deleterious effects of prostitution: "After a Telephux job, I desperately wanted to talk to somebody. I'd be like a deflated life ring, everything inside of me sucked out with a long tube" (Sakurai 2004: 39–40). Ami illuminates the sorrows of living only for the body, calling into question the theories of middle-aged men like critic Miyadai, who opined that in 1990s Japan, the body was the last bastion, the final indulgence. Miyadai looked to compensated daters—real-life versions of Ami and her friends—as those members of society who had figured out how to live by and for the body, reaping the financial rewards in the process. He argued that young girls selling their bodies were the most prepared for life without hope, expectation, or promise, arguing that, in Iida's (2002: 232) words, "the search for a 'deep self' beneath one's socially and commercially mapped surface is meaningless." In fact, at the end of the text, Ami makes a passing reference to "this man named Miyadai who's doing research at his university on girls who turn tricks" (Sakurai 2004: 123). Miyadai's appearance anchors the text to the material world and provides context for a deeper understanding of the issues it addresses. The text does not reaffirm his ideas on the pleasures of the body and the pursuit of meaninglessness, however. My contention is that while the idea of embracing meaninglessness and transgression is attractive, it is not a sustainable reality. Literary characters need to be anchored to something. For Ami, that something is the familial roles of daughter, wife, and sister.

Miyadai's disengagement with the world he critiques immunizes him from his own provocative theories. In other words, the pursuit of meaninglessness is itself meaningless for Japanese youth, like Ami, who have grown tired of the horizon of the limitless. Calling into question Miyadai's assertion that living by and for the body liberates oneself, Ami's investment in compensated dating is a divestment in herself and her self-image. "I couldn't forgive myself for feeling any pleasure at all with [my clients]. Still, no matter how much I vowed to become an unfeeling stone, in the end I'd be overcome by the conditioned reflexes of my own membranes and feel literally sick with self-contempt" (Sakurai 2004: 18). Late in the text, Ami is sexually assaulted and wonders if her violation is a form of punishment. Because she is pregnant with Takuya's child at this point, she wonders further: "Maybe the fetus was already dead and its rotting corpse wanted to drag me along with it into the world of nothingness—out of hatred for my irresponsible flesh" (2004: 79). Her child is unharmed, however, and Ami finds it to be symbolic of the new direction in her life.

In this way, the narrative reproduces the central conflict in Ōe's *A Personal Matter*, in which protagonist Bird attempts to flee the trappings of daily life, including his marriage, his job, and most importantly, his deformed baby. Bird dreams of escape—to Africa, and into the body of his lover, Himiko, who provides temporary catharsis. But in the end, Bird goes back to the life from which he fled, accepting his socially responsible role as husband and father. In *Innocent World*, the looming threat of the child, which, as the product of incestuous sex, is already marked as deformed, drives the narrative toward its resolution and points Ami in the direction of normalcy and responsibility. In the end, she has dropped out of school and shares an apartment with Takuya, on whom she is relying "to create [her]self anew" (Sakurai 2004: 122). Having successfully extricated themselves from the parental household, they are able to construct their new family in peace. Ami still turns tricks but has an exclusive contract with a wealthy playwright. Prostitution is a means to an end for Ami, a "source of income" she can use to build a life (Sakurai 2004: 120). The transgressive slant of teenage prostitution falls away here, and the weight of adult responsibility comes to the fore. "I can't go back to that side if I want to," she says, referring to the world of youthful recklessness (2004: 119). Rejecting home life and school, Ami finds strength in familial bonds and her new place to call home, a place to collect herself and start again.

Incest thus offers Ami a chance to embody singularly the dynamics of the family, to become the family herself. As a plot device, incest allows for the figuration and reconfiguration of the family in crisis. In *Innocent World*, adults do not protect the children: there are no decent mothers or fathers, and all of the adults are rotten, malicious, and selfish. Even when a woman seems to come to Takuya's aid after he gets lost, she tries to take him to a love hotel against his will. Thus, the children are left to their own devices to figure things out for themselves. Although incest threatens the moral and ethical boundaries of the family, which, in millennial Japan, is already under threat, it simultaneously opens a new familial space bound by DNA.

At the same time, however, incest's threatening nature makes it provocative entertainment. Allison draws our attention to a number of sensationalized incestuous affairs that took place in Japan in the 1980s involving mothers and their sons. The media villainized these mothers as deviants unable to control their sexual urges that unfortunately landed on their adolescent sons. As Allison notes (2000: 134), these stories of incest are ultimately stories about "frustration" and "disappointment." Incest thus works by first shocking and then calming, drawing readers in with taboo accounts of familial sex and then tempering expectation by offering a fitting antidote. In the midst of the fall of the family, the fitting antidote to the incest narrative is the emergence of a new family. *Innocent World* contributes to the tradition of the family romance, exploring its traumas and terrors before figuring out its resolution and restoration. Ami's desire for unity and wholeness, in the guise of the androgyne, speaks to a national struggle for cohesion and the neutralization of difference. Incest exploits not only this quest for cohesion but also, and even more importantly, the nullification of difference.

The crucial disparity between the mother-son incest Allison examines and the sibling incest of *Innocent World* is the contextual backdrop for the precarity of the lost generation. In the 1980s, citizens still clung to ideals of education and hard work, and, as Allison notes, mothers provided for their diligent sons in a variety of ways. *Innocent World* reminds us of the shifting nature of the state, illuminating the ways the state was dismantled and then put back together. Thus, in Sakurai's text, only by embracing transgression can the family/state relationship be redressed. Bound by blood now, mother/sister, father/brother, and child are linked and represent an even stronger iteration of that which started to crumble in the 1990s. Ami's hope is to build a new life around a conjugal family, symbolic of youth who are tired of struggling against Japanese hegemony and simply want a place to rest.

"A far-away illness from a far-away world." That is how Akari, the seventeen-year-old protagonist of Sakurai Ami's *Tomorrow's Song* (1997), describes her conceptualization of HIV.[1] Akari's reflection on HIV's proximity—or lack thereof—to her own world comes in the wake of her testing positive for the illness after taking an at-home test. "AIDS? What kind of illness was AIDS again? I remember being handed a pamphlet once in school. You lose a lot of weight, and the chances of death after a number of years are high. Homosexuals aren't the only ones susceptible; dentists and blood products can also cause infection. That's about all I remember" (Sakurai 1998: 32). Akari's limited understanding of the circumstances surrounding contagion reflects a broader cultural blind spot regarding the ways in which HIV transmission and containment have been historically understood in the Japanese popular consciousness. Through a close reading of *Tomorrow's Song*, this section examines the cultural space of HIV in Japan from the late 1980s through the publication of the text in the mid-1990s. The 1980s saw the infiltration of HIV into the social fabric via "three big commotions" (*sandai sōdō*), namely the Matsumoto, Kobe, and Kōchi incidents. While the following decade saw the emergence of compensated dating, the risks involved in the practice contributed to the spread of HIV/AIDS and formed the context for *Tomorrow's Song*.

Initially, during the early 1980s, the Japanese public largely envisioned HIV as an issue facing the American gay community (Oike 2014: 3). The Japanese media, eager to exploit the public's lack of understanding, portrayed the Japanese themselves as the vulnerable targets of this ostensible American problem. The media adopted a language of invasion that, as Elizabeth Miller has demonstrated, resonated historically. The "black ships" that brought US Commodore Matthew Perry to Japan in 1853–54, effectively ending the Japanese seclusion policy (*sakoku*) and contributing to the fall of the Tokugawa Shogunate (1603–1868), were calculated images used by the media to portray Japan as "an island under siege" (Miller 1994: 4). At the same time, some health care professionals argued for ethnic exclusion from the "problem" of HIV. As Miller says, one health-care professional suggested that the Japanese could not contract the illness "because [they] have a different body type" from Americans. Perhaps emphasizing the foreignness of this disease, most references to AIDS in the popular literature used the Roman alphabet "AIDS" rather than the Japanized term "*Eizu*."

However, the trajectory of this contagion discourse changed with the "three big commotions" that occurred in rapid succession between 1986 and 1989. The "Matsumoto Incident" in 1986 concerned a Filipina sex worker named "Suzy" who was said to be HIV-positive, shifting the discussion toward heterosexual women in the sex industry. Importantly, "Suzy" was foreign, and so

AIDS was still thought to affect fringe communities and marginalized individuals. Nevertheless, a mild "AIDS panic" ensued (Oike 2014: 3). The unstated reason was this: the infiltration of AIDS into "the water trade," as it is politely called, meant that heterosexual men were at risk and, therefore, so were their households. Meanwhile, a headline in a popular weekly magazine read: "This is just the tip of the iceberg. '*Japayukisan*' or 'AIDS prostitutes' are landing in Japan continuously and are going all over Japan, and foreigners who are HIV-positive are slipping into the country." The term "Japayukisan" refers to foreign migrant women. "Prior to the Second World War, poor Japanese women were sent abroad to Japan's outposts to work (often as sex slaves) and were called 'Karayukisan,' meaning 'China-bound.' The term 'Japayukisan' is a play on this historical term, meaning 'Japan-bound.'" The same article referenced above goes on to warn:

> If that Filipina woman you played with that night was an AIDS patient, it's no longer another person's problem. [...] Japayukisan are everywhere. This may come into your household as well. [...] If one thinks about the fact that the many men with whom she had relations while in Japan received a gift of American AIDS from her, that is really cause for huge panic.

Threats to Japan's borders, threats to the household from outside, the need to find infected people in order to protect the public, and the possibilities of heterosexual transmission through the sex industry (foreign women, in particular) were critical themes in these narratives. However, in this discourse persisted a conceptual divide between vulnerable Japanese men on the one hand and dangerous non-Japanese women on the other.

Prophetically, in January 1989, newspaper headlines announced the first *Japanese* woman thought to have contracted HIV through heterosexual contact. Media outlets were quick to emphasize that this woman, who was from Kobe, was sexually deviant. She was said to have had sex with over one hundred men, lived with a bisexual Greek sailor, and was "probably" a prostitute. As a result of this reporting, men in and around Kobe flocked to clinics in droves. HIV was poised to make the jump from the periphery to the center, with philandering Japanese men the unwitting victims of circumstance and desire. Shortly after this media buzz, the Kobe woman died. The Ministry of Health and Welfare expressed disappointment that now they would be unable to trace her contacts. Miller notes that, in the aftermath of her death, several weekly magazines sought out the site of her funeral and published a snapshot of the funerary photograph that accompanied her coffin, in the name of the "public good" and AIDS prevention. During this "panic," the central health center in Kobe fielded over sixty thousand calls, and over three thousand people (mostly men) came for testing. Hyōgo prefectural officials were at a loss and desperate. One official was quoted in the press: "If one is leading a normal life, then one is safe." Normalcy was a key term for these officials, who advanced the notion that HIV/AIDS circulated beyond the safety and sanctity of "normal" Japanese life.

Less than a month later, the idea of "normal" came under threat. A pregnant housewife from Kōchi was the next confirmed case to cause a buzz. Newspaper columnists launched into debates over whether or not she should continue to carry the child for fear of spreading HIV to the next generation, among other topics. The irresponsibility of this mother, the perceived dangers to the future generation of Japan, and the necessity of screening women for HIV were central to these discussions.

These "three big commotions"—the Matsumoto incident, the Kobe incident, and the Kōchi incident—reveal that while HIV began as a fringe concern, only when women were the vectors of contagion did the public consciousness pay critical attention. The Matsumoto incident underlined dangers of the "*Japayukisan*"—foreign women migrant workers. The Kobe incident further fueled concerns about dangers of contact with foreigners and the dangers of prostitutes (who sleep with foreign men) in general. And the Kōchi incident, through focus on this "irresponsible, unmother-like woman," reinforced social expectations about motherhood and women as guardians of the household. The fanfare that sprang from the "three big commotions" led to the discursive construction of three new risk groups: foreign women, Japanese prostitutes, and housewives.

What is important to note in the social readings of the above incidents is the complete lack of male involvement. In each case, men are positioned as victims of female contagion. In the first and second incidents, it is men who are vulnerable to the scourge of the infected female (foreign and Japanese) "prostitutes." In the third case, the female body—always already infected—is made out to be an incubator of HIV, ready to pass on the virus to the next generation. Where is the male body in these discussions? Where is male culpability?

What Sakurai accomplishes with *Tomorrow's Song* is to give voice to an as yet unexamined risk group: the teenager. It is significant, then, that her text should be published amid the fanfare surrounding the phenomenon of compensated dating. Research on the association between HIV/AIDS and compensated dating is lacking, but *Tomorrow's Song* establishes a connection between teenage transgression and contagion, filling a palpable silence regarding the potential and largely unacknowledged consequences of this phenomenon. Indeed, sex education was, at least in the 1990s, virtually nonexistent. This is particularly the case regarding recreational—and certainly transactional—sex. Ever since the Allied Occupation, educational content regarding sexual activity has tended to focus on the maintenance of female "purity." "Purity education" is a means of distilling "wholesome thought" regarding sex and providing guidance on "virtuous" and "correct" relations between men and women. Sound and healthy societal maintenance vis-à-vis reproduction within the context of the conventional nuclear family is central to the ways that sex and sexuality are discussed in Japan. One result is that out-of-bounds sex remains a fringe topic, as do issues of contraception and alternative expressions of sexual pleasure and non-hegemonic sexualities. *Tomorrow's Song* contributes to an urgent, if nascent, discourse on the dangers involved in certain risk-taking behaviors.

Tomorrow's Song is not critical of its protagonist, Akari. Narrated through Akari's eyes, the text takes readers from her realization that she is HIV-positive through her unplanned pregnancy and finally to a romantic reconciliation with her estranged partner, Sid. In this way, the narrative reflects the trajectory of the "three big commotions," intertwining stories of prostitution and pregnancy and the migration of HIV from periphery to center. It must be said at the outset that Sakurai's novel is not *about* HIV or AIDS. Rather, it is a pseudo-science fiction narrative about a subset of telepathic and empathetic Japanese, including Akari, who rally together to prevent a madman from destroying Tokyo. Akari possesses "flippers" which allow her to experience the thoughts and feelings of others. She works part-time for the EBO science lab, which is developing a device, called a "melon," that will help restore empathy to the human experience. The novel comments on the ways in which contemporary Japanese have become disconnected from themselves and each other. In this context, the textual presence of HIV is curious. Akari's initial concern for her health gradually gives way to concern for her emotionally distraught twin sister Misaki, the fate of Tokyo, and ultimately, to her unborn child. In this way, the novel is bracketed by the specter of HIV. Yet in my analysis of the novel, I aim to bring HIV into greater focus, for Japanese cultural artifacts that give voice to those struggling with this illness are few indeed. The text deserves our attention, at the very least, for this reason.

Early in the text, boyfriend Sid brings home an HIV test as a Christmas present for Akari. "In all of Japan, no one else has a toy [*omocha*] like this," he boasts before handing over a small gift (Sakurai 30). His words lack irony, but they could be meant to suggest the foreignness of HIV in 1990s Japan. Wrapped in a package, Akari first thinks his gift is a wedding ring. After opening it, Akari decides it is a pregnancy test, explaining that she has already had "two or three" pregnancy scares in the past (Sakurai 1998: 31). Sid laughs and clarifies that it is an HIV test that detects antibodies in saliva. Akari spits on the end, and a short time later a thin red line materializes in a small box. Note that this scene is initially contingent on the fantasy of marriage, a fantasy that gives way to the cruel reality of contagion. Indeed, the thin red line that symbolizes infection ruptures the life that Akari has worked hard to build. She and Sid live in a luxury apartment. Sid earns a handsome wage at a host club, while Akari is employed at EBO. Their combined income affords them an affluent lifestyle and a way of life in which HIV ostensibly has no place. After all, Sid's reference to the HIV test as "a toy" implies frivolity, as though it is a gag gift. Seriousness sets in, however, and Sid accuses Akari of contracting HIV when she worked at a "date club," a member-only club in which paying members go on "dates" with women who were sometimes schoolgirls. "Who knows what you could have caught from those old men," he admonishes.

By aligning contagion with teenage prostitution, Sakurai draws attention to the unacknowledged dangers inherent in this social practice. As we saw at the beginning of this section, Akari knows very little about HIV—commenting that it seems to be from a "far away world." Her supposition may speak to the lack of public discourse in Japan regarding sex education and disease prevention. Sid's accusation is a one-off, and no more textual space is given to the possibility that Akari's experience working at the "date club" could have led to her infection. However, this is an important moment in the text because it plants the seed of possibility. It also shifts HIV into the realm of middle-class sexual behaviors. Prostitution is sometimes thought of as a practice of the working poor or a necessity for impoverished women (Kinsella 2014: 98). Compensated dating had particular social resonance because the girls who ostensibly participated were seemingly "motivated by the desire for luxury and fun" (Kinsella 2014: 98). Kinsella (2014: 177 demonstrates that "the spread of lower-class female lifestyles across class boundaries" is not anomalous in 1990s Japan. Historical precedent was set by "the prewar notion of the pampered and licentious modern girl (*modan gaaru*)," with her interest in Western fashion, working, and financial and sexual independence. Kinsella draws a corollary between the modern girl of the 1920s and the sexy schoolgirl of the 1990s to demonstrate that financial freedom rather than financial necessity has been a motivating factor for Japanese women since at least the prewar era. Indeed, the media frenzy surrounding compensated dating in the 1990s was largely the result of fetishistic media outlets that portrayed the schoolgirls as brazenly selfish and sexually scandalous. What was left unsaid and unaccounted for, what our interest is here, is the relationship between disease and desire. Cultural artifacts such as *Tomorrow's Song* act as barometers, allowing us to explore the anxieties of the reading public at the time.

Sakurai's novel is not the only cultural artifact to shed light on this cloaked issue. In 1998, the year following the publication of *Tomorrow's Song*, Japan's public broadcasting network, NHK, aired a miniseries about a schoolgirl who contracts HIV through compensated dating. Called *Kamisama mō sukoshi dake* (*Precious Time*), the popular series concerns seventeen-year-old Kano Masaki (the same age as Akari) who engages in prostitution in order to buy concert tickets to see her favorite singer. This is how she contracts HIV. *Precious Time* follows Masaki from before her illness until after she dies from AIDS-related complications. Along the way, the television series addresses issues including school bullying (*ijime*), family relationships, HIV/AIDS stigma, and pregnancy. Like Akari in *Tomorrow's Song*, Masaki learns she is pregnant (reminding viewers of the third of the commotions, perhaps).

She carries the ultimately healthy child to term and even gets married (to a man who knows her HIV status) on her deathbed in the hospital.

I see an interesting parallel between *Tomorrow's Song* and *Precious Time*. Appearing within a year of one another at the height of the compensated dating hurly-burly, the text and miniseries approach the same questions of sexual health and sexual risk through prostitution. Neither pursues issues of safe sex or condom use. Furthermore, as with the three big commotions, male sexual desire as the vector for contagion is not explored at any length. Even so, Sakurai and NHK deserve recognition for their pursuit of a mild form of activism.

At its core, *Tomorrow's Song* is about humanity in the face of adversity. The reader learns early on that Akari's upbringing was rough. Her father was absent, and her mother was apathetic and philandering. Still a middle-school student at this time, Akari joined the "date club" to earn money and left home, leaving her twin sister Misaki behind. Such clubs are nominally illegal, and Akari's was raided by the police. Her mother, hoping to teach Akari a lesson in responsibility, had her daughter sent to a juvenile detention center, where she lived for a short time before escaping. During her imprisonment, the reader learns late in the novel, Akari was raped by an HIV-positive guard, which is how she contracted the illness. (More on this below.) Akari never went back home. Instead, she moved in with Sid. Recent academic work on precarity and homelessness in Japan focuses on the lack of an *ibasho*, or "place." "Everyone needs a place, identity, affiliation," Anne Allison notes, citing activist Amamiya Karin: "we need an *ibasho* that finds us necessary." *Ibasho*, Allison writes, is a human right. But this right is increasingly denied to individuals in Japan who find themselves robbed of their "zone(s) of comfort." The fractured home life Akari sought to escape is a reminder that citizens sometimes live under duress, finding their home lives intolerable. We find in *Tomorrow's Song* a near-perfect portrait of the family in decay: a father who is never home because of obligations to the company, and an antagonistic relationship between mother and daughter that culminates in the daughter leaving home in search of better comforts.

Denied the comforts of an *ibasho* (safety, sanctuary, belonging, and humanity), Akari strikes out on her own, using the allure of her body in a cultural moment fixated on the body of the teenage girl. The text centralizes the body with its evocation of HIV discourse. After taking the HIV test and reading the results, Akari binges on drugs and alcohol. She and Sid go to a club in Shibuya where she buys marijuana and methamphetamine ("S" in Japanese, for *shabu*, speed) from a "hippy Japanese." Sometimes, she explains, she buys from "an Iranian acquaintance" (*kao najimi no Iranjin*). She allows a Russian to flirt with her. He strikes up a strange conversation about syphilis in Russia, opining that the Japanese do not suffer from such problems because they are all "happy." He then tells her that "love is the best protection" from STDs like syphilis and HIV. Akari is irritated by the conversation: "Is this asshole hitting on me?" She invites him to the women's bathroom and has unprotected sex with him. Afterward, in blue lipstick, she scrawls on his t-shirt, "Welcome to the wonderful AIDS world" (in English). This scene emphasizes woman as contagion. As with the three big commotions, it is the woman's body that is a threat to the sexual prowess of man. Sid witnesses the event from afar. When Akari emerges from the bathroom, he strikes her across the face. Here, Akari's body is reaffirmed as the site of contagion, recklessness (drugs, unprotected sex), and domestic violence. Akari weaponizes her sexuality against the Russian while at the same time she is punished with home-grown masculine violence for stepping out of bounds.

This is not her first encounter with masculine violence. As mentioned, at the juvenile detention center she was raped by an HIV-positive guard. This act robs Akari of her sense of personhood and agency. At the same time, the act underscores the power imbalance embedded in the guard-prisoner relationship. Due to the traumatic nature of the event, Akari has suppressed it from her memory. She learns late in the text, as do readers, the true cause of her infection. It was not her participation in the date club that exposed her to HIV; rather, it was pure masculine aggression and sexual desire against which she had no defense.

Unprotected sex with the Russian, then, reads as an attempt to return HIV to the male sexual body. At the same time, the incident in the club carries the weight of an important moment in Japanese cultural history. Miller's work on HIV in Japan demonstrates that Japanese health officials were concerned with the cost of "internationalization." She writes: "In numerous discussions of AIDS in Japan, AIDS was represented as an inevitable consequence of 'internationalization' as well as an example of how Japan is becoming 'internationalized' as the number of HIV cases rises." Miller points out that notions of "internationalization" are mutable and include "the nation-state's powerful global position." Concurrently, however, "internationalization" implies "social disorder: crime by foreigners, migrant workers, AIDS." Miller positions HIV as a symptom of a "borderless age" (*bōdāresu jidai*), a term, she says, that was gaining currency in Japanese intellectual circles in the late 1980s and early 1990s. She explains that "the dissolution of borders raises questions about the maintenance of inside and outside through the manipulation of symbolic forms." In the early 1980s, as already described above, HIV was widely considered an "outside" problem. Miller also reads the "global reality of an AIDS epidemic" that "respects no borders" as equally symbolic of the borderless age of millennial Japan. The dance club reflects nicely Japanese "borderlessness." The foreigners that Akari and Sid encounter inhabit zones of insubordination. They lack dimension textually and are reduced to their outsider status in the narrative as "the Russian" and "the Iranian." Threat and degradation are marked as foreign; drugs and HIV in Japan carry associations of scourges and infiltrations from abroad.

Even the HIV test Sid brings home is of foreign origin. After the test reads positive, Akari attempts to contact the manufacturer. She finds, however, that other than an obscure reference to the USA as the test's place of production, there is no other identifying mark. This upsets her and causes her to feel helpless. We can conclude, then, that threats to Akari's insular world indeed come from abroad: the foreign HIV test brings with it confirmation of foreign illness. In this light, Akari's incident with the Russian reads as though she is also attempting to return HIV to the outside world and the body of an outsider.

We are reminded, then, of the difficulty of individuals relating to each other in the text. The premise rests on the conceptual division between those with "flippers" and those without. Although Akari has been dealt a difficult hand, she possesses empathetic abilities that allow her to experience the sufferings of others. This is an ability that she briefly chooses to ignore, in light of her HIV-positive status. She desires to live recklessly and to cause harm, to live as a "gidophiliac," one of the members of society that victimizes others.

In the process, she disavows the prospect of heteronormativity. In spite of her struggles as a young teenager, by the time Akari is seventeen she has acquired some symbols of normative middle-class existence. She lives with a partner, earns an income, and even expresses an interest in marriage, as demonstrated by her initial reaction to the box Sid brings home containing the HIV test. In fact, she envisions a closet bursting with clothes, as well as trips to the nail salon and leisurely drives in a Jeep, accompanied by an Irish Setter and Belgian Shepherd—her "children"—piled in the backseat. The regime of heternomativity offers stability and the prospect of a bright future. It is a "script" that provides means of orientation—a "straightening device" that aligns bodies in particular ways with the promise of particular rewards. With the intrusion of HIV, however, these fantasies of ordinariness are fractured by drug use, vindictive unprotected sex outside of a conjugal setting, and domestic violence. The specter of HIV clouds Akari's vision of ordinary life and with it, the future and its guarantees. She begins living only for the present, for HIV in an era before medical breakthroughs forestall the future. So why not live fast?

In this light, Akari is one of Japan's lost children, a figure whose body is marred with the scars of ontological struggle. The figure of the child in distress is powerful, for it asks us to question the state of things. Lee Edelman argues that children represent the communal efforts of adult citizens to provide for and watch over their young. In this paradigm, children are figures of potentiality. They are bodies to be inscribed by dominant cultural, social, political, religious, and philosophical (among other) discourses. Japan in the 1990s was awash in stories of youth gone wild. From schoolgirl prostitutes to child killers, young Japanese were portrayed as a demographic in crisis. Their actions seemingly reflected the erosion of traditional values and portended the collapse of the sanctity of the future. The "child or youth stands in for the past and future of the nation, in terms of the temporality imputed to their development, as well as the value assumed to be latent within." The family troubles that befell Akari early in life betray the tensions inherent in the nuclear family. Furthermore, her assault as a ward of the state speaks to the inability of social institutions to protect the young. HIV is therefore an appropriate symbol for the untenability of the future in a nation in crisis.

Crisis is the refrain of the novel at the level of the individual and the nation. It is not only Akari who is under duress. Her twin sister Misaki is also burdened. As a middle-school student, she became involved with one of her teachers, who impregnated her. She ultimately miscarried. As a result, Misaki retreated into herself and refused to leave her bedroom for two years. Misaki eventually decides to abandon the claustrophobic safety of her bedroom for the escapism provided by drugs, alcohol, and partying. Misaki has not seen her sister Akari since Akari left home, but the pair reunite in the club, where Akari spots Misaki dancing with a blind musician named Chiaki. Not without a sense of irony, the novel's emphasis on empathy and "seeing" into the lives of others is undercut by Chiaki's blindness. A good-natured individual, he cares deeply for the emotionally wounded Misaki. In spite of his efforts, she falls into a coma, where she remains for the majority of the novel.

For Akari, in contrast, pregnancy presents a turning point. Akari learns of her pregnancy when she goes to the doctor to confirm her HIV-positive status, and the child orients her away from expressions of self-harm and self-destruction and toward righting herself and her surroundings. In this respect, the child conforms to Edelman's ideas on futurity, influencing the ways in which Akari relates to Japanese society and offering her a new sense of bodily integrity and hope for the future.

She therefore begins to take measures to suture her family whole. With her child in mind, she and Sid reconcile. Akari also takes it upon herself to look after Misaki when the latter is comatose in the hospital. In an important moment in the text, Akari uses her "flippers" to "see" into Misaki's mind. There she discovers the context for Misaki's affair with Nagino, her middle-school teacher. Nagino manipulated Misaki and coaxed her into a sexual relationship. Misaki insisted she would carry the baby to term, with or without Nagino. Fearing for his job and the threat of alimony for his current wife, Nagino kidnapped Misaki and tried to murder her. She survived but lost the baby. This loss cripples Misaki, and she is unable to overcome the emotional distress caused by Nagino. This experience is partially to blame for Misaki's years barricaded in her room as well as subsequent struggles with drugs and alcohol. Sakurai uses the term *kyōshi* ("the teacher") to describe Nagino, certainly to diminish his personhood but, more importantly, to remind readers that the man is in a socially authorized role as an educator and instructor. Misaki was but one teenager victimized by Nagino. He strangled another junior high school student and convinced yet another to kill herself. Nagino is a predator, the worst kind of adult male, whose thirst for sexual conquest lures Misaki—the "good" daughter—into the worst corners of the adult world, where someone like her does not belong.

However, Sakurai renders Nagino a victim of circumstances. What amounts to a monstrous misogyny is the result of his own warped experiences as a child. As he explains to Akari after he has kidnapped her, his mother forced him into a sexual relationship when he was still a boy. She possessed a carnal love for her son that she was not able to replicate emotionally. He takes his displaced frustration out on girls rather than women because in his mind it is only a matter of time before they take on the sinister, affective shape of his mother. "All women are the same," he complains at one point. In this manner, the novel drives home sex as the site of pain and consequence: for Akari, it is HIV; for her sister, it is a miscarriage and emotional harm; even for Nagino, it is child abuse and incest. This is not to suggest that Sakurai excuses Nagino's behavior by placing him within the population of the disabused and sentimental subaltern; it is, however, to say that Sakurai contextualizes Nagino's injurious and warped behavior vis-à-vis the failures of his mother. In effect, he becomes like her, reproducing the gendered distress she caused him.

Tomorrow's Song thus coincides with Lauren Berlant's formulation of empathy as an affective, if ineffective, narrative device. She argues that narratives dedicated to trafficking in distress ultimately prove ineffective as demands for redress. The habitual, repetitive harm done to Japan's younger generation(s) emerges as their source of recognition and identification with each other. For example, the reader learns of Nagino's conditions of injury through what amounts to a confessional disclosure. Confessions are acts of attrition, gambits for acceptance and recognition. Nagino's disclosure of his antipathy and hatred for women—he wants to "erase" (*kesu*) the world's "irritating (*jama*) women"—is an attempt to publicize the anguish that governs his own private sphere and forge, warped as it may be, a lexicon of injury and harm that crosses genders and generations. According to Berlant, the logic of empathy risks becoming a goal in and of itself emptied of political potential. "Pain centered politics," she writes, are often compromised by the lie of "affective identification and empathy," in which "the capacity for suffering and trauma" is taken to be the "core" of individual and collective existence. (Berlant 1998: 636). We see this in *Tomorrow's Song*, in which every body (everybody) is damaged goods. (Akari calls herself "fallen girl" [*hametsu teki na onna no ko*].) Nagino's confession must be understood in the context of the novel's broader aims to illuminate the psychic anguish and affective struggles of young Japanese. As context for his deranged behavior, Nagino's disclosure of his damaged past offers up a platform for the illusion of knowing the other through the common identification of pain.

Berlant is critical of the ways in which empathy has been commodified in US popular culture. She looks to popular media platforms as examples of empathy's commodity value. She addresses the fantasy of empathetic identification as a consumer distraction: "The political as a place of acts oriented toward publicness becomes replaced by a world of private thoughts, leanings, and gestures" (Berlant 1998: 641). Here Berlant references talk shows, films, and novels that showcase injury in a passive fashion. Berlant wants political change and sees the indiscriminate airing of personal detriment to be a distraction from activism. Identification is possible, she argues, but not much else. Writes Berlant: "[W]hen sentimentality meets politics, it uses personal stories to tell of structural effects, but in so doing it risks thwarting its very attempt to perform rhetorically a scene of pain that must be soothed politically" (Berlant 1998: 641). Moreover, victimization is the thread of identification in the publicizing of pain: in *Tomorrow's Song*, for instance, all are victims of contemporary circumstance. Victimization within commodity capitalism is an especially pernicious enterprise, according to Berlant, for the underprivileged, abused, and downtrodden become spectacles. Suffering and its analogs are destinations in this formulation, a point of arrival, and, even better, one of departure.

In our case, the woes of the characters in *Tomorrow's Song* congeal to embody the detriments of Japanese social life at the turn of the century. Nagino's confession occurs alongside his attempt to project his psychic pain onto the whole of Japan. After he kidnaps Akari, he takes her on a killing spree in which he blows up the "Lifeway" factories scattered throughout Tokyo. In another confessional dialogue, Nagino explains that his father created the Lifeway brand food preservation product, and he achieved much success. Lifeway was proven to be detrimental to health, however, and Nagino's father lost his fortune and then committed suicide. Nagino's terrorist acts enact scenes of destruction are carried out in front of Akari so he can have an audience to witness his psychological turmoil (his anguish as a destination). His acts are also punctuated by his rape of Akari, in which he treats her like a "rubber doll" and "gouges" (*eguru*) her "womb" with his penis.

Akari eventually escapes and formulates a plan with Chiaki (Misaki's boyfriend) to stop Nagino. Akari lures Nagino to a middle school, where Chiaki and a group of youths are waiting to confront him. These youths are all, like Chiaki, mentally or physically challenged in some way. "Defect" or handicap, as we have seen in our earlier discussion of *Innocent World*, is an extended metaphor for the state of Japanese society at the millennial turn. The showdown between young Japanese and Nagino is therefore an attempt to protect innocence from further erosion. Akari's role in this confrontation is precipitated by her desire to leave innocence behind. Having experienced life beyond the warped safety of the schoolyard or the family and void of the comfort of friends (she mentions none), Akari attempts to make amends for stepping too far out of bounds.

Telepathically, Akari leads Nagino to the middle school. When he arrives, he is adamant that, unlike the misfit youth that have gathered to stop him, he has no need for connections. "Since I was thirteen, I've been completely free," he declares. He pulls a knife from his pocket and threatens to kill Akari. "You can't kill me, but I can kill you. That's how free I am," he says (Sakurai 1998: 178). The youth, including Sid and Misaki, surround Nagino and begin to sing to him. Misaki's presence among the group is particularly resonant given that her doctors predicted she would die. She speaks to him, affectionately calling him by his given named Shōji. She speaks of their dead child, envisioning him as a "boy" as beautiful as "Narcissus" (Sakurai 1998: 181). In anger, Nagino attacks her, but he is taken aback by a disembodied voice from his past: "I don't want to become a monster. That's why I killed my mother. Believe me. You have to believe me" (Sakurai 1998: 182). Thirteen-year-old Nagino continues to speak: "If I kill my mother, I'll be all alone in the world. But if I don't the two of us will turn into disgusting bug-like creatures that roll around in the dirt and feed off of the blood of humans. I don't want to see that happen to her. So I will kill her. That makes sense, right?" (Sakurai 1998: 182). Nagino wrestles with the specter of his teenage self, who continues to speak of his own guilt and burden: "I love my mother. But I'm scared.... It would be better to die. Someone, get me out of this prison. I want to be free. Kill me" (Sakurai 1998: 183). Nagino dies when these two halves of his psyche converge, and the voice from his past effectively grants his wish for freedom.

Nagino's death liberates Akari as well. She comments that she is now "just a little different" from who she was "in the past" (Sakurai 1998: 186). She notes that although her stomach has yet to show signs of pregnancy, her "receptors" are picking up something. "It's alive," she says. "It's breathing" (Sakurai 1998: 187). When Akari and Sid then go for a drive, she comments on the intensity of the sun's rays. "It's so bright and blurry (*nijimu*), I can't see anything" (Sakurai 1998: 187). The text ends here, with Akari squinting into the sun's brightness and thinking optimistically about the future. Akari's comment that she "can't see anything" speaks to her inability to know the future. And, like the blind Chiaki, Akari's own sense of blindness provides an antidote to her prior preoccupation with telepathic "sight."

There is hope in the glittering sun at the conclusion of *Tomorrow's Song*, a glint of optimism, as Akari emerges from her struggles bruised but not broken. Her unborn child reorients the text toward that which had seemed so far out of reach—the future. And yet, despite the optimistic presence of the sun, much remains unknown/unseen. The specter of HIV is left unresolved. Is Sid also infected? What of Akari's unborn baby? These are important issues, and *Tomorrow's Song* is frustratingly inconclusive here. Akari's myopic interest in her bourgeoning family eclipses the greater issues at hand and takes for granted the destructive potential of HIV. To her credit, Sakurai offers a quiet meditation on HIV, a social issue that has received little critical attention in the public consciousness. But she also sidesteps a teaching moment here in favor of a more streamlined and positive conclusion. Her rhetorical methodology reproduces the social complacency of HIV as an inconsequential nuisance.

Sakurai's fiction is ultimately about how young Japanese get unstuck, how they move forward, how they navigate the vicissitudes of recessionary Japan. These teenagers embrace transgression as a way to reject Japanese social life but in each case, transgression becomes a means to an end; transgression *is* the way forward, but their relinquishment of transgression speaks to a sense of "growing up." One cannot transgress forever, Sakurai seems to suggest, if one wants to find stability in unstable times.

Note

1 It should be pointed out that there is a perpetual issue with HIV-related terminology in Japanese discourse. "HIV" (in Japanese, *hito men'ekifuzen uirusu*) and "AIDS" (*Eizu* or *kotensei men'ekifuzen shōkōgun*) are often and mistakenly used interchangeably. The former is a virus, while the latter is the amalgamation of diseases and infections caused by the HIV virus.

WORKS CITED

Allison, Anne. 2000. *Permitted and Prohibited Desires: Mothers, Comics, and Censorship in Japan*. Berkeley, CA: University of California Press.

Allison, Anne. 2013. *Precarious Japan*. Durham: Duke University Press.

Berlant, Lauren. 1998. "Poor Eliza." *American Literature* (September), 70(3): 635–68. https://doi.org/10.2307/2902712 [accessed 30 May 2023].

Edelman, Lee. 2004. *No Future: Queer Theory and the Death Drive*. Durham: Duke University Press.

Etō Jun. 1993. *Seijuku to sōshitsu: haha no hōkai (Maturity and Loss: Collapse of the Mother)*. Tokyo: Kōdansha.

Hurley, Adrienne. 2011. *Revolutionary Suicide and Other Desperate Measures: Narratives of Youth and Violence from Japan and the United States*. Durham: Duke University Press.

Iida, Yumiko. 2002. *Rethinking Identity in Modern Japan: Nationalism as Aesthetics*. New York, NY: Routledge.

Kinsella, Sharon. 2014. *Schoolgirls, Money and Rebellion in Japan*. New York, NY: Routledge.

Kurahashi, Yumiko. 2015 [1998]. "An Extraterrestrial." In *The Woman with the Flying Head and Other Stories*, translated by Atsuko Sakaki, 3–28. New York, NY, Routledge.

Levi-Strauss, Claude. 1969. *The Elementary Structures of Kinship*. Translated by James Harle Bell and John Richard von Sturmer. Edited by Rodney Needham. Boston, MA: Beacon Press.

McLelland, Mark. 2003. "Review of *Men and Masculinities in Contemporary Japan: Dislocating the Salaryman Doxa*." *Intersections: Gender, History and Culture in the Asian Context* (9). Online at: http://intersections.anu.edu.au/issue9/mclelland_review.html [accessed 11 July 2018].

Miller, Elizabeth. 1994. *A Borderless Age: AIDS, Gender, and Power in Contemporary Japan*. PhD Dissertation. Ann Arbor, MI: UMI.

Nakamura, Karen. 2013. *A Disability of the Soul: An Ethnography of Schizophrenia and Mental Illness in Contemporary Japan*. Ithaca, NY: Cornell University Press.

Ōe Kenzaburō. 2002. *Rouse Up O Young Men of the New Age*. Translated by John Nathan. New York, NY: Grove Press.

Oike, Machiko. 2014. "Nihon no shōsetsu to HIV/AIDS." *Bunmei kagaku kenkyū* 9: 1–24.

Robertson, Jennifer. 2005. "Biopower: Blood, Kinship, and Eugenic Marriage." In *A Companion to the Anthropology of Japan*, edited by Jennifer Robertson, 329–354. Malden, MA: Blackwell Publishing.

Sakaki, Atsuko. 1999. "(Re)Cannonizing Kurahashi Yumiko: Toward Alternative Perspectives for 'Modern' 'Japanese' 'Literature.'" In *Ōe and Beyond: Fiction in Contemporary Japan*, edited by Stephen Snyder and Philip Gabriel, 153–176. Honolulu, HI: University of Hawai'i Press.

Sakurai Ami. 1996. *Innosento wārudo* (trans. *Innocent World*). Tokyo: Gentōsha.

Sakurai Ami. 1998. *Tumorozu songu* (Tomorrow's Song). Tokyo: Gentōsha.

Sakurai Ami. 2004. *Innocent World*, translated by Stephen Clark. New York, NY: Vertical Books.

Ueno Chizuko. 2009. *The Modern Family in Japan: Its Rise and Fall*. Melbourne: Trans Pacific Press.

5

THE TWO BODIES OF KIRINO NATSUO

Grotesque and *Real World*

In Kirino Natsuo's *Grotesque* (*Gurotesuku*, 2003) and *Real World* (*Riaru wārudo*, 2004), the fissures of Japanese social life are grafted onto women who are murdered by emotionally unstable and sexually frustrated men. In these texts, women must be erased, and Kirino's victims are the stereotypical and polarized images of whore (in *Grotesque*) and mother (*Real World*). In neither case does the central murder occur on the page. *Grotesque* opens after Zhang, the immigrant killer of prostitutes Yuriko and, presumably, Kazue, has already been captured; the events of *Real World* unfold after the protagonist, Toshiko, overhears her neighbor murder his mother with a baseball bat. These novels are not concerned with the violent acts themselves but rather with the aftermath. Both attend to the conceptual space of violence against women as a form of gendered revolt against the female subject that obfuscates a desire for Japanese identity and stability. While Kirino's earlier and widely acclaimed novel *Out* (*Auto*, 1997) is striking in its investment in women killers, the works discussed in this chapter turn to the familiar terrain of violent acts that reproduce gender codes and binaries. Indeed, the texts in question play on a number of familiar pop-cultural tropes around gendered violence, such as fallen or transgressive women and the representation of crime for public edification.

By focusing on crimes that have already been committed, Kirino questions the legitimacy of social life in millennial Japan. Beyond the complexities of male "violence and the right to it" (Copeland 2004: 250), Kirino takes particular issue with the deleterious effects of fraudulent meritocracy and rampant fetishization of adolescent female sexuality. Her texts align with others discussed in this study, all of which have harsh things to say about women's place in contemporary Japan. The fiction by Kanehara Hitomi and Sakurai

DOI: 10.4324/9781003231806-6

Ami discussed in Chapters 3 and 4 illuminates the experiences of growing up displaced and homeless (both figuratively and literally) in the lingering shadow of economic recession. Kanehara's pseudo-autobiographical *Snakes and Earrings* and Sakurai's journalism-inflected *Innocent World* offer stylized portraits of Japanese teenagers struggling to get by. As we will see in the discussion that follows, Kirino takes a different approach by drawing inspiration from real-life cases of violence and reworking them to prove many of the same points.

Grotesque is loosely influenced by the "Tōden OL satsujin-jiken" (the Tōden OL ["office lady"] Murder Case),[1] the 1997 murder of thirty-nine-year-old Watanabe Yasuko, a senior researcher at Tokyo Electric Power Company who also moonlighted as a prostitute. Media fascination swirled around Watanabe's supposed double-life, and in the process "evok[ed] a well-worn pornographic trope: the specter of a good woman with the hidden face of a whore" (Yoda 2006b: 186). Intellectual interest in the case, however, focused on Watanabe's turn to prostitution as a response to the double-standards that frame Japanese female subjectivity. Although well-paid and successful, Watanabe inevitably faced a cultural backlash for refusing to leave her career for the sake of family life, as is customary (and expected) of Japanese women. Also, for Watanabe, sex work may have been a means of negotiating the "dysfunction of corporate life and middle-class domesticity" in which she found herself ensnared (Yoda 2006b: 187). Kazue, the character in *Grotesque* most closely based on Watanabe, is similarly bound by the contradictions of Japanese social life. A graduate of the prestigious Q High School for Young Women (based on Keiō's Women's High School, where Watanabe matriculated) and a similarly elite college, Kazue is poised for corporate success. Frustrated by the social and professional barriers she continues to encounter, however, she turns to night-work, claiming prostitution as a means to rebel against gender norms and the male-oriented and male-dominated corporate world. Like Watanabe, Kazue keeps a detailed log of her customers and the amount of money exchanged. And like Watanabe, her body is found in an empty apartment, and one of her customers is arrested and charged with the murder. Zhang, a Chinese national in Japan illegally, maintains his innocence; but he admits to killing Kazue's friend, Yuriko, who is also a prostitute, because of a misdirected sexual desire for his own sister.[2]

Kirino deploys the murder trope in *Real World* as well, drawing inspiration from the real-life events surrounding the "Kōbe renzoku jidō sasshō jiken" (the Kobe Child Murders). As discussed in Chapter 2, in May 1997, Sakakibara Seitō, the pseudonym of a fourteen-year-old junior high school student, strangled and beheaded an eleven-year-old classmate, Hase Jun. While this was not the first instance of juvenile crime in Japan, it was regarded as irrefutable evidence that the Japanese family was in disrepair. While the education system had long been held responsible for the welfare of Japanese youth, the blame shifted to the family after the Kobe Child Murders.

As Andrea G. Arai has demonstrated, Sakakibara's actions provided sociologists and educators with a dangerous glimpse into Japan's future. Notwithstanding the disturbing violence of the murder (Sakakibara later confessed to killing ten-year-old Yamashita Aya and to attacking several other girls), commentators were concerned about the psychological and emotional welfare of Japan's juveniles, concluding that "the child" was now "an object either to be feared for or afraid of" (Arai 2006: 222). In other words, Japan's youth were regarded as the locus of the adult world's failures, as though there was a latent Sakakibara Seitō in every child just waiting to get out. In Sakakibara's 2015 autobiography, incomprehensibly titled *Zekka* (*Desperate Song*), he refers to himself as "Motoshōnen A" (Former Child A)—because he was a juvenile when he committed the murders; his real name was never made public—and writes of sexual depravity and finding beauty in his actions. Appropriately, the murderer in *Real World* (whom the other characters refer to as Worm—his actual name is never disclosed) is driven to kill by a combination of his hatred of the educational system, mental instability, and sexual frustration. Although he attends a prestigious high school, Worm is burdened by his mother's quest for status and her obsession over her son's academic pedigree. Her insistence that he devote himself to his studies at all costs compromises his social and sexual development. Worm's mother thus becomes the focal point of his anger and frustration toward Japanese social hegemony and his own stunted sexuality.

Grotesque and *Real World* are texts of complaint and critique, and the murders that foreground the narratives themselves afford Kirino a platform for social commentary. To this end, the point of these texts is not the violent acts against women (a mainstay of popular media), and the characters of import are not the agents of that violence; rather, Kirino's focus is on bonds between women and how, in contemporary Japan, those bonds are doomed to failure. In both texts, female relationships are compromised and diminished by the intrusion of, and ultimately the necessity for, male sexuality. *Grotesque* is concerned with the friendship and petty rivalries of Yuriko and her classmates Kazue and Mitsuru. Narrated by Yuriko's unforgiving (and unnamed) sister, the text tracks uncomfortably the inhospitable social climate of Q High School before addressing the paths that Kazue and Yuriko take toward prostitution. In *Real World*, four high school female friends help Worm evade capture by the police. All five principal characters take turns narrating the text, and while Worm's crime and its motivation set events in motion, of primary concern are the ways in which the girls' friendship unravels as a consequence of their involvement—and complicity—in Worm's actions.

The centrality of male sexuality and frustration in the grim outcome of these texts speaks to Lauren Berlant's observations on "complaint" as a literary mode. In women's complaint texts, Berlant argues, women repeatedly return to sites of pain, disappointment, and rage, not out of masochistic pleasure but because of social conditioning and the allure of unrealized personal, political, and affective potential. Men are often, though not always, the vector of women's complaints—directly or indirectly—and these kinds of narratives often address the vicissitudes of romantic love, gender inequality, and social immobility. Berlant theorizes the reasons why women are able to cling to heteronormativity and normative resolutions to instability and attrition, through what she calls "the juxtapolitical," or a cultural sphere that approaches but fails to achieve political discourse. In lieu of active dissent, aggression, and engagement with structural inequalities and the supremacy of male culture, these texts often privilege the emotional toll for women who form bad attachments to social life. Berlant (2008: x) writes that complaint narratives "act [...] as a critical chorus that sees the expression of emotional response and conceptual recalibration as achievement enough."

Kirino's critique of normative Japanese culture centers on the downward spiral and ultimate destruction of her female characters. My contention is that the bad decisions these characters make are precipitated by their attempts to navigate an unforgiving social terrain in which women remain in positions of inferiority. Prostitution (*Grotesque*) and matricide (*Real World*) can be read and theorized as transgressive acts of aggression and agency. As demonstrated in Chapter 4, middle-class women who willingly traffic in sex work complicate the typical association of prostitution with poor or indentured women. In *Grotesque*, Kazue and Yuriko do not see sex work in terms of potential upward mobility, driven instead by revenge and aspirations for social and professional agency. Similarly, violence toward the mother captures the youthful aggression and destructive desire of the teenage son in *Real World*. For the four female high school students in this latter text, involvement in Worm's murder affords them the opportunity to demonstrate dissent and displeasure toward the adult world and, more importantly, the women—and potential mothers—they will inevitably become.

These two novels are dependent on the figure of the "teenage menace," a term used by Adrienne Hurley (2011: 13) in her comparative study of youth violence in Japan and the US. Hurley draws attention to the methods through which Japanese and American mass media imagine young people as coercive threats to social cohesion. Hurley's concern is with the ironic and simultaneous cultural constructions and prohibition of violent crimes committed by young people. That is, she charts the ways in which children are harmed by US and Japanese culture and *turned into* killers and victimizers through processes specific to late-capitalist societies; at the same time, these killers are held responsible for their crimes, often at the expense of understanding and intervention.

Andrea G. Arai has similarly interrogated the figure of the "wild child" in recessionary Japan, looking at two specific examples from 1997 of youth gone wild: San, the feral heroine of Miyazaki Hayao's *Mononoke hime*

(*Princess Mononoke*, 1997), and media portrayals of Shōnen A, or Sakakibara Seitō. Kirino's texts offer snapshots of youth behaving poorly: truant, rebellious schoolgirls and a teenage boy who seemingly takes pleasure in murdering his mother. She taps into the anxieties surrounding the commercial success of narratives about wild Japanese youth who, at least in *Grotesque*, become wild Japanese adults. I read their endings as solutions to the problem of Japan's bad children: poorly behaved characters are punished.

While *The End of Transgression* as a whole is concerned with fictional representations of youthful rebellion and misbehavior, this chapter looks specifically at Kirino's figuration of the emergence and demise of the "wild" Japanese schoolgirl. Together, *Grotesque* and *Real World* comment on the conditions under which young Japanese women grow to rebel against the structures of their own social development. Drawing on the work of Judith Herman, Hurley (2011: 86) comments on the difference between lives that are disrupted by traumatic events and those that are "formed in a state of constant traumatic disruption." In the Japanese context, the recession, along with other social and political upheavals, upset the lives of those who grew up after the war and invested themselves in economic rebuilding. In contrast, youth who were born after the economic bubble burst have known only the trauma of a stagnant, empty reality. The primary characters in Kirino's novels do not know the affluence of the 1970s and 1980s and are immune to the lure of education and its potential payoffs. Similarly, they did not come of age during the reconfiguration of the Japanese home and ascent of the myth of the professional housewife (*sengyō shufu*), who existed in support of her breadwinning husband. Instead, these characters are invested in retaliating against the now empty signifiers of a once affluent Japan.

In *Grotesque*, characters' terrible experiences in school and at home foreground their later turn to sex work, which then leads to their murder. In *Real World*, friends equally dismayed by school and home life help Worm cover up his murder, a decision that proves disastrous for all involved. It is thus necessary to examine briefly the ways in which previously sanguine educational institutions turned Japanese youth against themselves. These themes were approached in the previous chapter's analysis of Sakurai Ami's *Innocent World*, with particular attention to teenage prostitution (compensated dating) as supposed retaliation against classroom boredom and the emotionally and physically abusive home life of protagonist Ami and her half-brother Takuya. My reading of Kanehara Hitomi's *Snakes and Earrings*, in contrast, focused on the lack of these institutions rather than their social detriment. Kirino's texts therefore contribute to a discourse of negativity and complaints regarding the social topography of recessionary Japan but fail to successfully transgress against it.

Until 1945, the Japanese school system was an indoctrination tool of imperial ideology. One of the primary goals of the Allied Occupation was the political reorientation of Japan, a crucial component of which was the dismantling and reassembling of Japan's education network and severing its connection to the military state. This complicated and not entirely successful process entailed nullifying the Imperial Rescript on Education, removing curricular decisions and textbook publication from State control, and extending compulsory education from six to nine years. The aim was to decentralize and "democratize" the education system and to liberate Japanese subjects from the weight of the government's failed imperial ambitions.

The Fundamental Law of Education introduced the concept of equal education, regardless of ability, transforming schooling from an honor for the elite to a privilege for all. Following the end of the Occupation in 1952, however, Japanese leaders reacted to the egalitarian approach to education advocated by the occupiers by instituting a rigid system of exams and promotion. Secondary and higher education were diversified in line with broader conservative trends in the political realm. Postwar emphasis on economic growth and human capital infiltrated classrooms to create the next generation of skilled workers. With the neoliberal turn in Japanese education from the 1960s, higher education again "became a sorting machine for the middle-class masses" (Gordon 2002: 119). Japanese leaders place a heavy emphasis on scholastic achievement, and exams took on special significance as a means to "slot young men and women into appropriate levels and roles in the work place" (Gordon 2002: 120). Indeed, Ronald Dore's (1976) observations on Japan's "diploma disease" speak to a cultural moment in which education was the nexus of—and solution to—national, cultural, political, and economic concerns.

The demand for a competitive edge, unsurprisingly, surged. Personal wealth and a social preoccupation with credentialism fueled the emergent cram school, or *juku*, industry, which intensified the demand on children to succeed academically. Education, rather than a gateway to opportunity, was repurposed as a means to status and prestige, with social emphasis not on the acquisition of education itself but rather what school one attended. The toll on Japanese youth was great, drawing the attention of social critics who were concerned that the cost of academic elitism overshadowed its rewards. Too much was being asked of Japanese children too soon, and the ramifications were extreme. Violence, bullying, suicide, and reports of students refusing to go to school were topics widely publicized in the media from the 1970s that continue to dominate headlines today. These developments painted a grim picture of the contemporary education landscape, and from the 1990s the classroom was increasingly portrayed as being on the verge of "collapse" (*hōkai*).

At the center of the educational web was the mother, whose dedication to the advancement of her children led to the title "*kyōiku mama*" or education mother. Everything depended on a child's success at school—social success, family prestige, and even a mother's identity. A woman was expected to invest so exclusively in her children that nothing else mattered—not her husband, not even her own happiness. The pressure to protect and promote the child was so great, that in extreme cases women slipped into incestuous relationships with their sons, as noted in Chapter 4. The all-loving mother transforms into a monster.

The collapse of the economy in the late 1980s and early 1990s exposed the extent to which the Japanese education system reproduced social inequality rather than offering the opportunity for upward mobility. The façade of credentialism was undermined by extensive job loss and sociocultural stasis, throwing into disarray the tenets of duty and sacrifice that shaped familial relationships since the Meiji period. Thus, the rise and fall of education mirrors the rise and fall of the family, as well as the nation. Following the promulgation of the Imperial Rescript on Education in 1890, philosopher Inoue Tetsujirō argued that "a people's position as subjects is just like children's position to their parents, which means that a nation is an extended family and that commands and orders given by the monarch of the nation to his subjects are no different from instructions given [...] by the parents of a family to their children" (qtd. Ueno 2009: 64). These sentiments are echoed in Kawaji Toshiyoshi's proclamation that "the nation is a family, the government the parents, the people the children, and their police their nursemaids" (qtd. in Gluck 1985: 187). The Meiji government drew from Confucian ethics to inform its conceptualization of a new nation for new times, advocating an ideological paradigm in which the emperor was the symbolic father of the family-state. Filial piety and monarchic loyalty, two distinct concepts in Confucianism, were compressed into a single idea, *chū-kō*, to subsume family responsibilities under national responsibilities. The notion of the family state (*kazoku kokka*) was a crucial ideological construct that effectively bound citizens to the emperor, who was portrayed as both father of his nation of children and nucleus of the national body or polity (*kokutai*). In this paradigm, all citizens had clearly articulated roles that would benefit the home and the nation. Women in particular—denied rights as citizens—were asked to become citizens by proxy, raising and educating their children and dutifully serving their husbands, who were charged with advancing capitalist enterprises.

The end of the Pacific War left the mythology of the family state in ruins. The Occupation-enforced Civil Code of 1948 codified into law the abolition of the prewar family system and dislocated the primogeniture at its core. In law (if not practice), women were granted voting and property rights and other social freedoms. As Yumiko Iida explains, however, the resulting social environment left many Japanese in a state of confusion and anxiety. She writes: "With the emergence in the postwar period of new values that often exacerbated conflicts between the sexes, and with the collapse of the extended family into the nuclear family, the traditional Japanese family system suffered a serious erosion that altered both the role ascribed to each family member and the dynamics of husband-wife relations" (2002: 134).

The question of postwar progress and structural rebuilding was, as in the Meiji period, grafted onto the new postwar family. In conjunction with reified conservative thought in the 1950s and 1960s, men were to advance the nation's interests outside of the home while women were to uphold the integrity of the family within it. The unprecedented growth of the economy circa 1955–1970 legitimated the reconstructed and bifurcated Japanese household. Nevertheless, the failure of the economy in the following decades jeopardized the aspirations of many middle-class households. Corporate restructuring meant the end of white-collar job security, the masculine ideal of the salaryman, and postwar visions of leisurely consumerism. It meant, too, that families were stripped of their nucleus. What were families to do once the aspiration of social mobility seemed infeasible and, to a new generation, not worth the effort?

Kirino's work delineates this emergent pointlessness of ordinary Japanese life. Her female characters circulate unwillingly through social institutions that have lost their practical value. Their home lives are dysfunctional, and their school lives are similarly troubled. They rebel—turning against family, friends, and themselves. And like other characters examined in this book, Kirino's women revel in their own mediocrity, embracing strategies of laziness, defiance, and ego. Their worlds revolve around their desires, impulses, and bad choices. In this way, Kirino's narratives follow a formulaic trajectory in which girls behave badly simply because they are not supposed to. My argument is thus invested in exploring the ways in which transgression in her texts is itself a stereotypical manifestation of life in recessionary Japan. Her texts can be and are frequently read as reactive discourses against feminine comportment and expectation. I read Kirino in the opposite direction, as a voice that capitalizes on casualties of transgression while lamenting the decision-making processes that lead young Japanese women to their own destruction. By drawing from real-life instances of murder, Kirino plays to readers' expectations for, and fascination with, the morbid aspects of millennial Japan. At the same time, the somber conclusions to her texts are, in my formulation, a jarring reminder that there is no safe place beyond the frame of normativity.

Grotesque is overrun with citizens of diminished confidence in the state and warped expressions of affection and sympathy for those close to them. This tension between public and private spheres manifests in lives crippled by the vicissitudes and pressures of Japanese social life, illustrated most poignantly by the murders of the narrator's sister and her childhood friend. In a lengthy and eloquent confession that belies his rural and impoverished upbringing, Zhang Zhe-zhong, an illegal immigrant from China, explains what drove him to kill Yuriko, the narrator's sister. Although he maintains that he did not kill Kazue, the other victim, he frames his crime in terms of love, loss, and isolation. These motivating motifs speak to the life situations of all of the characters in the text, who lack intimate connections, familial stability, and aspirations of upward mobility. In this light, Zhang is simply a casualty of his own inability to cope, and his incarceration animates Kirino's exploration of crooked citizenship. In this way, the novel is devoted to characters who have resigned from expectation and responsibility, who have ostensibly embraced transgressive ways of living. However, all is not lost. The specter of the family emerges if but momentarily as a beacon of normality and equilibrium for the catty and manipulative narrator. Ever the antithesis of parenthood and maternity, this nameless narrator's *volte-face* speaks to the draw of stability and the end of transgression. Accordingly, *Grotesque* cultivates an ethos of adult corruption and resignation—packaged in Kirino's use of the grotesque—before offering the family as the antidote.

In her analysis of the novel, Rebecca Copeland (2018) encourages a "'grotesque' reading ... [that] encourages multiple interpretations and celebrates the confusion and uncertainty the novel invites" (2018: 148). In keeping with a grotesque reading, I turn to Mary Russo (1995:1) and the obvious linguistic correlation between grotesque and the cave-like "grotto-esque," which conveys historically gendered associations regarding the female body as "dark, material, immanent, [and] visceral." It is from the depths of the female body, in other words, that a woman's incongruous nature ruptures forth. Sexual difference is at the core of conceptualizations of women's bodies as maligned. According to Barbara Creed (1993: 6), women across national cultures and historical eras have been uniformly "constructed as 'biological freaks' whose bodies represent a fearful and threatening form of sexuality." Thus, what is grotesque here is that which is culturally, socially, physically, and psychically freakish. The grotesque is the mysterious female body, but so, too, her latent instability lurking below the surface.

As an innately corrupt form, messy and uncontained, the female body is also potentially threatening to discourses of convention. Russo (1995: 3) states that "the grotesque body is the open, protruding, extended, secreting body, the body of becoming, process[,] and change. The grotesque body is opposed to the classical body, which is monumental, static, closed and sleek, corresponding to the aspirations of bourgeois individualism; the grotesque body is connected to the rest of the world." Russo's conceptualization of the female body draws on Bakhtinian theories of the grotesque as inversion and antithesis. According to Bakhtin, "The grotesque body [...] is a body in the act of becoming. It is never finished, never completed; it is continually built, created, and builds and creates another body" (1965 [1984]: 317). While Russo criticizes Bakhtin for what she sees as a negative formulation of the female grotesque, she nevertheless finds that he ascribes to the female form an ethos of transgression. "In the everyday...world, women and their bodies, certain bodies...are always already transgressive" (Russo 1986: 217). For Russo, it is the negative, fearful implications of the female body as excess that affords its transgressive properties.

Of course, it is only because the female body has been coded in negative terms that it possesses transgressive properties in the first place. Hegemony dictates our ability to rebel, and the coding of the female body as unpleasant, unpredictable, and unruly grants female grotesqueness the possibility for rebellion. The Bakhtinian grotesque body is closely linked to notions of the "carnival" as a space of unrestricted play, performance, and excess where the social hierarchies of official culture are violated. Bodies coming together, if but momentarily, disrupt distinctions between class, race, and gender, even blurring dichotomies that separate human from animal, master from slave, and high culture from low. Chris Jenks identifies the transgressive potential of the carnival thus: "It is style unrestricted, method without parameter or rigour, decentered identity and a continuous broken chain of signifiers" (2003: 164). As a collection of oppositional stances, the carnival represents the breakdown of order and the attendant carnivalesque bodies as an affront to society. In this way, feminist interpretations of the female body might focus on empowerment through hedonistic impulse, exploiting social, historical, and cultural fears of female physicality.

Carnivalesque populism, as formulated by Bakhtin, fails to account for "the social relations of gender," however (Russo 1995: 63). Beyond the safety of academic theories regarding the carnival as a site of release and reconfiguration, it stirs the sobering reality that the unrestricted comingling of bodies presents a danger for women. Russo calls attention to the fact that women's bodies are concurrently dangerous and in danger; in danger because of their dangerous nature. Furthermore, carnivals constitute *permitted* disruption. As Terry Eagleton (1981: 148) writes: "Carnival [...] is a licensed affair in every sense, a permissible rupture of hegemony, a contained popular blow-off [that is] relatively ineffectual" as a political expression. His observation illuminates the contradictory nature of transgression. As an experience of authorized misbehavior, the carnival underscores the extent to which rebellion occurs with institutional permission. Eagleton (1981: 149) continues, "From one viewpoint carnival may feature as a prime example of that mutual complicity of law and liberation, power and desire." Here Eagleton evokes the words of Michel Foucault and Georges Bataille, examined at length in the introduction to this study, both of whom remind us of the short-lived nature of transgression as well as the necessity of rebellion for the sustained dominance of official culture. In this light, theories of the female body as a medium of subversion are fraught with tension. The carnivalesque female body of literary and feminist theories elides the extent to which that same body is often vulnerable, exploited, and entrenched outside of academe.

The body need not be *either* free or imprisoned, of course, transgressive *or* well-behaved. Rather, attention to their interplay between rebellion and submission is necessary to understand the narrative flow of Kirino's *Grotesque*. The novel showcases contemporary Japan as a "grotto-esque" space: dark and inimical.

Bodies come together in ways that are antithetical to official culture. For example, prostitution is a prominent theme that governs the interactions of the major characters. The narrator's beautiful sister Yuriko and their bookish classmate/friend Kazue both take to the streets, where they are eventually killed by Zhang, an illegal immigrant from rural China. Zhang's younger sister Mei-kun, too, becomes the victim of a human trafficking ring. She eventually dies when the siblings are sneaking into Japan aboard a rickety boat. The bodies of these women are impure and carnal, "public spectacle" (Russo 1995: 213). Russo argues that the careful maintenance of "boundaries" between self and other, subject and object, and agent and victim (among other binaries) are necessary for women's self-preservation (1995: 213). "Making a spectacle out of oneself seem[s] a specifically feminine danger," she reflects. "Any *woman* could make a spectacle out of herself if she [is] not careful" (1995: 213; emphasis in original). Kirino's vector of female spectacle is prostitution, her focus on women negotiating cultural landscapes in which their bodies determine their social and financial worth, and in which they are always in danger of slipping into spectacle. The novel is bleak, putting on display bodies that exist vulnerably outside of bounds. The ramifications of living beyond measure reestablish order, however, and Kirino's novel ultimately reminds readers of the necessity of Russo's "boundaries." It is those who refuse to live by the rules of official culture that are punished. But this is not immediately obvious.

Grotesque reads like a celebration of the antithetical and the contrary. And Kirino's narrator—the most manipulative and underhanded of all of the characters (about whom I say more below)—functions as a guide of sorts, leading readers into an inhospitable and potentially unfamiliar social landscape. As such, the novel's aims echo those of the other texts analyzed in *The End of Transgression*, illuminating the degeneration of recessionary Japan. The sense of loss and failure that came with the collapse of the economy seems to permeate all aspects of life. Authors such as Kirino—but also Sakurai Ami and Kanehara Hitomi, both analyzed in earlier chapters—ridicule and mock nearly every aspect of Japanese social life. The family, in particular, is the object of Kirino's scorn, and *Grotesque* implies that the illusory nature of prostitution has taken the place of familial bonds.

Grotesque accordingly opens with a lengthy exposition in which the narrator describes a favorite pastime of hers: envisioning having phantom babies with random men. "Whenever I meet a man, I catch myself wondering what our child would look like," she says. "It's practically second nature to me now. Whether he's handsome or ugly, old or young, a picture of our child flashes across my mind" (Kirino 2007: 3). The narrator boasts of her resistance to heteronormative culture, claiming little interest in men, marriage, or motherhood. As a thirty-nine-year-old woman who does not conform to typical Japanese conceptualizations of femininity, she exists in an antithetical space of selfishness and subtle defiance. In addition, she lacks stable employment and instead works a number of temporary jobs. None of this bothers her, of course. "I'm really proud to be a middle-aged, part-time, unattached freelancer," she brags (Kirino 2007: 16). She rejects aspirations of upward mobility, romance, and, perhaps most importantly, motherhood. Although contemporary Japanese women experience a greater sense of cultural autonomy compared to their mothers and grandmothers, including advances in the workplace, "a vast array of ideological and institutional pressures that engender women through their association with domesticity has not shown much sign of abating" (Yoda 2006b: 267). To this end, Kirino's narrator represents a countervailing way of life that rejects nearly every pillar of postwar Japan. Her strange pastime relegates maternity to a fantasy, something to experience from afar. At the same time, she undermines cultural imperatives for domesticity and procreation: through a phantom union with a phantom man, she produces a phantom child; in reality, however, she does nothing at all. This is not incidental. Because Kirino's text is devoted to exploring social life after the collapse of Japan's economic dream, her narrator's hobby can be interpreted as a mockery of ideals of productivity and aspirational living: she produces nothing.

Kirino's warped model of female citizenship offers a critical assessment of the family. Consistent with her devaluation of maternity, Kirino is most aggressive toward contemporary conceptualizations of the Japanese family and familial dynamics as repositories of personal strife. As demonstrated in previous chapters of this study, the family has long been subject to ridicule and mockery in Japanese literature, particularly following the emergence of the ethos of enterprise (*kigyō*) in the 1970s, which imbricated familial life and economic policy. Anne Allison explains the dynamics of Japan's "enterprise society" (*kigyō shakai*): "For a man, this meant providing for family; for a woman, it meant raising children and running the home; and for a child, it meant studying hard, excelling academically, and acquiring a job and family of one's own as an adult" (Allison 2013: 22). Here, Allison demonstrates that individual adult male and female lives were relegated to public and private spaces, while children circulated between private realms of study and public efforts for academic ascension. The end of the age of economic prosperity ushered in an era of critical reflection, and the family was accordingly served up for ridicule.

The family is thus the cause of and solution to the problems afflicting Kirino's characters. The vacuous space beyond hegemony is initially enticing, before ultimately proving detrimental. In the process, the family is produced as a site of safety and sanctuary, and characters' desire for autonomy and individuality beyond that site is punished. In the close readings that follow, I suggest that while Kirino can criticize the family sphere and its effects on the men, women, and children who circulate within it, and figure its dissolution, she cannot envision a replacement. Early in the novel, Kirino's narrator wonders if "we are attracted to what frightens us" (2007: 4). It is a prescient observation, made in response to her thoughts on the primordial, almost instinctual, drive to procreate; prescient because Kirino's narrator is frightened by the family, yet it is what she ultimately seeks out.

It is in this context that the grotesque and the monstrous take their shape. The narrator explains that growing up, her younger sister Yuriko struck her as "monstrous" (Kirino 2007: 7). Although Yuriko was "terrifyingly" and "diabolically beautiful," her perfect features were also "tiresome" and "unnerving" (Kirino 2007: 7, 9). This interplay between attraction and repulsion is an obvious textual motif and source of fascination for the narrator. It is also of grave importance for grotesquery as a theoretical mechanism: "The grotesque provokes conflicting responses," write Justin Edwards and Rune Graulund. "In this, the grotesque is disturbing because it incites seemingly incompatible emotions through its representations of abjection and possibility, limitations and becomings, compassion and rejection, attraction and repulsion" (2013: 78). The narrator saw Yuriko's angelic features as a manifestation of her innate evil. Their mother committed suicide after moving to Switzerland with her husband, a Swiss national of Polish descent (Kirino 2007: 41), and the narrator wonders if she "die[d] because she gave birth to the monster Yuriko" (Kirino 2007: 7). Furthermore, because neither their mother nor their father was particularly attractive, the narrator—also of plain face and unimpressive features—fears that Yuriko is an unnatural abomination (Kirino 2007: 6). The narrator fixates on Yuriko's youthful beauty as the origin of her evil nature, commenting that her perfect face looked like a "mask" (Kirino 2007: 19); but she is also convinced that her younger sister "had been a monster all her life," a terrible "mutation" (Kirino 2007: 8, 20).

In the narrator's eyes, Yuriko was responsible for the imperiled dysfunction that assailed their family. For example, the narrator says that Yuriko's radiant beauty turned mother and eldest daughter into "enemies" (Kirino 2007: 23). Reflecting on her childhood memories, the narrator contends that it was Yuriko who did not resemble her, while her mother felt the opposite, that Yuriko was the standard of comparison. In either case, Yuriko did not belong, and her extraordinary looks intensified the "mediocrity" of the rest of the family, while exploiting the conditions of female rivalry (Kirino 2007: 23). "Jealousy, envy, and competition," writes Karen Hollinger (1998: 207), regularly inform "antiquated stereotypical representations of female relationships." As a result, women learn to "beware of and fear one another" (Hollinger 1998: 207). The narrator's portrayal of the sibling dynamic in *Grotesque* is informed by the constellation of negative effects Hollinger mentions. Hollinger argues persuasively that antagonistic relationships between women obfuscate and excuse the role men have in constructing female rivalries. She writes that female rivalries "relieve men of any responsibility for women's problems, and suggest, instead, that women should grant men primary importance in their lives because they are the only ones upon whom women can rely" (1998: 207). Her words are inflicted with a particular feminist impulse that is absent from

Kirino's book. Kirino's concern is nevertheless with frayed bonds between women. And although the narrator is quick to accuse her sister of an innate sinister evil, Kirino's point seems to be addressing the latent monstrosity hidden within everyone in millennial Japan, particularly its women. In this regard, the narrative speaks to Russo's (1995: 7) contention that "the grotesque" is a physical manifestation of a troubled and warped "interior event." Yuriko's supposed grotesqueness is therefore hardly anomalous, and neither is she solely responsible for the failure of their family. She stands out because her flawless features contradict the possibility of a dark, flawed core.

In other words, the other principal characters are *clearly* malfunctioned and maladjusted, their less-than-ideal physical features betraying similarly ugly inner selves. Unsurprisingly, the narrator is preoccupied with ugliness. She notes, for example, that if she and her boss, a "section chief," had a child, it would be "crude and hideously ugly" (Kirino 2007: 13). Elsewhere, commenting on a diary Yuriko left behind (which constitutes Chapter Three of the novel), the narrator remarks on her sister's "ugly" handwriting (Kirino 2007: 123). She says, too: "Here I am, beautiful Yuriko's ugly older sister, the blight on Yuriko's life" (Kirino 2007: 188). As a final example, reflecting on the death of her friend Kazue, who, like Yuriko, became a prostitute, the narrator remarks, "Kazue grew hideous and exposed her ugly body to others" (Kirino 2007: 530). The novel is a constant interplay between beauty and its inverse, and throughout the narrator insists on emphasizing what is ugly. Russo writes that the "positioning of the freak as an illustrative detail and as a pictorial object requiring narration" is central to notions of the grotesque (Kirino 2007: 87). Kirino's narrator takes up this role, emphasizing the lack of aesthetic discourse in millennial Japan. Perhaps understandably, then, Yuriko's beauty is particularly unnerving because it simply does not belong in such an ugly world.

Grotesque feels like a celebration of the unsightly, crowning victorious the most hideous of the female characters. Kirino departs from normative creative contexts by writing a novel in which her female characters are all largely monstrous. Sandra Gilbert and Susan Gubar (1979: 17) have discussed the bifurcation of female characters where women are represented as "angels" or "monsters." The angel is the "aesthetic ideal" to which all women are held (Gilbert and Gubar 1979: 17). As the angel's "necessary opposite and double," the monster strikes fear into the hearts of men with her "Medusa-face" (Gilbert and Gubar 1979: 17). Although Gilbert and Gubar's concerns are with Western literature, their observations are prescient, for the combative images of an angelic or monstrous femininity are readily found in Japanese texts. Copeland (2005: 16) has shown how the trope of the monstrous female has origins in early Japanese myth and expressions of male dominance; she writes that through motifs of "the corpse, the crone, and the snake," "mythmakers rescripted female potency and consigned it to positions of abjection and debility." Abjection is theoretically aligned with the grotesque. The maternal body, "ugly and aberrant," "refuses [to] stay beautiful and domesticated" (Covino 2004: 30): in contrast to the "closed, smooth, and impenetrable" civilized body (Bakhtin 1965 [1984]: 317), the maternal body leaks, oozes, and secretes.

For all of its grotesque elements (theoretically speaking), *Grotesque* is bereft of the so-called maternal body. Yuriko gives birth to a son named Yurio, who is then raised by his father. The *act* of maternity is not textually important. The characters are always already grotesque, needing not the acts of expulsion, excretion, and excision that are important to theoretical permutations of the grotesque female body. Kirino's deployment of the motif of prostitution serves to mark each character as grotesque as well as to figure the grotesque body in ways that are similar to the textually absent maternal body. The prostitute's body, in contrast to that of her chaste and morally upright sister, stands apart from order. Alain Corbin's observations on public and commercial sexuality are relevant here. He writes that "excessive sexual relations threaten [social] equilibrium," and therefore the prostitute—the symbol of excessive and morally derelict sexuality—is subject to ostracizing and regulation (1987: 210). Regarding commercial sex in nineteenth-century France, he argues that the prostitute "does not just symbolize moral rot; she is literally a putrid woman, as demonstrated by the odor she emits. By frequenting her, one risks the living corruption of [disease]" (Corbin 1987: 210–211). The borders of the prostitute's body are easily broken, penetrable, and her place on the street represents her uncontained nature. Corbin paints a striking image: "The prostitute enables the social body to excrete the excess of seminal fluid that causes her stench and rots her" (Corbin 1987: 211). He sees her as a corpse: "the stinking body of the prostitute, given over to living putrefaction, prefigures death" (Corbin 1987: 211). Corbin's attention is on a particular manifestation of the poor streetwalker, and certainly not all prostitutes fit this model. Importantly, in *Grotesque* they do.

Yuriko's venture into prostitution begins in school (when she is fifteen years old), where she conspires with a classmate named Kijima to profit from the selling of sex. As her pimp, Kijima constructs an economic marketplace based on the circulation of Yuriko's body (Kirino 2007: 159). In her diary, Yuriko suggests that her fervent interest in sex from a young age primed her for a life of prostitution: "For a nymphomaniac like myself, I suppose there could be no job more suitable than prostitution: it is my God-given destiny" (Kirino 2007: 136). She continues: "I'm like a vagina incarnate—female essence embodied. If I ever were to deny a man, I would stop being me" (Kirino 2007: 136). Yuriko says that she became aware of "the lust that linger[s] in [the male] gaze" while she was still a child (Kirino 2007: 129). "Before I even began to worry about homework or any of those school things, I began having secret liaisons with men. And it is men who give me the proof I need now to feel alive" (Kirino 2007: 134). Yuriko envisions herself as a version of the angelic woman about whom Gilbert and Gubar, among others, have written. She exists only to please men; she is only a sexual body. She writes that Kijima "was the first male who did not feel desire for me. […] He was also the second person to hate me, the first of course being my sister. Both my sister and Kijima were able to make me feel that in their presence there was no purpose to my existence" (Kirino 2007: 152). Kijima, who is gay, is a misogynist. His efforts to lead Yuriko into prostitution serve to denigrate her existence and place her in harm's way. Yet because Yuriko desires all men, she finds value and self-worth in her role as a fallen figure of public sexuality. Here, Kirino evokes heteronormative economies of power, positioning the beautiful nymphomaniac as an object of male desire and nearly pornographic fantasy. Not only does Yuriko flaunt the sexual body, she is also "half" (Kirino 2007: 153), the offspring of a Japanese mother and Swiss father. Her DNA marks her as exotic while simultaneously placing her in a discourse of sexually aggressive outsiders. Japanese men, "on account of their supposedly stronger sex drive [vis-à-vis Japanese women]" (McLelland 2015: 197–198), see foreign women as potential outlets for sexual aggression and desire. Because Japanese women are held to rigid standards of maternity and matrimony, foreign women can be seen as sites of recreational sex. Yuriko thus embodies fantasies of male sexual prowess.

Her worth, however, is bound to the youthful and beautiful version of herself, and as Yuriko ages her body betrays her, rendering her "a shabby whore" by novel's end (Kirino 2007: 505). In her diary, Yuriko reflects on the inevitability of the aging process: "It is quite clear to me now. When I was a girl I was abundantly endowed with that certain something that attracts older men. […] As fate would have it, though, the older I've become the harder it is to retain this charm" (Kirino 2007: 128). Her diary is a record of her descent from teenage vixen to common streetwalker. It is also a record of the trappings, ruination, and expiration of male sexual desire. Yuriko realizes that boys/men her age are not drawn to her. Rather, she has an inexplicable sexual power over older men. She details the ways in which male family friends and even relatives began seeing her as an object of desire when she "was still just a little girl" (Kirino 2007: 125). Yuriko initially discusses the flirtatious relationship she had with an American named Johnson, when she was twelve and he was twenty-seven. When she was fifteen, Yuriko moved in with Johnson and his Japanese wife Masami, after which Yuriko and Johnson began sleeping together. Masami uncovered the affair and divorced Johnson, accusing him of taking advantage of Yuriko (Kirino 2007: 127). Yuriko goes on to discuss the first sexual relationship she had, which was with her uncle Karl, who, in his words, "raped" her when she was fifteen (Kirino 2007: 131). According to Yuriko, she was too young to understand why Karl's attraction to her was "taboo" (Kirino 2007: 130). She recalls vividly the moment his sexual desire turned against her, however: "That was the first time I noticed that the men who embrace me, every single one of them, end up with an expression of emptiness when they are done as if they have lost something. Maybe that is why I am always in search of a new man. Maybe that is why I am now a prostitute" (Kirino 2007: 131). Yuriko's acceptance of her own disposability, in concert with her awareness of the limits of her own abilities to attract men (who, as she gets older, are less interested), demonstrates how she develops a warped sense of her own sexual and individual positionality.

Her story is the inverse of Kazue's, who decides to pursue an afterhours life of prostitution. While Yuriko was defiant and troublesome (her exquisite beauty affording her freedom from academic expectation), Kazue was a model student. She was studious throughout high school, matriculated to the prestigious Q University, and became a successful executive at G Architecture and Engineering Firm. According to court documents indicting Zhang of the murder of Yuriko and Kazue (which comprise Chapter Five of the novel), Kazue began moonlighting as a hostess and escort before turning to "full-fledged" prostitution (Kirino 2007: 250). If Yuriko's attraction to prostitution is due to nymphomaniacal desire ("I loved sex so much I wanted to screw as many men as I could" [Kirino 2007: 7]), Kazue's is a deliberate and calculating reaction to gender politics in recessionary Japan. In her diary—a record of her sexual encounters with men and money received—she writes of feeling frustrated by her inability to get ahead and to attract men. All brains and no beauty, Kazue finds it impossible to succeed in the workplace where men are promoted and women are judged by their fashion choices and "marriagability." Simultaneously deflated by the constraints that Japanese society has placed on women as well as her inability to attract men, she gravitates toward prostitution as a means of freedom and retaliation. Kazue writes gleefully of her dual identity: "By day I was respected for my brains; by night I was desired for my body. I felt like Superwoman! [...] By day a business woman; by night a whore. [...] I was capable of using both my brains and my body to make money" (Kirino 2007: 409, 427). This is a conditional kind of desire; men want Kazue not for her potential as a romantic partner but rather as a sexual object.

Nevertheless, Kazue realizes that manipulating male sexual desire is a woman's sole avenue of power. She admires Yuriko for this reason: "In her treatment of male desires of all kinds, she had built a world entirely out of men—even if only for the briefest of moments. [...] She didn't have to study; she didn't even have to work. She was able to bring the world to her feet by one method and one alone—because she was able to make men ejaculate. Now I would do the same" (Kirino 2007: 475). Kazue's association of the sexual body with power is pernicious, insofar as it coopts female sexuality as an instrument of patriarchal power. Indeed, one wonders if selling the body is as powerful a demonstration as Kazue would like.

Rather than prostitution as such, she finds power in revealing her dual identity to potential customers. Kazue's version of middle-class prostitution gives her a sense of pride (Kirino 2007: 412). She offers to show these men her corporate ID card (Kirino 2007: 431), desperate for a sense of validation as a woman who has *chosen* to pursue prostitution.

In this study, I already have examined the political implications of prostitution as a middle-class hobby rather than lower-class financial necessity. I examined the trope of the teenage prostitute as a rebellious daughter from an upwardly mobile and socially aspirational family, demonstrating that the edicts of power governing the selling of sex are reversible in situations not governed by socioeconomic precarity. My aim here is not to bifurcate the prostitute into *either* an agent *or* a victim, of course; the politics of commodified sex are far too complex for such a reductive view. Instead, by drawing attention to acts of prostitution that are not dictated by lower-class struggles, I have broadened the theoretical scope, discursive construction, and subversive potential of sex for sale. For example, Kazue sees herself as an agent of "revenge" against patriarchal power (Kirino 2007: 431, 432, 489).

She is able to make this claim against presumptions of prostitution as an involuntary occupation, reproducing stereotypes—especially prevalent in Asia—about vulnerable women and difficult choices. Intentionally or otherwise, Kazue's celebration of her own sexual agency occurs vis-à-vis a broader context of human trafficking and gendered exploitation. For many women in Asia, indentured sexual servitude is a sobering reality. Indeed, as Louise Shelley (2010: 153) notes, "With Japan's postwar affluence [...] more than 100,000 women from Thailand and the Philippines [are] trafficked into the Japanese sex industry." It is in this context that Kazue stakes her claim. Kirino's novel does not address at length sex slavery or prostitution as a grim reality; readers should be mindful of the broader cultural context in which Kazue, as well as Yuriko, manifest their own sense of agency. Because prostitution is generally conceived as coercion, Kazue is able to celebrate the ways in which she is not like the other women who walk the streets. Indigenous sex workers are often portrayed as passive, beautiful, innocent, and poor, but the body of the middle-class prostitute can be readily configured as a site of transgression and, as Kazue believes, "revenge." Even the narrator suggests that prostitution is "the means [Kazue and Yuriko] had for waging war on the world" (Kirino 2007: 50).

The extent to which Kazue and Yuriko take revenge on anyone or anything is debatable, however. For Kazue, prostitution is a reactive and retaliatory mechanism undertaken as a response to her feelings of inadequacy and her anger at the myth of meritocracy. She attempts to make a mockery of the subjugated position of ordinary Japanese women. She attempts to see sex as a source of power by behaving in ways incongruous with typical permutations of gender and class. In grotesque fashion, she makes a spectacle of herself, reveling in the confused reactions of her customers when she tells them of her day job. As the narrator reflects, comparing the major difference between Kazue and Yuriko's turn to prostitution: "If a woman who is beautiful but has no other redeeming value turns tricks until she's ancient, no one gives it a second thought. But Kazue's turn to prostitution left everyone racking their brains to figure out why. A career woman by day, a prostitute by night. Men everywhere were beside themselves trying to work that one out" (Kirino 2007: 16). But saying yes to sex and bodily autonomy does not mean saying no to authority. In fact, this is rarely the case. Kazue's non-existent sex-life prior to her venture into prostitution) and Yuriko's nymphomaniacal tendencies reveal the theoretical gap between sex and sexuality in general. Kazue's determination to upset expectation through sex and Yuriko's inability to control her sexual desire demonstrate the ways in which decision and compulsion are nearly antithetical practices: Kazue has gone to lengths to attempt to marginalize herself while there is no place for Yuriko in the sexual landscape of millennial Japan. As the narrator's words suggest, men are puzzled by Kazue's decision, but her actions are ultimately of little consequence to anyone.

Kazue's investment in her body as a sexual commodity betrays the extent to which she is expendable. This logic extends to Yuriko as well. The deaths of both women reflect the ways in which prostitution codes women as largely unnecessary. Their deaths similarly mark the sexually transgressive female body as a site of punishment. Prostitution can be interpreted as the inverse of sexual monogamy as well as the antithesis of the institution of marriage. Venality has no place in the domestic sphere, and women who conduct themselves in suspect ways can be subject to social scorn and censure. Sexually aggressive women upset gendered expectations for comportment, but by the end of Kirino's novel, those same women are punished for their transgressions. Note that although Kirino portrays two women with different sets of motivations for prostitution (framed in terms of compulsion and decision), she writes them into the same fate.

When both women are murdered, they manifest Corbin's association of the prostitute with the corpse. He reasons: "Prostitutes...appear...dangerous for the same reason as corpses or carrion. ... [:] the ambiguous status of the woman's body, at once menace and remedy, agent of putrefaction and drain... female bodies at the beck and call of the bourgeois body" (Corbin 1987: 212–213). Corbin's interpretation of the prostitute as a diseased, dangerous corpse can be contextualized in terms of social discourses of containment and surveillance. He continues: "The first task of regulation is to bring the prostitute out of the foul darkness and remove her from the clandestine swarming of vice in order to drive her back into an enclosed space, under the purifying light of power" (Corbin 1987: 215). Corbin's words, of a different time and place of course, speak to legislative efforts to control the in-hock body, to prevent its diseased flesh from compromising the health of the social body. Like the corpse, the prostitute exists as body only: she is flesh through and through. Yuriko makes this point clear when she describes Kazue's appearance the first time she sees Kazue walking the street. Failing to recognize her, Yuriko sees Kazue as but another prostitute: "What was remarkable about the woman was her appallingly impoverished body. She was so thin as to be nearly one-dimensional, a skeleton covered in skin" (Kirino 2007: 164). Yuriko portrays Kazue as a living corpse, a sickly creature stuck between the world of the living and that of the dead.

Kazue sees a rival prostitute named the Marlboro Hag in this same light. The Marlboro Hag is an aging streetwalker who has staked her claim in front of a statue of Jizō, "the gentle Buddhist bodhisattva, a protector of those condemned to hell and all who wander between realms" (405). Kazue first sees the Marlboro Hag when Kazue is working as a call girl at an escort service. Once she leaves the escort service, she decides to start a turf war with the Marlboro Hag. According to Kazue, the Marlboro Hag possesses a kind of freedom that Kazue envies. Accordingly, the Marlboro Hag "was a woman to be respected, a woman among women" (440). The Marlboro Hag is undeterred by Kazue's attempts to take over her spot in front of Jizō, claiming that her customers will never betray her because she has "a body men will pay to see" (442). She then reveals to Kazue her supposedly desirable body, forcing her hand to her chest: "The Marlboro Hag pressed my hand up under the right side of her bra. … Instead of a saggy breast she had just a ball of tattered cloth" (442). Cancer, the Marlboro Hag explains, took her right breast ten years ago, after which she decided to stand in front of Jizō and proposition men. This aging, diseased prostitute best exemplifies Corbin's thoughts on the figure of the prostitute as walking death. The Marlboro Hag is indeed both "corpse" and "carrion" (Corbin 1987: 212), her "fetid flesh" marking her body as an object of decay and disease (Kirino 2007: 442). The Marlboro Hag eventually dies from illness (448), effectively becoming Corbin's corpse.

In drawing from the real-life murder of Watanabe Yasuko, Kirino plays to existing tropes and stereotypes rather than formulating something more transgressive. Kirino's text is not a retelling of Watanabe's murder, but readers would find in Kazue's portion of the novel obvious affinities and parallels with the well-known "Tōden OL Murder Case." Nevertheless, Kirino writes Watanabe's death, which, as Hurley argues, had already been treated as sensationalistic fodder by news outlets, into the sphere of fiction. Hurley examines the "storytelling quality" of reports from the weekly periodicals. *Shūkan Post* reports drew on Watanabe's double-life to "inspire in readers a desire to know" (Hurley: 200). Another weekly, *Shūkan Gendai*, stated: "The gap between her pedigree as an elite graduate of the private Keiō University and the reality of her life as a 'woman of the night' is attracting attention to the murder of [Watanabe Yasuko]" (Hurley: 200). Hurley points out the linguistic similarities between these reports: namely, mention of Watanabe's middle-class background and her seemingly incomprehensible turn to prostitution, as well as the "attention" paid to her personal life. Hurley suggests that in portraying her as a sexual spectacle, the media wrote Watanabe's life (and death) as a source of voyeuristic fascination from which readers could not look away.

Accordingly, Kirino's novel promises readers a familiar story about prostitution as a form of middle-class rebellion and the grisly fate that awaits the woman who steps too far beyond the boundaries of acceptability. Simply put, we have seen it all before, and readers find pleasure not in learning Kazue's fate (which is predetermined), but in watching her die. The spectacle of the middle-class whore draws readers in with her sexuality before she is punished. In this way, the ghost of Watanabe Yasuko haunts the novel's other female prostitutes, all of whom share Kazue's fate.

For this reason, I argue that Kirino's novel profits from and advances a rhetoric of conservative sexual politics by killing off the women who become sexual spectacles. The narrator, the vector through which the entire novel is filtered, maintains a position of proud sexual abstinence up until the very last pages of the novel. She prefers, as demonstrated earlier, to envision phantom babies with strangers and colleagues, with no attention to "the part about the sex act" (Kirino 2007: 5). In fact, she speaks of "living forever as a virgin, a woman who would have no contact with men" (522). At the same time, she eschews conventional societal norms by remaining single into her thirties and investing herself only minimally in her work. On the surface, the narrator ostensibly occupies an oppositional space of selfishness, shirking social and cultural duties of maternity and domesticity.

But to what aim? The narrator's resistance to the kinds of personal connections that are central to home and corporate life leaves her bereft of intimate connections. Yuriko, Kazue, and Zhang are all tangled in the web of personal and familial ties. Only the narrator circulates alone. Her sole meaningful connection is with her kooky grandfather, with whom she lives after her father moves the rest of the family to Switzerland, just as the narrator is entering high school. "All I wanted was to preserve the quiet life I had with my grandfather," she says when she learns of Yuriko's plans to come back to Japan to finish high school (105). Later she reflects, learning of her grandfather's romantic desire for the mother of her classmate: "Love … love … love … everyone was tangled up with love" (200). The narrator prides herself on her disengagement with the trappings of intimate connections.

It is somewhat ironic, then, that at the end of *Grotesque* the narrator clings so tightly to her nephew Yurio, whom we first glimpse in Chapter Six during Zhang's trial. Yuriko's son with the American Johnson, Yurio is raised by his father in Japan, but Johnson leaves his son with Yuriko's former classmate and pimp, Kijima, when he returns to the USA after Yuriko's death. Once the narrator learns this, she is eager to raise Yurio on her own. She notes her "instinct[ual]" draw toward Yurio, and she promises to buy him a computer if he comes to live with her (375, 377). "I would replace Yuriko and be the mother he never had," she tells herself, noting that her "maternal instincts bubbled up within" (380, 381). The narrator envisions "a life with Yurio" and, at Yurio's suggestion, considers becoming a prostitute in order to provide for him the things he desires (528, 529). In the novel's closing scene, the narrator imagines herself being murdered by Zhang and joining Yuriko and Kazue in the afterlife, a sisterhood of prostitutes. This finale hints at the inevitability of transactional relationships, even quasi-maternal ones, while simultaneously positioning the narrator as yet another dead whore. In suggesting that his aunt "go out and earn money … like [his] mother," Yurio catalyzes female sexual commodification while the narrator plays the role of the surrogate mother figure who will do anything for her adopted son. Yurio's presence gives the narrator a sense of validation, pride, and purpose. So quick to dismiss "love" as a frivolous emotion, she inexplicably feels "a new emotion. .bud within [her]: love" (526).

Or does she? Her affection for Yurio is driven by her innate competition with Yuriko, and her "motherly instincts" allow her to let Yurio join her on the prostitute's stroll. In a way, he assumes the position his mother had occupied earlier, always besting the narrator at her own game. Yurio is a much more successful prostitute, popular with both women and men. He earns so much money; he could easily buy himself whatever he wants. The narrator has no need to turn tricks. But, like Kazue before her, she cannot back down once she has entered the "water trade."

Long critical of romantic entanglements, the narrator had also never invested in maternal love. She had rebuffed her own mother's attempts to bond with her. When she learns of her mother's suicide, her immediate thoughts turn to how her death might jeopardize the coveted distance she had put between herself and her sister. Neither romantic love nor familial ties carry significance for the narrator. Recall that at the beginning of the narrative she is pondering what kind of child she would produce with different sorts of men—phantom children drifting through the sea of her imagination like prehistoric monsters. It is fitting, then, that the novel should conclude with the narrator's acquisition of a surrogate child with freaky attributes. Yurio becomes her ideal child. And like her vision of the ideal child, he soon turns monstrous. He is as avaricious as any of the other characters. In fact, he gestures toward the "teenage menace," mentioned above. In Yurio, we have yet another iteration of the self-focused, misguided, unruly youth. Yuriko's true heir, the cycle of prostitution continues.

Kirino's prostitutes do not overthrow the system. Families in *Grotesque* are broken and menacing, hardly bastions of comfort or protection, and yet they survive. Fathers are tyrannical and narcissistic. Mothers have abdicated their positions as nurturers and, with the exception of Mitsuru's mother (who has the power to embarrass her daughter with her lower-middle-class honesty), drift through the narrative as shells of their former selves. Rather than bonding together in support against destructive parents, siblings squabble over what little access to power they may grasp. It is the female siblings who are discordant—the narrator and Yuriko, Kazue, and her younger sister.

By contrast, Zhang and his sister Mei-kun have a relationship that gestures toward incest. It is Yuriko's resemblance to the dead Mei-kun that attracts Zhang in the first place. In Chapter 4, I demonstrated the ways in which incestuous attraction between brother and sister actualizes a space of safety away from the terror of the conjugal family. Ami and Takuya, in Sakurai Ami's *Innocent World*, see their sexual relationship to its logical conclusion: a child. Kirino, in contrast, does not allow the same sense of closure for Zhang and Mei-kun. Instead, Zhang's desire for his sister's body and his concurrent denial of the inappropriateness of that desire lead to Mei-kun's death and eventually to Yuriko's. Like the narrator, he ends up alone, the corruption of his family manifested not in dysfunction but rather sexual taboo. The incest taboo is introduced early in the story when Yuriko, still an adolescent, has sex with her father's brother, an experience (statutory rape) that indoctrinates her into inappropriate sexual encounters. Like all the other tropes in the novel, which circulate and mutate with each iteration, by the time we reach the end and arrive at the narrator's attraction to her nephew, we are poised for a replay of incestual desire.

Kazue's family sits uncomfortably between the psychological abnormality of the narrator's family and the sexual aberration of Zhang's relationship with Mei-kun. Kazue criticizes her mother (despite her having a more exalted pedigree than her husband), noting that "she wasn't smart enough to get into med school" and blames her gender for her inability to succeed outside of the domestic realm (Kirino 2007: 99). In contrast, Kazue exalts her father, who is a near parody of the *teishu kanpaku* or "husband ruler." A man with little social capital himself, he nevertheless lords it over his family when he is home. Kazue lives to please him, seeing him as the pinnacle of success and the model for her own aspirations. Ironically, after Kazue's father dies prematurely, Kazue finds herself foisted into his role as the sole provider for her mother and younger sister as she trolls the streets looking for a father-like figure to stay her from her unhappiness.

Once the family loses its financial stability, Kazue comes to find that hard work and determination matter little in a world ruled by men and male desire. "If she should ever set eyes on a girl like Yuriko and her monstrously perfect beauty," the narrator claims, "Kazue's efforts—no matter how prodigious—would just be laughable" (99). Regardless of her intellectual abilities, Kazue soon learns, a woman like Yuriko will always come out ahead. Prostitution is proffered as an egress to equality between rivals, for the intellectually gifted Kazue and Yuriko—"dumb as a doornail" (111)—walk the same dirty streets and proposition the same questionable men. And, of course, they share the same fate, presumably at the hands of Zhang. Kirino seems to be lamenting women's inability to transcend public fascination with their bodies. In the process, she demonstrates that familial pressure for success is an integral part in establishing unrealistic expectations for women like Kazue, whose professional potential and personal sacrifice cannot make up for gender inequality. Kirino argues that the price of academic and corporate ascent (namely, the erosion of familial stability) is not worth the cost: Kazue, like the other characters, ends up alone, and her attempts to rebel against the social system that rewards a woman's sexuality but little else reaffirms the extent to which she is simply a body.

Grotesque, then, is not an example of "oppositional storytelling" (Hurley 2011: 12). It is not a celebration of female sexual agency. The novel rests on trapping women in an endless cycle of struggling to be desirable and then punishing them for their sexual transgressions. In the process, Kirino not only demonstrates the inescapability of cultural hegemony, but she also advocates for the endurance of the very institutions she initially appears to mock.

Monstrosity giving way to normality also informs the narrative trajectory of *Real World*. The novel begins as a meditation on the monster next door, unfolding after the principal narrator, Yamanaka Toshiko (who goes by the alias Hori Ninna), overhears her next-door neighbor murder his mother. Worm, as she decides to call this neighbor, emerges as an object of fascination for Toshiko and her three high school classmates, who rally together to help him evade the police. The narrative trajectory echoes that of *Snakes and Earrings*, in which protagonist Lui goes to extremes to cover up a murder committed by Shiba. At the same time, the matricide at the core of *Real World* pushes the text in the direction of Sakurai Ami's *Innocent World*, which similarly concerns itself with the death of the mother. As a symbolic affront to one's origin, one's place, even oneself, the desire for matricide in these texts underscores the desire for renewal and rebirth. It is a desire shared by all of the primary characters in *Real World*, though only enacted by the sole male figure among the four high schoolgirls. The novel afflicts each teenage character with a variety of personal problems (ranging from family and education to sex and sexuality) and frustration with contemporary Japan. In this way, Worm's murder of his mother suggests a collective adolescent retaliation against authority and Japanese social life while simultaneously, and more importantly, providing a temporary outlet for youthful rebellion. In other words, the monster next door unleashes the monster within.

In both *Real World* and *Grotesque* the mother is an impediment. In *Real World* her nagging catalyzes her son's decisive act. She wants him to toe the line, to study, and to become the mythic success. In *Grotesque* as well, maternal figures are either erased or silenced. Yuriko abandons her son; the narrator's mother does not defend her and ends up isolated in Switzerland, where she kills herself. Kazue's mother, though educated and capable, "disappears" into anonymity when her tyrannical husband declares himself her superior.

In *Real World* the mother is permanently silenced by the heir, who is abetted by other women.

My contention is that although the death of the mother can be read and theorized in transgressive ways, the outcome for Toshiko and her friends—Kaibara Kiyomi (Yuzan), Terauchi Kazuko (Terauchi), and Higashiyama Kirari (Kirarin)—is anything but liberating. In the end, Yuzan runs away, Terauchi kills herself, and Kirarin dies. Only Toshiko is left to pick up the broken pieces of their friendship. This jarring turn of events causes Toshiko to accept the conditions of adult life from which she had attempted to run. The novel is thus defined by woeful acquiescence. The four high schoolgirls' contribution to Worm's escape is easily coded as a form of revenge against the cultural construction of Japanese womanhood. Worm's mother foreshadows the women Toshiko and her friends will inevitably become, and in joining together to protect Worm from capture, they collude in symbolic violence against their future identities as Japanese adults, and Japanese women more specifically. That each female character has constructed an alias behind which she hides conveys a sense of escape, protection, and reinvention, a means to forestall the inevitability of adult life. As Rebecca Copeland (2004: 265) observes, Kirino's novels often address the concerns of women living amid "false [pretenses] and disguises." In the present work, Kirino reveals the challenges of holding too tightly to the mask.

The text frames itself in terms of this kind of disguise and misdirection. Chapter One of the novel opens with Toshiko, the chapter's narrator, applying make-up—both a disguise and prerequisite for typical feminine identity. She is distracted by the neighborhood goings on, and her train of thought shifts from the droning of the air pollution advisory alarm to the high school boy next door who "reminded me of a worm" (Kirino 2008: 5). Toshiko comments on his awkward nature that betrays a desire to "hide from the world" (5). Worm, as we come to know him, is not alone in his pursuit of anonymity, for the duration of the novel is concerned with why each character has constructed her own false identity. Toshiko, for example, as a teenage schoolgirl, is acutely aware of her status as a commodified object of adult fascination and, more specifically, male sexual fascination. "Horny men, both young and old[,]" see her as a sexual commodity, while marketing firms view her potential purchasing power as an asset to their commercial success (12).[3] In an effort to deflect attention from herself, she constructs her Hori Ninna persona and maintains a "nothing sort of look" (9). Although Toshiko leads a relatively normal life, with plans to attend a prestigious college, and she is the beneficiary of emotional support from both parents, she feels suffocated and frustrated by the pressures of Japan's intensely meritocratic society. Her Hori Ninna persona is a means to cope as a cog in a machine that is, to her, badly flawed. The narrative's concern, then, is not in overhauling the existing mechanisms of Japanese social life, but in the ways Japanese youth survive the present and come to terms with roles as victims of circumstance. In the novel's closing moments, Toshiko—also the final chapter's narrator—decides that she is "through with using a fake name," a gesture symbolizing her acceptance of the conditions of the real world, a symbolic removal of her disguise (208).

Each chapter reveals the conditions under which Toshiko and her friends live. Yuzan, for example, lives with her father and grandparents; her mother died of cancer when she was in middle school. Yuzan is a closeted lesbian; although she frequents lesbian bars in Shinjuku, she feels she must keep her sexual identity hidden from family and friends. Kirarin has an active but secret sex life to compensate for a broken heart suffered in middle school. She travels to Tokyo after school to meet men she finds on the Internet, using sexual encounters to compensate for a lack of self-confidence. Terauchi, who, like Toshiko, continually fends off sexual advances from strangers, struggles to reconcile her feelings toward her parents; she is angry at her mother for having an affair but also resents her father for making her commute to an expensive private school, among other reasons.

The lives of Toshiko and her friends are mediated by the heterocentric social structure of millennial Japan. Toshiko, Kirarin, and Terauchi are all attuned to the sexual commodification of their daily existence. "When the media was going nuts over schoolgirls getting old guys to be their sugar daddies for sex," Toshiko explains, referring to the popularity of compensated dating in the early 1990s,[4] "that was the time when high school girls like us had the highest price as commodities" (16). Toshiko and Terauchi are irritated by male attention and, by adopting their aliases, go to lengths to deflect the eyes of men. Kirarin, on the other hand, feels compelled to indulge in that same attention as a means to cultivate a sense of self-worth. She and several like-minded girls at her high school have developed an elaborate system to "get guys to pay attention to us" and like to "get picked up by guys, go with them to a karaoke place, go drinking, [and] spend the whole night having fun" (92, 93).

Meanwhile, the sexual closet in which Yuzan is trapped is a stern reminder of the demands of normative sexual identities. She is adamant that her friends not learn the truth about her sexual orientation (although Kirarin and Terauchi both know), concerned that if her secret got out her problems would simply worsen (45). For Yuzan, the closet offers protection while concurrently reinforcing sexual binaries. The invisibility of Yuzan's queer identity offers a space of protection to which the other characters do not have access. At the end of the novel, she disappears into the labyrinthine and secretive nightlife of Shinjuku, finding ironic escape in what Elizabeth Grosz (2001: 8) calls the "containment of gayness." Grosz (2001: 8) finds that the metaphor of the "closet" is both imprisoning and nurturing, for those who are (trapped) in it. In this way, she explains (2001: 8), hetereocentric and gay communities benefit from the isolationist rhetoric that informs gayness in contemporary society. In *Real World*, the safety of the gay community allows Yuzan to, in Toshiko's words, "come out of the closet" among her nightlife friends and to find a sense of belonging, even if that means living on the margins (Kirino 2008: 54).

Invisibility is crucial to the ways in which these characters navigate the sexual topography of contemporary Japan. Toshiko and Terauchi disappear into their respective personae. Yuzan lives a silent life of cloaked sexuality. And Kirarin gets sucked into the vastness of online chatrooms devoted to finding sexual partners. In short, these women are all faced with crises of sexuality that dictate the ways in which they relate to society at large. In situating her text amid high schoolgirls navigating Japan's sexual landscape, Kirino writes for an audience already familiar with a discourse of gendered sexual frustration. Because Japanese schoolgirls have long been objects of domestic and international sexual fetishization,[5] her novel attempts to give dimension to the experiences of teenage girls living under incessant and often unwanted attention. Her female characters, then, represent a range of archetypes: those who shy from male companionship, those who seek it out, and those who exist on a different sexual plane. Each character is burdened with the consequences of living as a sexual being in contemporary Japan.

Similarly, Worm's violent acts are partially catalyzed by his own sexual frustration. Worm is preoccupied with his unpopularity with women. His nickname, coined by Toshiko, brings to mind images of a slithery asexual organism. He "was a lanky, stoop-shouldered boy with small, gloomy eyes. Reminded me of a worm," Toshiko explains. "He had a sluggish way of walking with his head tilted to one side, and zero in the way of spirit" (5). This unflattering portrayal is reminiscent of that of the introverted and reclusive protagonist of Murakami Ryū's *Kyōseichū* (*Symbiotic Worm*, 2000)[6] who identifies *himself* as a worm, "a nonreflective, silent 'body'...—a living, spatially extended thing" that exists but does not exist really (Szafraniec 2007: 128–129). In Murakami's novel, Worm's response to the traumatizing nature of Japanese life is to barricade himself inside his home. In contrast, Kirino's Worm responds to that same trauma by destroying the central symbolic figure (the mother) of his own home. In Chapter Three of *Real World*, which Worm narrates, he explains that he first entertained ideas of killing his mother after she interrupted a sexual fantasy. Worm realizes that from the veranda of his house he can spy on Toshiko when she is in the bath. He is watching her undress when his mother catches him. She scolds him, exclaiming that he is "scum," and she reveals that the family has had to move in the past because of similar behavior (Kirino 2008: 78). "Something's wrong with you," she says (79). Her words draw attention to the latent sexual deviancy of her reclusive son, discussed further below, as well as the growing idea that Japanese youth are somehow dysfunctional.

Perhaps the most jarring example of youth dysfunction in millennial Japan is that of Sakakibara Seitō, aka Shōnen A, as he was referred to in the media, on whom Worm is loosely based and whose physical appearance is similar to Worm's. As described in Chapter 2, in 1997, Sakakibara (an alias that he created for himself; his real name was reportedly Azuma Shinichirō), then fourteen years old, committed two extremely violent acts. Afterward, he sent a letter to the *Kobe Newspaper*, blaming compulsory education, and the society that gave rise to it, for his actions and his "transparent existence." He goes on to express a desire to be acknowledged as "a real, living human being." Yumiko Iida has astutely suggested that Sakakibara's desire for validation depended on reconciling his own feelings of alienation. He "seems to have attempted to view the world from…the eyes of the monster" (Iida 2000: 446). Sakakibara ostensibly blames adult society for his monstrosity, and, in his letter, writes of seeking "revenge" against those who had robbed him of his humanity. His implication that Japanese adults have turned their children into monsters is not uncommon. For example, Satoshi Kotani (2004: 32) argues that, in light of crimes like Sakakibara's, in Japan "adults have created dreadful monsters out of youth."

To a certain extent, Kirino plays off social fears of what Kotani calls the "youthphobia" that afflicted the Japanese in the 1990s (Kotani 2004: 32). Kotani argues that the mass media capitalized on the morbid interest in juvenile crime in the wake of the Sakakibara murder. While there were a handful of copycat crimes throughout the late 1990s and early 2000s, he states that juvenile crime is not cause for mass concern (2004: 32). Adrienne Carey Hurley (2011: 155, 199), too, notes that "the seemingly ubiquitous teen killer of the late 1990s" was largely a product of popular culture that depended on "a simultaneous fascination and repulsion in response to violent behavior in children." She reminds us that the discourse surrounding teenage killers—in which youth are portrayed as unstable and maladjusted—is not particular to the contemporary moment. Hurley points to literature from the 1950s and 1960s by acclaimed author Mishimia Yukio, for example, to demonstrate the resilience and longevity of "intergenerational conflict" expressed through the motif of the violent adolescent boy (2011: 156). Kirino's text is thus part of a cadre of fiction—including, as Hurley points out, works by popular authors Murakami Ryū and Yū Miri (2011: 156)—that uses the familiar trope of the teenage killer to advance its transgressive agenda. Although Worm's violent act is not the novel's main event, its narrative arc seems to need masculine aggression and disappointment. In this sense, *Real World* is a narrative we have read before.

Kirino pulls from more than just the Sakakibara narrative. By drawing attention to Worm's sexual misgivings, Kirino introduces the stereotypical image of the reclusive sexual deviant. Since the arrest of twenty-seven-year-old Miyazaki Tsutomu in 1989 for the murders of and necrophiliacal acts performed on four young girls, male antisocial behavior and sexual frustration have been linked in the Japanese popular consciousness. Miyazaki's arrest came at an already anxious time in Japanese cultural history (see the Introduction), and the public readily saw this "otaku killer," as he was colloquially called, as a symbol of decaying social bonds and the deleterious effects of physical and psychological escapism. As Sharon Kinsella explains, manga artists and those who consumed their works "had no fixed identities, no fixed gender roles, and no fixed sexuality. Ultimately, they symbolized a group of young people who had become so literally anti-social they were unable to communicate or have social relationships with other people at all" (Kinsella 2000: 137). Because the primary producers and consumers of this type of media were men, the implicit fear here was of men who did not know how to be men. In this light, Miyazaki was the nexus of fears regarding the new generation of failed Japanese masculinity.

In *Real World*, when Worm's mother catches him spying on Toshiko and disrupts his voyeuristic sexual fantasy, she effeminizes him. He is already concerned that she has robbed him of his personal agency, therefore leaving him better off dead: "As long as she's around I'll never be free. She'll decide which university I should go to, pick out who I should marry, and wind up bossing my kids around" (Kirino 2008: 79). In other words, in the context of millennial masculinity, boys do not know how to become men and must be conditioned and cajoled by their mothers. Worm says that his mother "led… [him] around by the nose" (117). Worm does not feel the same antagonism toward his father. "He doesn't scare me," Worm says. "I'm taller than him, and stronger" (79). His father, like nearly all fathers in the texts analyzed in *The End of Transgression*, is a non-entity. In killing his mother, Worm attempts to establish control over his life by enacting control over her right to live.

Real World therefore treats violence toward the mother as the transgressive solution to the problem of selfhood. Worm's mother is a barrier to her son's self-assertion and autonomy, and this single act of aggression affords Worm a means to oppose locations of domestic power. At the same time, Worm's crisis of masculinity is an opportunity for Toshiko and her friends to stage their own revolt against Japanese social life. They are not agents of their own destructive acts but rather accomplices in Worm's construction of a post-matriarchal world. Because the text's events are catalyzed by matricide and the son's fantasy of independence, *Real World* offers violence as the only means of reparation for young Japanese men and women. Worm, Toshiko, and the others effectively gang up on the matriarchal figure, casting the latter as the repository of their collective anxieties and frustrations.

The text echoes Julia Kristeva's thoughts on the ways that matricide is necessary for successful individuation. In *Black Sun*, she posits (Kristeva 1989: 27), "For man and for woman, the loss of the mother is a biological and psychic necessity, the first on the way to becoming autonomous." She goes on to suggest that once the mother is abjected—through violent means—a period of mourning must follow. Otherwise, depression, self-hatred, and melancholia will set in. Most provocatively, Kristeva (1989: 28) argues that this process of radical abjection is more difficult for women to enact than men: "For a woman, whose specular identification with the mother as well as the introjection of the maternal body and self are more immediate, such an inversion of matricidal drive into a death-bearing maternal image is more difficult, if not impossible." Women are thus burdened with the psychological consequences of remaining attached to the maternal figure. At the same time, women—many of whom become mothers themselves—are destined to become that which they hate. Kristeva (1989: 28) writes: "In order to separate from their mother's bodies females must separate from themselves as women." Women must therefore also bear witness to their own potential matricide. This is why women are not capable, Kristeva says, of killing the mother; to do so would be to kill the self.

Real World's relationship to Kristeva's work comes from the centrality of the death of the mother, of course, but also the fate of the female characters in general. Worm's mother comes to stand for every mother in the text. Moreover, because each girl ends up worse off by the end, they are abjected themselves, having inadvertently fulfilled Kristeva's theory. Worm's liberation from the mother is also a liberation from repressed—and eventually warped—sexuality. Because Worm's mother catches her son spying on Toshiko, her gaze exposes his latent sexual deviancy. Until this point, his attempts to mask his erotic desires had largely been successful—at least according to Worm, who denies his mother's contention that the family has had to relocate in the past because of his behavior. In this way, then, Worm is similar to the text's other central characters, who hide behind facades and false personae. The mother seals her fate by inadvertently catching her son in a moment of authenticity.

His overwhelming disgust toward his mother for her own apparent transgression sets in motion the collective collapse of the other characters' false lives. The novel, then, initially offers violence and deception as a temporary solution to the problems afflicting Japanese youth, insofar as characters are afforded a means of escape. But the ability of the young escape artists to remain uncaged is compromised by the intensity of Worm's will to freedom. The girls' collective insistence on finding liberation not in their own actions but rather in those of Toshiko's next-door neighbor is a similarly unstable and ultimately unwise decision.

On the morning that Worm kills his mother, he follows Toshiko to the train station and steals her bicycle and cell phone, which he uses to call her friends Kirarin and Yuzan. Both girls are intrigued by Worm and bond with him over the phone. Yuzan, for example, talks to him at length about the death of her own mother. She jokingly tells him that she, too, murdered her mother, even though the woman actually died from cancer. Toshiko, calling her friend from her home phone, is irritated to learn this, especially because Yuzan was initially distraught by her mother's death. Toshiko, trying to talk some sense into her friend, tells her what Worm did to his mother. Yuzan responds coolly: "It's not our business. Worm killing his mother has nothing to do with us"

(Kirino 2008: 34). Toshiko replies: "I know. I don't care about that at all. I just want my bike and phone back" (35).

Japan's post-bubble generation is often characterized in terms of this sort of apathy and indifference. Kanehara's *Snakes and Earrings*, for instance, shocked readers with the casualness with which its characters view murder, recreational sex, sexual violence, and body modification. Kanehara's characters simply do not care about anything or anyone but themselves. The apathetic pulse that courses through Kanehara's novella is shaped by a generational pessimism regarding Japanese social institutions. *Real World*, published the same year as *Snakes and Earrings*, although by an author from an earlier generation, contributes to the discursive construction of self-centered Japanese youth. Toshiko's contention that she cares less about murder than her possessions goes a long way in establishing her and her friends as poster children for all that is wrong with millennial Japan. By constructing each character in this way, Kirino cultivates an ethos of nastiness, egotism, and transgression.

We might argue that Kirino's deliberate construction of female unpleasantness is in response to misdirected social and political discourses intended to protect Japanese youth. The 1999 Child Solicitation and Child Pornography Prevention Act (*Jidō poruno jidō kaishun kinshi hō*) codified into law attempts to end both sex tourism internationally and compensated dating domestically. Kirsten Cather points out, however, that the *Jipohō*, as the law is colloquially called, was formulated under international pressure and criticism regarding the Japanese government's relatively lax view of child pornography (Cather 2017: 78). Nevertheless, in order to combat the exploitation of women and children, the law reconceptualized the nature of prostitution by placing blame on the buyer (*kaishun* in the law's title) rather than the seller. Kinsella (2014: 94–98) suggests that the *Jipohō* and other similar legislations aimed not at the crimes of solicitation or exploitation but rather at the preservation of girlish innocence. It is worth noting that the bill did little to end—or even address—sex trafficking or change the stigma against compensated dating, given that the girls rather than their clients continued to be punished and castigated in the media. Central to the conservative agenda against compensated dating was the protection of girlhood through the punishing of monetized sex and female sexual deviancy and the simultaneous construction of the angelic and virginal *shōjo*.

"The rejection of the code of Japanese *shōjo* innocence," Kinsella (2014: 139) explains, has been a crucial component of Japanese female identity in modern culture. She calls attention to the *ganguro* and "B-girl" subcultures, which emphasize tan skin in a manner that contradicts stereotypical and historically rooted expressions of Japanese femininity (2014: 134). Since at least the Nara Period (710–784), white, translucent skin has represented idealized feminine beauty in Japan (Wagatsuma 1967: 407). Laura Miller (2006: 75) further suggests that the "bust-consciousness" trend in Japan in the 1980s "may…represent a rebellion against the cult of cuteness and ineffectual innocence still endorsed by many Japanese men." In this light, what Kirino offers vis-à-vis youthful deviance and rebellion is in line with widespread ideas about the agency of Japanese women. Schoolgirls, burdened with the weight of the past, are especially vulnerable to social coding since they are simultaneously seen as embodiments of a cute and sweet present and blueprints for an obedient and docile future. For this reason, schoolgirls are attractive vessels for discursive transgression and discord and for social commentary. In *Real World*, Worm is not the central character, after all, and neither is his crime of great importance. Rather, matricide facilitates the emergent viciousness of Toshiko's cohort, who are ostensibly only concerned with themselves.

In this light, their willingness to help Worm is uncharacteristic and upsets the dynamic of the friendship. Toshiko claims that although she does not "want to be an accomplice," she nevertheless craves "a taste of adventure" (Kirino 2008: 37). Her inexplicable attraction to Worm and his crime is echoed by her friends, who feel compelled to help him. "I'm pretty surprised myself," Yuzan says about her own role in Worm's escape. After Toshiko reprimands Yuzan for her complicity in the theft of Toshiko's belongings, Yuzan buys Worm his own cell phone and offers him her bicycle. Yuzan feels drawn to Worm because, like her, he seems lonely (39). In killing his mother, she suggests, he has "perfected his solitude" (39). Furthermore, because Yuzan's own mother is dead, she sees something of herself in Worm's actions. "I don't really know how to put it," she explains, "but it was like I didn't want him to come back to stupid boring reality, but instead create a new reality all his own" (41). She hopes for him what she cannot have for herself—a place to start over. The death of Yuzan's mother has compounded the displacement she already feels because of her sexual identity. She seeks out lesbian bars in Shinjuku's 2-chōmei's district, gravitating to the most "radical" bars that allow entry only to gay people. "I guess I wanted to make sure I wasn't the only one who was like me," she says (42). Her search for a so-called lesbian identity depends on constituting herself as distinct from heterosexual women. Kakefuda Hiroko (1992), a prominent gay-rights activist in the early 1990s, has argued that Japan's patriarchal social structure makes it challenging for women to pursue their own identity, let alone their own *sexual* identity. Sexually marginalized persons such as Yuzan are thus doubly bound by the social and cultural limitations of two strands of self-identification. Since Kakefuda's writings, queer identities have achieved a greater degree of social recognition and acceptance. Yuzan, however, understands that as a "girl who likes other girls," she will always struggle for a sense of place and belonging (Kirino 2008: 47). After she is attacked in 2-chōmei because of her sexuality, her awareness of her marginal status becomes more acute, and she grows fearful of *herself* for the "hatred" she "stirs up…in others" (48). Her attack brings to light the complexities and dangers of living as a lesbian in Japan and affords her insight into the reasons why Dahmer, a friend and fellow lesbian, vanished one day (49). At the end of the novel, Yuzan follows suit, disappearing into the lesbian nightlife in pursuit of acceptance by those who have been rejected by Japanese society.

Of all of the teenagers in *Real World*, Yuzan carries the heaviest burden. She learns of her mother's illness just as she is becoming aware of her sexuality (57). Her mother's violent and unpredictable mood swings make it difficult for Yuzan to confide in her. Her father, moreover, is rarely home, leading Yuzan to conclude that he is having an affair. This personal crisis complicates Yuzan's ability to study for her college entrance exams. She thus feels drawn to Worm, who seems to be suffering from his own crisis of subjectivity. Not only is his home life in understandable disarray, his aspirations for getting into Tokyo University are now ruined (60). Both characters understand that without a clearly delineated future or place in Japanese society, their lives are all but over. Indeed, Yuzan's sexual orientation precludes her from marriage and, presumably, motherhood, while her inability to plan for the future prohibits her from mapping her contributions to Japanese society. In her eyes, Worm has enacted a kind of self-alienation that mirrors the ways in which she has been alienated by the norms and expectations governing contemporary Japan.

In concert with several other works discussed in *The End of Transgression*, *Real World* attends to the middle-class melancholia that afflicts Japanese youth. Much scholarly attention has been paid to the economic woes of Japan's lower classes, but Kirino's concern is with the emotional precarity of those from decently affluent families. Like Sakurai Ami, Kirino demonstrates that the middle-class dream of ordinary Japanese families belies a crisis of belonging that is shared by Japan's displaced youth. "What Kirino...captures," writes Kristina Iwata-Weickgenannt (2015: 33) regarding another of Kirino's texts, *Metabola* (2007), "is the complete 'lack of reserves,' a deficiency that is symptomatic of contemporary forms of poverty," including a lack of "basic financial resources, close relationships[,] and mental stability." The latter two "reserves" take precedence in *Real World*, given that the comfortable communities in which Toshiko and her friends live contribute to their shared sense of displacement and alienation. These communities are comfortable in appearance only, and each character is dismayed by what lurks beneath the façade of ordinariness. Until Worm kills his mother, household problems remain relatively self-contained and isolated. The severity of his actions, however, exposes not only his problems but also those of the girls who come to his aid.

Their respective chapters read almost like confessions, illuminating the depths of their individual struggles.

In Chapter Four of the novel, for example, Kirarin uses her encounter with Worm—with whom she shares a hotel room while he is on the run—to reveal her anxieties about being caught between two social groups at school. Toshiko, Terauchi, and Yuzan are the studious, aspirational group, while a cohort of nameless girls Kirarin calls the "Good Times group" are more interested in "clothes, make-up, and guys" than academics (Kirino 2008: 93). Kirarin feels too sexually experienced to relate to Toshiko and the others, but too intellectual for her friends in the Good Times group. She decides to help Worm partially for the excitement of flirting with him. Their conversation turns serious, however, when Kirarin tells him about an affair her father had when she was in middle school. Of all of the primary characters, only Toshiko and Worm do not mention the sexual misdeeds of their parents.

David Bayley (1976: 111) contends that because marriage in Japan has historically been based on the familial obligations of both husband and wife rather than romantic attraction, "[i]nfidelity is not a source of guilt to men… Nor do wives feel that [their husband's] infidelity necessarily threatens their marriage." While there may be truth to this statement, and although Bayley says nothing about the indiscretion of wives, it is worth noting that young, unmarried Japanese such as Kirarin do not grant their parents the same degree of leniency. While Kirarin enjoys her sexual freedom, she holds her parents to a different standard. That parental philandering is something Kirarin, Yuzan, and Terauchi comment on suggests that the institution of marriage is somewhat of a mockery in millennial Japan, at least to the younger generations. In a novel devoted to façade, *Real World* offers up matrimony as yet another empty signifier of the instability of heteronormative culture. Because of Kirarin's father's infidelity, as well as her own troubled dating history, she views nearly all men with a mixture of disdain and suspicion. (She thinks poorly of her mother as well, concluding that she has bad taste in men.) Worm, however, seems neither sexually profligate nor particularly menacing, at least to her (Kirino 2008: 103). He lacks the sexual urgency and masculine bravado that Kirarin is used to, which makes him inexplicably harmless—even though he murdered his mother with a baseball bat! She feels comfortable enough around him to rent them both a hotel room for the night.

Kirarin is unaware of Worm's sexual proclivities, including his spying on Toshiko. Worm insists, however, that murdering his mother neutralized his aberrant sexual tendencies (114). He claims that he is "transforming" or "evolving" into a different person, an autonomous and largely asexual being (114). Worm's rejection of his sexuality, in concert with this rejection of maternal authority, suggests a grander attempt at erasure, a reset. Worm wants only to start from zero, not unlike the novel's other characters. However, Worm is unsettled by what he sees as Kirarin's "pornographic" behavior. "Now that I had done my mother in, I had to mow down all of the rest of the pornographic women in the world. Somebody's got to give order," he says (114). It is as though he sees female sexuality as a threat to the world in which he lives. A short time later he refers to Kirarin as a "noisy…slut" (127). He is caught off guard by unexpected sexual tension between them and, inexperienced with women, reacts by taking Kirarin hostage with a knife. She eventually falls asleep while he talks to her friends on the phone. In conflating his mother with all women, Worm also aligns her sexuality with that of female sexuality in general. Kirarin, who is the most sexually experienced of her friends, is therefore threatening to Worm's masculinity, and his attraction to her reads like a misdirected attraction of his dead mother. Nobuko Anan (2016: 56) argues that in the typical familial formation, mother-son incest "is implied in its very prohibition." Worm ostensibly desires a world without women, which is an ironic twist given that four high schoolgirls come to his rescue.

Of the four high schoolgirls, Terauchi stands alone in her eventual criticism of Worm. Worm calls her from the hotel room he is sharing with Kirarin and demands that Terauchi write a "criminal manifesto" (Kirino 2008: 143). Terauchi shrugs off his demand and, following the formula of the novel, uses her chapter (Chapter Six) to reflect on the conditions of her "self-induced depression" (148). The reader learns of her experiences commuting to an elite school when she was a child and, as she got older, her growing awareness of herself as a sexual object. Terauchi goes on to comment on the conditions of her home life, emphasizing her mother's festering resentment of her family. "I'm not sure when my mother...began to change," Terauchi reflects (153). She continues: "Every time Mom went on a trip I was afraid she'd never come back" (154). Terauchi eventually discovers that her mother is having an affair with a colleague, but buries her pain, afraid of a life without her, should her mother choose the other man over her family. Terauchi explains how her mother's affair changed the dynamic of the household, turning father against daughter and daughter against parents. Ever resentful of her mother, she says: "In my heart, I murdered my own mother long ago, over and over" (157). Feeling unimpressed by Worm's twisted bravado, she calls the police.

The central paradox of the novel is this divide between feminine passive-aggressive acceptance of the status quo and masculine retaliation against it. Toshiko, Yuzan, Kirarin, and Terauchi can only devise temporary solutions to their problems. Each girl feels anger and frustration toward her parents, and toward Japanese social life in general, but finds no liberation in her means of coping. Terauchi, for example, may despise her mother, but she accepts her mother's extramarital lifestyle and what it has done to their family. Killing her mother in her mind does not provide a permanent solution; on the contrary, because her mother "rule[s] at home" (154), Terauchi still needs her for familial stability. Toshiko enjoys masquerading as Hori Ninna in order to mock those who see her as a sexual and commercial commodity. She is only able to find temporary reprieve from behind this mask, however, because she will eventually have to take it off (which she does at the end, as I discuss later). *Real Life* hinges on this kind of psychological progress, with each character coming to accept the conditions of her life as a woman in contemporary Japan. Kirarin shows flashes of a more permanent change, claiming to have "discovered [her] real identity" as a "bad" woman who is "stronger" than her other friends (Kirino 2008: 166). Nevertheless, she remains heartbroken over her middle-school romance and wants only to return to Wataru, the boy who broke her heart. "This world," she says, is the one in which she is an accomplice to murder (174); in "that other world," she and Wataru are happy (171). Kirarin's dependence on heteronormative romance betrays the extent to which she is bound to institutional femininity. Her fear is to be cast into the abyss of the undesirable.

Kirino devotes each chapter to illuminating the afflictions of young middle-class Japanese, giving them understandable reasons to retaliate against society at large. But she also shows that the urge to rebel is sometimes counterproductive. In Kirarin's case, only after implicating herself in Worm's crime does she yearn for the safety of the conventional romance narrative. She does not get it, however. On the run from the police—thanks to Terauchi's anonymous tip—she and Worm hijack a taxicab to make their escape. She sees a successful getaway as her means to "escape this world" (174). But the taxi crashes after Worm slashes the driver's throat. Worm ends up in the hospital, and Kirarin, ejected from the taxi, is killed (180). "Flying through the sky," she says. "Such a wonderful, wonderful feeling" (180). This sense of levity reminds Kirarin of the "other world" of juvenile romance. She, like her friends, has been betrayed by the instability of the adult world. In Kirarin's case, it kills her.

Kirarin's death brings an end to the novel's exercise in transgression. The final chapter, narrated by Toshiko, explains the collapse of the main characters' collective rebellious vision. Toshiko reflects on a suicide note written by Terauchi, in which Terauchi examines her residual hatred for her mother and her feelings of guilt over Kirarin's death. This sense of guilt affects the remaining members of the cohort (Toshiko and Yuzan), both of whom had been eager to help Worm. Yuzan disappears after Terauchi's funeral, finding acceptance in Tokyo's underground gay nightlife. Toshiko finds herself alone, but not before detectives question her about her friends' involvement in Worm's crime. The detectives deduce the ways that Toshiko and her friends helped him escape, even reasoning that it was Terauchi who called the police. "I was taken aback," Toshiko reflects. "It sounded so stupid when someone else put it into words" (205). Their plan was indeed, in a word, "stupid," the brainchild of angry teenagers lacking the foresight to consider the broader consequences. Of the two surviving friends, only Toshiko remains "in this world," and she feels changed. "No more Ninna Hori," she tells herself, referring to her alias (208). Toshiko symbolically accepts the parameters of this world. Her friends are gone, casualties of transgression gone awry, and she is seemingly left with two choices: disappear like Yuzan, or grow up. Unlike Yuzan, she has nowhere to disappear to. Toshiko decides to take off her make-up, reminding us of the beginning of the text and her fateful encounter with the monster next door.

The two novels discussed here demonstrate how female characters are punished for acting in ways that are incongruous with Japanese hegemony.

Grotesque and *Real World* ostensibly advocate for female malevolence; both texts celebrate the extent to which Japanese women can be terribly cruel to others. At the same time, the novels read like instruction manuals for how to rebel against patriarchal authority and hegemonic governance over the female body. As I have demonstrated, however, what is important to understand is not the mechanics of rebellion, but what happens to those who insist on living too far out of bounds. Nothing good happens to the women who populate these novels. Kirino's novels, then, are about starting over after transgression has run its course.

Notes

1 "OL" (an abbreviation for "Office Lady") is a popular but ambiguously defined term used to refer to young working women who are generally understood to be single and engaged in low-level administrative or clerical work. Its use in this case is evidence of the ill-defined nature of the term because the woman in question was not only older but a senior researcher and less likely to have been performing tasks conventionally relegated to young women who, it is assumed, only intend to stay employed until they marry.
2 An immigrant from Nepal was arrested for Watanabe's murder. Although acquitted for lack of evidence, he was subsequently convicted on appeal by the Tokyo High Court and imprisoned for fifteen years before new evidence led to his release. He was deported back to Nepal to await a retrial, but, in 2012, he was absolved of guilt and in 2013 awarded compensation for wrongful imprisonment. https://japantoday.com/category/features/kuchikomi/back-in-nepal-govinda-mainali-adjusts-to-life-on-the-outside [accessed 14 July 2022].
3 Since at least the 1970s, marketing and advertising firms have focused on Japanese schoolgirls to set trends (Allison 2006: 139).
4 See Chapter 3 for a detailed discussion of "compensated dating" (*enjo kōsai*).
5 See Sharon Kinsella 2014: 18–19.
6 The title of the book is a play on the term *kiseichû*, meaning parasite. The characters Murakami uses—共生虫 rather than 寄生虫—are meant to highlight a certain degree of symbiosis (共) in an otherwise parasitic relationship. In *Tokyo Cyberpunk: Posthumanism in Japanese Visual Culture*, Steven T. Brown translates the title as *Symbiotic Worm* (Brown 2015: 213, n. 32).

WORKS CITED

Allison, Anne. 2006. *Millennial Monsters: Japanese Toys and the Global Imagination*. Berkeley, CA: University of California Press.
Allison, Anne. 2013. *Precarious Japan*. Durham: Duke University Press.
Anan, Nobuko. 2016. *Contemporary Japanese Women's Theatre and Visual Arts: Performing Girls' Aesthetics*. New York, NY: Palgrave Macmillan.
Arai, Andrea G. 2006. "The 'Wild Child' of 1990s Japan." In *Japan After Japan: Social and Cultural Life from the Recessionary 1990s to the Present*, edited by Tomiko Yoda and H. D. Harootunian, 216–238. Durham: Duke University Press.
Bakhtin, Mikhail. 1984 [1965]. *Rabelais and His World*. Translated by Helene Iswolsky. Bloomington, IN: Indiana University Press.
Bayley, David H. 1976. *Forces of Order: Policing Modern Japan*. Berkeley, CA: University of California Press.

Berlant, Lauren. 2008. *The Female Complaint: The Unfinished Business of Sentimentality in American Culture.* Durham: Duke University Press.
Brown, Steven T. 2015. *Tokyo Cyberpunk: Posthumanism in Japanese Visual Culture.* New York, NY: Palgrave MacMillan.
Cather, Kirsten. 2017. "Must We Burn Eromanga? Trying Obscenity in the Courtroom and in the Classroom." In *The End of Cool Japan: Ethical, Legal, and Cultural Challenges to Japanese Popular Culture*, edited by Mark McLelland, 70–93. New York, NY: Routledge.
Copeland, Rebecca. 2004. "Woman Uncovered: Pornography and Power in the Detective Fiction of Kirino Natsuo." *Japan Forum* 16(2): 249–269.
Copeland, Rebecca. 2005. "Mythical Bad Girls: The Corpse, the Crone, and the Snake." In *Bad Girls of Japan*, edited by Laura Miller and Jan Bardsley, 15–32. New York, NY: Palgrave MacMillan.
Copeland, Rebecca. 2018. "Lost in the Grottos: The Subversive Allure of Kirino Natsuo's Murder Mysteries." *Japanese Language and Literature* 52 (1): 145–160.
Corbin, Alain. 1987. "Commercial Sexuality in Nineteenth-Century France: A System of Images and Regulations." In *The Making of the Modern Body: Sexuality and Society in the Nineteenth Century*, edited by Catherine Gallagher and Thomas Walter Laquer, 209–219. Berkeley, CA: University of California Press.
Covino, Deborah Caslav. 2004. *Amending the Abject Body: Aesthetic Makeovers in Medicine and Culture.* Albany, NY: State University of New York.
Creed, Barbara. 1993. *The Monstrous Feminine: Film, Feminism, Psychoanalysis.* New York, NY: Routledge.
Dore, Ronald. 1976. *The Diploma Disease: Education, Qualification, Development.* Berkeley, CA: University of California.
Eagleton, Terry. 1981. *Walter Benjamin: Or, Towards a Revolutionary Criticism.* New York, NY: Verso.
Edwards, Justin and Rune Graulund. 2013. *The Grotesque.* New York, NY: Routledge.
Gilbert, Sandra and Susan Gubar. 1979. *The Madwoman in the Attic: The Woman Writer and the Nineteenth-Century Literary Imagination.* New Haven, CT: Yale University Press.
Gluck, Carol. 1985. *Japan's Modern Myths: Ideologies in the Late Meiji Period.* Princeton, NJ: Princeton University Press.
Gordon, Andrew. 2002. "The Short Happy Life of the Japanese Middle Class." In *Social Contracts Under Stress: The Middle Classes of America, Europe, and Japan at the Turn of the Century*, edited by Olivier Zunz, Leonard Schoppa, and Nobuhiro Hiwatari, 108–129. New York, NY: Russell Sage Foundation.
Grosz, Elizabeth. 2001. *Architecture from the Outside: Essays on Virtual and Real Space.* Cambridge: MIT Press.
Hollinger, Karen. 1998. *In the Company of Women: Contemporary Female Friendship Films.* Minneapolis, MN: University of Minnesota Press.
Hurley, Adrienne Carey. 2011. *Revolutionary Suicide and Other Desperate Measures: Narratives of Youth and Violence from Japan and the United States.* Durham: Duke University Press.
Iida, Yumiko. 2000. "Between the Technique of Living an Endless Routine and the Madness of Absolute Degree Zero: Japanese Identity and the Crisis of Modernity in the 1990s." *Positions* 8(2): 423–464.
Iida, Yumiko. 2002. *Rethinking Identity in Modern Japan: Nationalism as Aesthetics.* New York, NY: Routledge.
Iwata-Weickgenannt, Kristina. 2015. "Kirino Natsuo's *Metabola*, or the Okinawan Stage, Fractured Selves and the Precarity of Contemporary Existence." In *Visions of Precarity in Japanese Popular Culture and Literature*, edited by Kristina Iwata-Weickgenannt and Roman Rosenbaum, 24–42. New York, NY: Routledge.
Jenks, Chris. 2003. *Transgression.* New York, NY: Routledge.

Kakefuda Hiroko. 1992. *"Rezuibian" de aru, to iu koto*. Tokyo: Kawade Shobō Shinsha.

Kinsella, Sharon. 2000. *Adult Manga: Culture and Power in Contemporary Japanese Society*. New York, NY: Routledge Curzon.

Kinsella, Sharon. 2014. *Schoolgirls, Money and Rebellion in Japan*. New York, NY: Routledge.

Kirino Natsuo. 2007. *Grotesque*. Translated by Rebecca Copeland. New York, NY: Alfred A. Knopf.

Kirino Natsuo. 2008. *Real World*. Translated by Philip Gabriel. New York, NY: Alfred A. Knopf.

Kotani, Satoshi. 2004. "Why Are Japanese Youth Today So Passive?". In *Japan's Changing Generations: Are Young People Creating a New Society*, edited by G. Matthews and B. White, 31–46. New York, NY: Routledge Curzon.

Kristeva, Julia. 1989. *Black Sun: Depression and Melancholia*. Translated by L. S. Roudiez. New York, NY: Columbia University Press.

McLelland, Mark. 2015. "How to Sex'? The Contested Nature of Sexuality in Japan." In *The SAGE Handbook of Modern Japanese Studies*, edited by James Babb, 194–209. United Kingdom: Sage Publications.

Miller, Laura. 2006. *Beauty Up: Exploring Contemporary Japanese Body Aesthetics*. Berkeley, CA: University of California Press.

Russo, Mary. 1986. "Female Grotesques: Carnival and Theory." In *Feminist Studies, Critical Studies*, edited by Teresa De Lauretis, 213–229. Bloomington, IN: Indiana University Press.

Russo, Mary. 1995. *The Female Grotesque: Risk, Excess and Modernity*. New York, NY: Routledge.

Shelley, Louise. 2010. *Human Trafficking: A Global Perspective*. Cambridge: Cambridge University Press.

Szafraniec, Asja. 2007. *Beckett, Derrida, and the Event of Literature*. Stanford, CA: Stanford University Press.

Ueno Chizuko. 2009. *The Modern Family in Japan: Its Rise and Fall*. Melbourne: Trans Pacific Press.

Wagatsuma, Hiroshi. (1967) 'The Social Perception of Skin Color in Japan', *Daedalus* 96(2): 407–443

Yoda, Tomiko. 2006b. "The Rise and Fall of Maternal Society: Gender, Labor, and Capital in Contemporary Japan." In *Japan After Japan: Social and Cultural Life from the Recessionary 1990s to the Present*, edited by Tomiko Yoda and H. D. Harootunian, 239–274. Durham: Duke University Press.

6

CONCLUSION

Chaos, Schizophrenia, and Reconciliation in Millennial Japan

The close readings in previous chapters considered the ways in which transgression facilitates a return to normalcy. In these final pages, I consider this return to normalcy within its historical context. If literature is a barometer for culture, what are we indexing? My close readings have depended on addressing how a cluster of works of Japanese fiction reveals how female protagonists invest themselves in state institutions that, at best, are seen as wastes of time and, at worst, harmful to citizens entrenched within their paradigms. The conservative political climate in Japan is dominated by the legacy of former Prime Minister Abe Shinzō's agenda: his aggressive stance in East Asia, his resistance to state acknowledgment of sexual war crimes, and his demand for a greater national presence on the global stage. It all carries, for some, a neoconservative aura. This chapter (and this study as a whole) argues that texts from the millennial turn offer insights into the neoconservative underpinnings of the contemporary milieu. To conclude, then, I want to briefly consider the insights that literary products today reveal about this neoconservative turn in Japanese social life and in Japanese literature.

Abe's predecessor Prime Minister Nakasone Yasuhiro (1982–1987) inaugurated the shift toward neoconservatism through nationalist policies, the repercussions of which reached a critical mass during Abe's tenure as the longest-serving prime minister in Japan's history (2006–2007; 2012–2020). Nakasone's 1978 monograph, *Atarashī hoshu no riron* (A New Theory of Conservativism), offered *shinhoshushugi* (neoconservativism) as a means of restoring a sense of Japan's prewar national identity. He argued that the Japanese no longer needed the US or the constitution it imposed after World War II. As Prime Minister, Nakasone fought, unsuccessfully, to overturn Article 9 of Japan's constitution, which prohibits military aggression beyond defensive

DOI: 10.4324/9781003231806-7

measures by the Japan Self Defense Forces. His calls for a strengthened military echoed the Meiji-era ambitions of "rich nation, strong army" (*fukoku kyōhei*). The Meiji era was a time of acute national anxiety as the Japanese government sought to vivify a sense of Japanese identity vis-à-vis the Western colonial powers. The ambitions of Nakasone's cabinet were analogous to those of the Meiji state, especially in terms of its stake in identity politics: Nakasone envisioned the Japanese as the leaders of Asia, arguing that the Asia-Pacific War was fought in the name of Asian liberation from Western imperial enterprise. Channeling the rhetoric grounded in Japan's wartime pursuit of a Greater East Asian Co-Prosperity Sphere, Nakasone saw the Japanese as the leaders and liberators of East Asia. Accordingly, Nakasone established the controversial practice of visiting Yasukuni Shrine to pay homage to Japan's war dead, including its convicted war criminals.[1] This is a practice most subsequent LDP-affiliated prime ministers have continued despite widespread opposition from the Japanese left as well as citizens and governments from other Asian nations.

The end of the Cold War and the implications of Japan's shaky economy stoked national anxieties that, by the 1990s, produced calls for vigilance over Japanese national identity. To be sure, the recession coincided with the emergence of Chinese and South Korean economic prowess on the global stage. Japanese leaders were forced to ask difficult questions regarding Japan's place in a world that seemed to be leaving the Japanese behind. One response, carried out by Prime Minister Koizumi Jun'ichirō (2001–2006), was to challenge the limitations of Article 9 by bringing the nation into the United States' post-9/11 War on Terror. Enhanced Japan-US ties, however, worsened relations with China and Korea, which were already deteriorating as a result of neoconservative chauvinism about the legacy of Japan's armed forces during the Pacific War. From inadequate apologies for Japan's use of sexual slave labor to yearly trips by Koizumi to Yasukuni Shrine to memorialize the war dead, many Japanese felt unable to move out of the shadow of their wartime history and had grown weary of constantly being asked to apologize for it. In this context, the neoconservatism of the contemporary moment can be felt acutely and can help us understand this ontological struggle over Japanese history and identity. Masaru Tamamoto explains that "while nationalism commonly serves to distinguish a nation from other nations, Japanese nationalism today does not have a national other, and nor does it need one. The other of Japanese nationalism is itself, its own contemporary history which began on 15 August 1945 [the day of surrender]. The nationalist other is Japan's post-war" (Tamamoto 2018: 178). If the Japanese national psyche has been bifurcated for nearly a century, one wonders whether it is possible to construct a unified national consciousness.

Tamamoto's observations are astute. The resolution of this bifurcation was central to the neoconservative agenda, as seen particularly in Abe's commitment to rewrite the postwar constitution, which he saw as something "imposed upon the vanquished Japanese" by the Americans in order "to prevent Japan from ever again rising as a great power" (Tamamoto 2018: 179). In this view, the constitution was an empty signifier, an illegitimate document that has anchored the Japanese to a war from which they were not legally al lowed to move. Abe became "intent on clearing Japan of what he sees as wrongful accusations" of Japanese wrongdoing during the war. (Tamamoto 2018: 180). Because of the constitution, these wrongdoings—including war crimes—have been "internalized" and have shaped Japanese consciousness domestically and Japanese self-consciousness internationally. Abe was therefore aggressive in pursuing his own antidote to "guilt fatigue," including denying the "Nanjing Massacre" and the use of Korean "comfort women" during the war (Tamamoto 2018: 180). Abe's politics cannot be separated easily from his ethno-political orientation, which represented the cresting of national schizophrenia that has plagued the Japanese since the end of the war.

Efforts to reconcile this sense of national schizophrenia have, according to Kinhide Mushakoji, left the Japanese vulnerable to "a resurgence of the Japanese claim to ethnic-superiority developed since the Meiji State-building [which] reached its paroxysm in the 1930s" (Mushakoji 2015: 39). Mushakoji is concerned that fascism lurks just below the surface of Abe's policies and politicking (Mushakoji 2015: 39). Mushakoji speaks of historical fascism, the *in toto* sublimation of the Japanese populace. If Mushakoji's words are true, and the Japanese are potentially on the brink of a fascist turn, one wonders how and why Abe—"a grudging reformer" (Bridges 2010: 77)—could so easily rise to and maintain power. Here I am reminded of Gilles Deleuze and Felix Guattari's theoretics of political desire. "The fundamental problem of political philosophy," they argue, is this: "why do people still tolerate being humiliated and enslaved, to such a point, indeed, that they actually want humiliation and slavery not for others but for themselves?" (Deleuze and Guattari 1983: 29). Deleuze and Guattari trace "this perversion of the desire of the masses" to problems within the individual. Japan's long recession nurtured a pervasive sense of isolation, ennui, rootlessness, and anxiety that has rendered Japanese youth susceptible to the ramifications of the crumbling artifice of contemporary society and the rise of a kind of affective chaos that has left many vulnerable to the siren sound of what Foucault calls "the fascist within"—the individual who desires his or her own repression.

Frederic Jameson identifies schizophrenia as an apt metaphor for the influx of empty signifiers that pepper the contemporary landscape. He argues that "the schizophrenic…does not know personal identity in our sense, since our feeling of identity depends on our sense of the persistence of the 'I' and the 'me' over time." The schizophrenic suffers from a crisis of identity and lacks temporal continuity; the *meaning* of self is foreclosed on he/she who is unable to differentiate between oneself and the self of others. The schizophrenic is nobody, an anti-subject whose self-imposed oblivion is emblematic of the experiences of contemporary life—isolated and disconnected. "Isolated, disconnected, discontinuous material signifiers which fail to link up into a coherent sequence" contribute to the erosion of temporal continuity (Jameson 1985: 119). The implications of this are embedded in a discourse of the end of transgression. The current postmodern montage desensitizes and disorients citizens to subversion and transgression. Art, for example, used to occupy a critical social space: "[M] odernism functioned against its society in ways which are variously described as critical, negative, contestatory, subversive, oppositional[,] and the like." (Jameson 1985: 125). Jameson then asks: "Can anything of the sort be affirmed about postmodernism and its social moment?" (Jameson 1985: 125).

Schizophrenia and capitalism are the two rhetorical pillars of Deleuze and Guattari's *Anti-Oedipus*. Schizophrenia, for them, is opposed to, but coeval with, capitalism. If, in Jameson's formulation, consumer capitalism decenters the individual and his or her ego, for Deleuze and Guattari the schizophrenic has no center/ego to begin with. They thus turn to the "schizo," or someone who is unaware of herself, someone who has no sense of self or autonomy; there is no "me" and there is no "you." As such, schizophrenics are resistant to the psychoanalytic process; they are perpetually "somewhere else, beyond or behind or below" the familial pulses and fluxes that are at the root of Freudian psychoanalysis. Mark Seem (1983: xvi) explains that such individuals "escape [the] coding" of the psychoanalytic process and "flee in all directions" (Deleuze and Guattari 1983: xxi). Like the "schizo," capitalism knows no cultural, historical, or ethnic limitation; it heeds no rules, and behaves no master. But capitalism and schizophrenia are not the same in their analysis. Capitalism *produces* schizophrenics "the same way it produces Prell shampoo or Ford cars" (Deleuze and Guattari 1983: 245). The schizophrenic cannot be sold, of course, and therefore must be "confined [as a] clinical entity" (Deleuze and Guattari 1983: 245). The schizophrenic represents the limits of capitalism—something that is created but cannot be sold: "Hence schizophrenia is not the identity of capitalism, but on the contrary its difference, its divergence, and its death" (Deleuze and Guattari 1983: 246).

Jameson and Deleuze and Guattari occupy different theoretical positions regarding the schizo. We have seen that Jameson (1985: 125) implicates schizophrenia into the reproductive processes of consumer capitalism. For him, the schizophrenic is complicit, a harbinger of the fall of transgression and the dominance of postmodern montage. For the latter two theorists, however, schizophrenia disrupts this same montage and disturbs the incessant stream of signifiers that is symptomatic of contemporary social life. They call for a celebration of schizophrenic sensibilities as the antidote to the malaise of life as we know it. Schizophrenics are transgressive individuals in an age when transgression's efficacy has worn. Nevertheless, all three theorists agree that human experience has become disrupted through contemporary life.

For Jameson, schizophrenia results when isolation, ennui, etc. (the postmodern condition) erode bonds between individuals. His emphasis on signifiers emptied of content is emblematic of lives emptied of meaning.

The fiction of the contemporary milieu emerges from a sense of national schizophrenia regarding what it means to be Japanese. The imbrication of fascism, schizophrenia, and capitalism, I argue, contribute to the current affective crisis afflicting today's Japanese as reflected in a particular brand of neoconservative literature. Where does this literature come from? What are the conditions under which it emerges? In my final discussion, I return to Japan and its literature, but I do so with an eye toward the above theoretical strands; to best understand this literature, we must be mindful of how fascism, schizophrenia, and capitalism intersect.

I have already demonstrated the ways in which schizophrenia manifests itself at the political level; the nationalistic policies of Abe Shinzō and his predecessors are grounded in visions of *return*—a return to an autonomous (prewar) state of existence that echoes in the hollows of a dead fascist narrative. For ordinary citizens, what it means to be Japanese is a different, more abstract inquiry that takes the form not of policy but of subjectivity. Earlier in this study, I traced the ascent of a public consciousness dedicated to consumer capitalism. I used Tanaka Yasuo's best-seller, *Somehow, Crystal*, as evidence of a mass fascination with wealth as a gateway to successful living and to successful Japaneseness. At the height of the economic bubble, to consume was to be Japanese; to be middle-class was to be Japanese.

The transgressive literature of the 1960s and 1970s raged against these imperatives. Emblematic works of fiction include Kōno Taeko's 1962 short story "Yōji gari" (Toddler Hunting) and Kanai Mieko's 1976 "Usagi" (Rabbits), both of which are invested in broke, unruly women who behave in ways that were decidedly un-Japanese. In the first instance, middle-aged protagonist Akiko enjoys being childless and is content with her low-level desk job. She hates little girls—ever unaware of the harsh gendered realities that await them; she loves little boys for the same reason. Akiko represents a critique of both the gendered divisions of labor and the ubiquitous dreams of material mobility. At the same time, she enjoys a masochistic relationship with a man her junior and asks him to beat her during sexual play. Because material wealth was crucial to postwar visions of Japaneseness, the family unit was extolled as the pinnacle of the affective labor of the nation, for upward mobility and middle-class security demanded devotion to the family unit. As such, recreational sex—particularly for a woman—had no place in the national narrative. A masochistic relationship was a waste that contributed to nothing but the manifestation of (female) pleasure and desire. In the context of Kōno's narrative, masochistic sex also serves as a critique of the gendered violence with which women live every day, as Gretchen Jones (2000) and Julia Bullock (2010) have shown in their readings of the story.

Kanai Mieko's story, "Rabbits," contributes to this rhetoric of class-based transgression via the destruction of the family unit, which is replaced by a pseudo-sexual relationship between a young girl named Sayuri (the secondary narrator/protagonist) and her father, who bond over the butchering and devouring of rabbits. One day the girl wakes to find that everyone in her family has disappeared except her father. She hardly notices their absence and begins staying home from school to eat rabbits with her father. Their house falls into disarray and squalor, and soon her father succumbs to health problems. His daughter is left to do the butchering. Although she struggles at first, she grows to take sexual pleasure in the slaughter. The narrator/protagonist decides she wants to dress up as a rabbit and have her father enact a fantasy of strangling and butchering her—an unsubtle euphemism for incest. Her plan does not come to fruition, however. When she dresses in a large rabbit suit and hops into his room, her father panics. He throws something at her, wounding her eye, and then promptly dies of a heart attack. She eventually puts out her other eye and dies as well. As in "Toddler Hunting," there is a hint of gendered subjugation in the story. But in contrast to Kōno's work, Sayuri in "Rabbits" dies and her story of resistance to normative Japaneseness is "inherited" by the frame narrator. Kanai's text offers an illuminating contrast to Kōno's, in which protagonist Akiko has to negotiate the real-world consequences of her actions and resistance to Japanese hegemony.

The 1960s and 1970s were exciting times, and literary endeavors such as those by Kōno and Kanai demonstrate the fragility and vulnerability of Japanese subjectivity during the era's upheavals. In the above-mentioned texts, transgression is a means to challenge the boundaries of Japanese female subjectivity; Kōno and Kanai explore undiscovered and unknown possibilities for new ways of being: unmarried, childless, sexual, somehow escaping expectations. These two narratives were part of a politically charged agenda by many authors to reject dominant ideologies. We see no schizophrenia here, no confusion or waffling on the part of protagonists, who are self-confident and bold. "Toddler Hunting" and "Rabbits" are not necessarily representative currents in all of Japanese letters. After all, Tanaka's best-selling *Somehow, Crystal* was published in the early 1980s. However, what politically oriented fiction offered was an *alternative* conceptual space through which the possibilities of transgression could be explored. Indeed, "revolutionary forms of activism and critique emerged to challenge official forms of politics and daily life" (Marotti 2013: 2). Student radicalism from the 1960s, for example, has been well documented, while William Marotti's (2013: 3) study *Money, Trains, and Guillotines* draws attention to "a diverse group of young artists [who] worked to repoliticize daily life through interventionist artistic practices." He writes: "Their critical focus and organizational strategies *anticipated many of the more commonly known practices of activists in the late 1960s*, both in Japan and around the globe" (Marotti 2013: 3; emphasis added).

What I emphasize here speaks to the observations Bullock has made regarding women's fiction of the same era: "While explicitly political expression of radical feminism did not emerge in postwar Japan until the women's liberation movement of the 1970s, women writers of fiction began to challenge normative discourses of gender.... well in advance of these developments in the second wave-feminist movement" (Bullock 2010: 4, 23). In short, Bullock reads fiction of this era with an eye toward the anticipatory space it occupied, one shared by other creative enterprises. Literature (as well as the arts) was simpatico with the broader goals of the political left regarding Japanese subjectivity and personal agency.

These short stories are open-ended, unfinished at the end. Where "Toddler Hunting" concludes with protagonist Akiko's bewilderment at an unexpected gift (of a flesh-like slice of watermelon) from a small boy, "Rabbits" ends with the frame narrator climbing into the fetid rabbit flesh suit the Alice-like protagonist has left behind in her death. These texts might be read with an eye toward the open-ended and unfinished work of feminist activism in the dynamic postwar milieu. What space does literature occupy now vis-à-vis its cultural and political contexts? If literary works can be seen as a barometer of sorts that reflects—and anticipates—social trends, is the fiction I have analyzed in this book emblematic of an incipient nationalistic (re)turn? Does it reveal a certain anxiety and ambivalence regarding the direction of the Japanese national consciousness? The recession, of course, crippled the ambitions of many Japanese and, in some ways, did the political work of activists, artists, and authors of prior generations. The recession rendered meaningless those institutions against which women raged in the 1960s and 1970s. Rather than actively resist the trappings of hegemony, young Japanese found the hegemonic state stripped of its power: middle-classness was less a conceptual status to challenge than an unattainable pursuit, for example; educational credentialism, too, slid from an object of derision to one of apathy—*why bother?* The fiction I have discussed in the previous chapters is apathetic on the one hand but also anxious and fidgety on the other. I contend that the characters in these works are similarly burdened with a sense of confusion regarding the unstable future before them. Kirino and her contemporaries offer case histories of women figuring out how to get by, for theirs is a milieu sustained not by insurrection (a la the 1960s and 1970s) but rather by desperation and exhaustion. In other words, theirs is a search for stability rather than a rallying cry for its opposite.

As I have argued, stability is readily found in visions of a dormant Japanese essence and the flight from perversity. Alan Tansman (2009: 4) sees this trend in fascist terms, arguing that fascism is the obliteration of difference, the construction of "timeless uniformity" at the expense of "messy variety." How interesting, then, that many of the texts I have analyzed should end in the same way: visions of men and women forging connections. If women's fiction of the 1960s and 1970s is distinct for its lack of finitude, millennial fiction (if Kanehara et al.

are any indication) leaves little room for ambivalence. Perhaps we can say that authors are tired of the promises of an unknown future and yearn for something more substantial, and concrete. The uniformity here is unmistakable, even predictable. I am reminded too of Nina Cornyetz's (2009: 323) words: "As a reactionary modernism, fascism has a specific politics of time… [;] it is palingenetic, moving forward toward "regeneration" as it looks nostalgically backward toward a mythic past." Her observations are coterminous with Tansman, insofar as both scholars argue that repetitive homogeneity is a crucial dimension of conservative thought. Their observations provide an important framework for understanding and interpreting literary works that follow the same narrative trajectories. Cornyetz (2009: 326) notes the importance of the "image of the same." That is, fascism is "an attempt at fixing signification" through "a combination of images of sublation" (Cornyetz 2009: 326). Thus, we see protagonists gravitate toward familial, heterosexual/normative expressions of social life. Romance is of the utmost importance, as is the codification of gender roles. This is not to claim that the repetition of images/motifs in and of themselves constitutes a fascist aesthetic. Cornyetz (2009: 343) points out, and I agree, that "the aesthetics and politics of [fascist] representation…might not seem particularly sinister in the absence of" an extratextual political reality. Thus, the political context of contemporary Japan offers important insights into how neoconservative fiction can be read. Important here is homogeneity *at the expense* of difference—the *destruction* of alterity.

I would argue, then, that the end of transgression in women's fiction portends a fascist turn—aesthetically if not literally. "[F]ascism masquerades as that which it is not," Cornyetz (2009: 326) writes. So does transgression. In Chapter 2, I demonstrated that transgression ultimately is not subversive; it reaffirms the boundaries that it ostensibly crosses; it stabilizes boundaries as it tests the limits of their fortitude. The end of transgression means a return to a time of limitation and normativity. Evident in the literature I have analyzed in this book is the primacy of heterosexual love. This is an idealized love, for Kirino's narrator in *Grotesque* simply imagines herself dying by Zhang's hand and joining a sorority of sisters similarly dispatched, while the teenage romance of *Tomorrow's Song* and *Snakes and Earrings* is cloaked in sunny symbolism. With these observations in mind, consider Rey Chow's (1998: 26; cited in Cornyetz 2009: 325) thoughts on fascism: "The most important sentiment involved in fascism is not a negative but a positive one: rather than hatefulness and destructiveness, fascism is about love and idealism. Most of all, it is a search for an idealized self-image through a heartfelt surrender to something higher and more beautiful." Is this not what is going on in the fiction I have discussed here? One might argue that fiction is often about idealism, that it represents realities yet unattained. Women's fiction has long been sustained by this notion. Writing *against* aggressive hegemony has been of utmost concern for women writers, as has offering new configurations of female subjectivity and alterity.

What differentiates fiction from the millennial turn—with Kirino, Sakurai, and Kanehara as representative authors—is its dismissal of alterity and investment in, to use Chow's word, surrender: to men (the murderous Zhang, the unstable Sid, the vicious Shiba, the terrible Niizaki, and so on); to familiarity (heterosexual romance, normative figurations of gender); to a script against which women's fiction ostensibly stands. This fascism is quiet, creeping, invested in "mov[ing] forward while gazing backward" (Cornyetz 2009: 330).

This fascism is predicated on desire, but this desire is shaped by political and social contexts. So, although the fascism about which I have been writing is not political per se, the literary products are themselves embedded in the larger political field. This is an example of micropolitics. Deleuze and Guattari (2004: 227) rely heavily on the notion of "microfascisms," the personal desire for order, rule, and coherence that is derived from greater political, social, and cultural currents. This is the answer to their question: why desire your own oppression? Desire "results from a highly developed, engineered setup rich in interactions: a whole supple segmentarity that processes molecular [private] energies and potentially gives desire a fascist determination" (Deleuze and Guattari 2004: 237). Their interest in the interplay between the molar and molecular speaks to the interplay between public and private desire, which cannot be separated from one another.

Thus, the fascist longings evident in Japanese millennial fiction are imbricated in larger processes of fascistic desire. Reason, consensus, normality—these used to be the objects of scorn and suspicion in women's fiction, carrying, as they did, implications of gendered oppression and inequality. The fiction I have analyzed here suggests an openness to these same avenues of oppression. The reason is not because heteronormativity is no longer oppressive: Kirino's novels show us the inherent dangers in female prostitution; Kanehara's reveal the consequences of sadomasochistic desire; Sakurai's index rape and emotional violence. There is no reason to suppose that the gendered worlds in which these authors' protagonists circulate are better or fairer than that of Kōno Takeo's Akiko or Kanai Mieko's Sayuri.

Certainly, inroads have been made in leveling gender imbalance in the political and economic spheres of Japanese social life. However, the conservativism of the contemporary moment has the potential to nullify feminist progress. The falling birthrate alone has brought to the surface recalcitrant appeals for women to return to the home to repopulate the nation. It is easy to blame women for the population decline, and a stigma against unmarried, childless women persists. However, Sachi Sekimoto and Yusaku Yajima (2017: 37) contend that demographic concerns are rooted in issues of economic stasis rather than gender upheaval: "The general political solution to population decline primarily concerns the rhetoric of 'we want to get married and have kids, but cannot.'" Sekimoto and Yajima (2017: 37) note that young people continue to desire institutional heteronormativity in spite of the challenge that "normative lifestyle[s are] increasingly difficult to fulfill." These scholars are correct in their assertion that "population decline becomes a women's issue" when reproduction "becomes a target of national policy" (Sekimoto and Yajima 2017: 37). In the contemporary moment, reproduction is coded politically as a woman's biological goal and route to personal fulfillment. Although they do not use this term in their discussion, Sekimoto and Yajima are referring to the insidious operation of fascist desire and the sublimation of personal interest to the demands of state doctrine.

The recession has redirected desire and created a generation of citizens who are vulnerable to the pull of hegemony and the safety it provides: this is comfortable subordination. In the Introduction, I referred to the political edge of hegemony, and here I return to that discussion. Antonio Gramsci (cited in Beasley-Murray 2010: 1) has argued famously that hegemony is underpinned by "the 'spontaneous' consent given by the great masses of the population to the general direction imposed on social life by the dominant social group." The failure of the economic system amplified the "domestic pathologies" within Japanese social life (Tozzo 2017: 114). At the same time, however, it exposed the fragility of life beyond bounds. If prior generations refused boldly institutional hegemony and found pleasure in navigating the undiscovered country of a new Japanese subjectivity, today's Japanese are burdened by the reality that they cannot afford, economically and effectively, the risks.

Sekimoto and Yajima remind us that young Japanese are excluded from the ritual of marriage simply because they cannot pay for it. They are correct in their understanding of marriage as a highly gendered issue. Yet they might also ask why, in the face of economic hardship and middle-class impossibility, young people continue to desire what they cannot have. The answer might lie with Lauren Berlant's notion of "cruel optimism," in which individuals desire paradoxically that which is personally detrimental. Questions of desire are central to Berlant's concept, especially what she calls a "scene of desire:"

> Cruel optimism names a relation of attachment to compromised conditions of possibility. What is cruel about these attachments, and not merely inconvenient or tragic, is that the subjects who have x in their lives might not well endure the loss of their object or scene of desire, even though its presence threatens their well-being, because whatever the content of the attachment, the continuity of the form of it provides something of the continuity of the subject's sense of what it means to keep on living and to look forward to being in the world.
>
> (2011: 21)

The scene of desire is important in orchestrating longing for, faith in, and attachment to a particular life mode. Allegiance to this scene of desire demands that "[o]ne make affective bargains about the costliness of one's attachments" (Berlant 2011: 21). In the context of recessionary Japan, "the costliness" of fidelity to hegemony has already been well-established. Certainly, the Japanese *know* what is at risk; indeed, the genealogy of Japanese women's fiction has articulated substantively the potential downfall of clinging to "gendered scripts" (see Chapter 3 of this study), a term Sarah Ahmed (2010: 59) uses to describe the ways in which women bargain themselves into predetermined spheres of desire. Ahmed writes of the preponderance of "happiness" in social discourse; few would contest the idea that happiness is the ubiquitous signifier of successful living. As such, Ahmed (2010: 6) demonstrates the means through which happiness becomes a gendered issue: marriage, for example, is "defined as 'the best of all possible worlds' as it maximizes happiness." This observation contributes to an answer to the query Sekimoto and Yajima pose: why do young people continue to pursue life modes that are largely unattainable? An observation especially true for women, who shoulder the burden of a specific manifestation of heterosexual happiness and hegemony.

Ahmed (2010: 145) rightly points out that "[n]arratives of rebellion can involve deviations" from hegemonic scripts "if they return us to the origins of heterosexual desire." Her keen observation illuminates the mechanics of transgression that I have been discussing in this study: transgression is allowed so long as it dissipates. Is it any surprise, then, that the works of fiction I analyze here end in a celebration of heterosexual desire? This can be sexual desire, as in the case of *Grotesque*, whose protagonist eschews until the very end any suggestion that she possesses desire, or it can be the desire for heterosexual normativity, as we see in *Tomorrow's Song* and *Snakes and Earrings*. In these latter two narratives, it is consequential that those chasing after normativity are teenagers, as if they realize the uselessness of prolonged rebellion. In other words, young Japanese should be the citizens who are most suspicious of hegemony's empty promises. Akari's and Lui's return to normative heterosexuality neutralizes narratives that had been sustained by pages of drug use, alcoholism, promiscuity, and trouble-making. By the end of their respective narratives, readers get the sense that these teenage protagonists are ready to leave rebellion behind, realizing that their individual desires for transgression are supplanted by the desire for normativity. Their stories once again become narratives of convention, reconciliation, and place.

Note

1 Yasukuni Shrine is a Shintō shrine in Tokyo founded by Emperor Meiji in 1869. It commemorates individuals who died serving Japan during the Meiji, Taishō, and first half of the Shōwa Periods, including convicted war criminals. Exhibits at the Yūshūkan War Museum espouse a revisionist history of World War II that glorifies Japan's prewar and wartime aggressive, expansionist military agenda.

WORKS CITED

Ahmed, Sarah. 2010. *The Promise of Happiness*. Durham: Duke University Press.

Beasley-Murray, Jon. 2010. *Posthegemony: Political Theory and Latin America*. Minneapolis, MN: University of Minnesota Press.

Berlant, Lauren. 2011. *Cruel Optimism*. Durham: Duke University Press.

Bridges, Brian. 2010. "Japan: Political Longevity and Troubled Governance." In *Public Governance in Asia and the Limits of Electoral Democracy*, edited by Brian Bridges and Lok-song Ho, 77–88. Northampton, MA: Edward Elgar.

Bullock, Julia. 2010. *The Other Women's Lib: Gender and Body in Japanese Women's Fiction*. Honolulu, HI: University of Hawai'i Press.

Chow, Rey. 1998. *Ethics after Idealism: Theory–Culture–Ethnicity–Reading*. Bloomington: Indiana University Press.

Cornyetz, Nina. 2009. "Fascist Aesthetic and the Politics of Representation in Kawabata Yasunari." In *The Culture of Japanese Fascism*, edited by Alan Tansman, 321–354. Durham: Duke University Press.

Deleuze, Gilles and Felix Guattari. 1983. *Anti-Oedipus: Capitalism and Schizophrenia*. Translated by Robert Hurley, Mark Seem, and Helen R. Lane. Minneapolis, MN: University of Minnesota Press.

Deleuze, Gilles and Felix Guattari. 2004. *A Thousand Plateaus: Capitalism and Schizophrenia*. Translated by Brian Massumi. London: Continuum.

Jameson, Frederic. 1985. "Postmodernism and Consumer Society." In *Postmodern Culture*, edited by Hal Foster, 111–125. London: Pluto Press.

Jones, Gretchen. 2000. "Subversive Strategies: Masochism, Gender and Power in Kōno Taeko's 'Toddler Hunting.'" *East Asia* 16 (4): 79–107.

Kanai Mieko. 1982 [1976]. "Rabbits." In *Rabbits, Crabs, etc.: Stories by Japanese Women*, translated by Phyllis Birnbaum, 1–16. Honolulu, HI: University of Hawai'i Press.

Kōno, Taeko. 1996 [1962]. "Toddler Hunting." In *"Toddler Hunting" and Other Stories*, translated by Lucy North, 45–68. New York, NY: New Directions Publishing Corporation.

Marotti, William. 2013. *Money, Trains, and Guillotines: Art and Revolution in 1960s Japan*. Durham: Duke University Press.

Mushakoji, Kinhide. 2015. "Ethno-politics in Contemporary Japan: The Multi-Occasion of Orientalism and Occidentalism." In *Making and Unmaking Japan: Protosociology*, vol. 32, edited by Ritu Vij, 36–58. Frankfurt am Main: Gerhard Preyer.

Nakasone, Yasuhiro. 1978. *Atarashī hoshu no riron*. Tokyo: Kōdansha.

Seem, Mark. 1983. "Introduction." In *Anti-Oedipus: Capitalism and Schizophrenia*. Translated by Robert Hurley, Mark Seem, and Helen R. Lane, xv–xxiv. Minneapolis, MN: University of Minnesota Press.

Sekimoto, Sachi and Yusaku Yajima. 2017. "The Affective Politics of the Feminine: An Interpretive Analysis of Japanese Female Comedians." In *Intercultural Communication in Japan: Theorizing Homogenizing Discourse*, edited by Satoshi Toyosaki and Shinsuke Eguchi, 27–40. New York, NY: Routledge.

Tamamoto, Masaru. 2018. "Towards True Independence: Abe Shinzo's Nationalism." In *Identity, Trust, and Reconciliation in East Asia: Dealing with Painful History to Create a Peaceful Present*, edited by Kevin P. Clements, 179–200. New York, NY: Palgrave Macmillan.

Tansman, Alan. 2009. "Introduction: The Culture of Japanese Fascism." In *The Culture of Japanese Fascism*, edited by Alan Tansman, 1–30. Durham: Duke University Press.

Toivonen, Tuuka and Yuki Imoto. 2012. "Making Sense of Youth Problems." In *A Sociology of Japanese Youth: From Returnees to NEETs*, edited by Roger Goodman, Yuki Imoto, and Tuukka Toivonen, 1–29. New York, NY: Routledge.

Tozzo, Brandon. 2017. *American Hegemony after the Great Recession: A Transformation in World Order*. New York, NY: Palgrave.

EPILOGUE

Nina Cornyetz

David Holloway's *The End of Transgression* is thick and rich. It is a visceral read; he probes his primary texts from one angle after another, circling and re-circling back with multiple interpretations and analyses, having recourse to secondary sources as diverse as Slavoj Žižeck and Michel Foucault. *The End of Transgression* argues that for a particular group of contemporary Japanese women writers, transgression of a variety of gendered norms fails in any attempt to rethink such gendered norms and, in the end, reinstalls those very norms. Or as Holloway maintains, transgression deals in the reciprocity between limitation and subversion. "[It] is not the complete transcendence of a norm, boundary, or limit, but rather the creation of new knots of confinement" (Introduction, 4).

The End of Transgression is, first and foremost, a work of literary history. There is a sweeping contextualization and historicization of modern Japanese literature, which sets the stage for the close textual analyses that follow. These, in my mind, are the requisite parameters for solid literary analysis. In other words, Holloway provides extensive and concrete material, socioeconomic, and sociocultural dissection of the historical circumstances leading up to and during the period when the writers he analyzes were writing, and a similarly broad and deep overview of the Japanese-language literature leading to those writers. This historical material is followed with close readings of the texts themselves. In this epilogue, I will not attempt to summarize the work that the text does, but prefer to use this space to engage with some of the broader theoretical implications of Holloway's argument that are part of my response to his study. Were he alive today, I would love to engage him in discussions of the points that follow.

DOI: 10.4324/9781003231806-8

In the works Holloway analyzes, the female characters transgress with the body as the privileged site of such transgressions: "in the form of incest, prostitution, illicit love affairs, body modification, self-starvation, and other corporeal acts" (Introduction, 13). Hence, one might postulate that they transgress in normative ways for women—masochism, prostitution, eating disorders, compensated dating, etc.—unlike Yoshimoto Banana, who, by substituting food for sex, moves away from such complicity with tired models of male constructs of women (Chapter One). But these transgressions end up being, paradoxically, what we might think of as post-feminist—in its most pejorative sense—capitulations to a neoliberal or neoconservative concept of female personhood under mature capitalism and, to use Holloway's terminology, a schizophrenic attempt at individual stabilization. Holloway writes: "I make the claim that women writers of the millennial turn are less interested in pushing boundaries and making 'noise' than they are in finding moments of affective quietude for their characters" (Introduction, 4).

He expounds:

> I would argue that in the pages of this fiction there is a critical engagement with the *idea* of normativity. Characters establish families, pursue romantic relationships, and even approach marriage, but in each case something is off and abject. On the contours of these crooked unions, choreographed by crooked citizens, stirs the end of transgression. Central to these works of fiction is the seemingly paradoxical longing for confinement and containment provided by the status quo, for a time orchestrated by rule and regulation (Introduction, 7).

In his *The Alienated Subject*, James A. Tyner borrows Erich Fromm's notion of the authoritarian (sadistic) and passive (masochistic) personality to describe the positions of and the relations between, respectively, the capitalist and the worker (2022:19–20; Fromm, 1957: 3-4). Discussing the alienation of the workers from their labor, the products of their labor, and the loss of meaningfulness of their lives in general, Tyner writes, "as a political philosophy, sadomasochism directs attention toward concrete social relations as embedded in hegemonic structures of production, distribution, and consumption, that is, in particular modes of social organization, and, as such, offers a particularly salient vantage point from which to interpret alienation" (2022: 19). To summarize, the "exploitative and alienating conditions of capitalism are effectively sadomasochistic in orientation" (58).

Holloway cites the boredom, the absence of a "place to belong to," the disenfranchisement and relegation to the margins of society that make themselves known as affective states throughout the novels he writes about. This too can be attributed to the nature of consumer-oriented capitalism in which there is only a trompe l'oeil of freedom:

> Whereas spiritual emptiness was of grave concern for prior generations, emptiness was, in the context of a materially affluent Japan, cause for celebration. The void left by history could be filled with consumer goods while at the same time extolled as proof of Japan's mastery of contemporary living (Chapter Two, 33).

When labor no longer has dignity, purpose, and meaning, *existing* is all that is left; necessitating a kind of violence to cut through the state of nothingness—as Holloway notes most powerfully in the case of Lui of *Snakes and Earrings* (Chapter Three). Citing David Harvey, Tyner avers that in the process of alienation in the United States the disenfranchised blue-collar, but not poor, white workers turn their rage and frustrations not at the capitalist system, but on the scapegoats offered up as compensation for the unfairness of the system itself: minorities, women, and immigrants (2022: 69). This same deflection of rage can certainly be seen in many of the Japanese texts discussed by Holloway: women, of course, but also others, like those with tattoos or piercings and Chinese immigrants who occupy abjected positions in contemporary Japan and who may be either intratextual perpetrators or targets of violence.

As Tyner also reminds us, we must be aware that the alienation of women is *specific* to their status as women, and further particularized by race, ethnicity, economic status, age, and other copresent material conditions of each individual woman's existence (2022: 96–103). In Sandra Lee Bartky's take on a type of alienation specific to (white, North American, and Western European) women, she asks how might the structure of the female unconscious reproduce differently alienated modes of existence (1982: 131)? She notes the problematic whereby a male factory worker is markedly unenthusiastic about going to work, whereas many women enthusiastically and paradoxically embrace the very conditions of alienation of their lives as women. She writes (and this is certainly applicable to the contemporary Japanese context):

> There is no dearth of contenders for the title of "Miss America." Most teenage girls would rather be Bo Derek than Madame Curie. "Playmate of the Month" is an enviable status. Thousands of women have been attracted to movements like "Fascinating Womanhood" which aim both to safeguard and to promote the more objectionable norms of femininity. Women of all classes buy large numbers of books and magazines which teach them how to be better, that is, more "feminine" women.
>
> (131)

Bartky argues that in her sexual objectification, a woman must introject what others have called the male gaze and see herself as both observer and object to be evaluated by socially constructed ideals of beauty. Bartky notes the gratification and pleasure that women may experience when regarding themselves as sexual objects; she links this to the Freudian concept of narcissism and to the fact that the first object of our primary narcissism is ourselves. This, she argues, further infantilizes women (1982: 134–135).

Following Sigmund Freud while historicizing his argument with her "fashion-beauty complex," the introjection of the male gaze sets women up with an impossible goal and a perpetual sexualized failure:

> Overtly, the fashion-beauty complex seeks to glorify the female body and to provide opportunities for narcissistic indulgence. More important than this is its covert aim, which is to depreciate woman's body and deal a blow to her narcissism. We are presented everywhere with images of perfect female beauty—at the drugstore cosmetics display, the supermarket magazine counter, on television. These images remind us constantly that we fail to measure up. Whose nose is the right shape, after all, whose hips are not too wide—or too narrow? The female body is revealed as a task, an object in need of transformation. "There are no ugly women," said Helena Rubinstein, "only lazy ones" (Quoted in "Fashion, Beauty and the Feminist," *The Freewoman* (Sept.-Oct., 1978).
>
> (Bartky, 1982: 135)

I would amend Bartky's observations to note that narcissism is not just about "love of self," but more accurately, love of one's ideal self, which one can never actually be. Therefore, there is inherent in narcissism a malevolence toward one's failure to live up to the ego ideal (Freud 1959). Hence, it should come as no surprise that the female characters in the works Holloway explores are filled with self-doubt, take on false personas, engage in masochistic sexual activities, choose the wrong men, and end up back where they started.

One might characterize the novels discussed in *The End of Transgression* as constituting a lover's complaint, as theorized by Lauren Berlant: "the complaint is a performative plea that implicitly holds no hope for change in the condition of the author's misery—apart from whatever response the complaint itself might elicit from the audience" (1988: 243). And this very complaint originates as a statement that is turned into such a performative plea. "It is not the woman who first calls her self-articulation a complaint, a whine, a plea: rather, the patriarchal social context in which she makes her utterance hystericizes it for her, even before she speaks" (1988: 243). The description of her material conditions of existence is turned into a hysteria that confirms her status as victim.

Here I want to invoke the blunt words of Amia Srinivasan: "Desire can cut against what politics has chosen for us and choose for itself" (2021: 96). How does one liberate desire from politics? Is such a thing even thinkable? If indeed we are born into a discourse and system that precedes us, we are always already structured by that structure, even as incrementally perhaps that system transforms over history, and as Freud argued throughout his lifetime, desire leaks out in unplanned and sometimes politically incorrect cathexes. To quote Slavoj Žižek:

> The point of "inherent transgression" is not only that resistance is immanent to Power, that power and counter-power generate each other, it is not only that Power itself generates the excess of resistance which it can no longer dominate; it is also not only that—in the case of sexuality—the disciplinary 'repression' of a libidinal investment eroticizes this gesture of repression itself, as in the case of the obsessional neurotic who derives libidinal satisfaction from the very compulsive rituals destined to keep the traumatic jouissance at bay.
>
> (Žižek, 1997: 35)

As I am fond of reminding my students, the symptom itself is the sexual activity of the neurotic, and the neuroses are the negative of the perversions. While the pervert transgresses sexual norms, the neurotic has headaches, spasms, and rituals. The pervert cannot know his own desire because he disavows lack and instrumentalizes himself under the law of sadism, which stipulates how he will relate to jouissance (Lacan, Kant, and Sade). The neurotic represses his desire and substitutes it with the symptom. For the pervert, there is a failure to acknowledge that the desire of the Other, no more or less than that of the self, can only be in the form of a question and never filled by a specific content (Lacan, 2002; Zupançiç, 2000). It seems to me that one tragedy for the perverse female characters analyzed by Holloway's study is that they are convinced there is an answer to both, or at least one, of these questions. And they cannot find that answer.

WORKS CITED

Bartky, Sandra Lee. 1982. "Narcissism, Femininity and Alienation." *Social Theory and Practice* 8(2): 127–143.

Berlant, Lauren. 1988. "The Female Complaint," *Social Text* 19/20 (Autumn): 237–259.

Freud, Sigmund. 1959. "On Narcissism: An Introduction." In *Collected Papers IV*, 30–59. New York, NY: Basic Books.

Fromm, Erich. 1957. "The Authoritarian Personality." translated by Florian Nadge. *Deutsche Universitätszeitung*, Band 12 (9): 3–4.

Lacan, Jacques. 2002. "Kant with Sade." In *Écrits*, translated by Bruce Fink, 645–670. New York, NY, and London: W.W. Norton.

Srinivasan, Amia. 2021. *The Right to Sex: Feminism in the Twenty-First Century.* New York, NY: Farrar, Straus and Giroux.
Tyner, James A. 2022. *The Alienated Subject: On the Capacity to Hurt.* Minneapolis, MN: University of Minnesota Press.
Žižek, Slavoj. 1997. *The Plague of Fantasies.* London and New York, NY: Verso.
Zupançiç, Alenka. 2000. *Ethics of the Real: Kant and Lacan.* London and New York, NY: Verso.

INDEX

Note: Page numbers followed by "n" refer to notes.

For Product Safety Concerns and Information please contact our EU
representative GPSR@taylorandfrancis.com Taylor & Francis Verlag GmbH,
Kaufingerstraße 24, 80331 München, Germany

Printed and bound by CPI Group (UK) Ltd, Croydon, CR0 4YY
18/04/2025
01848358-0001